THE SPEED OF RISK
Lessons Learned on the Audit Trail

2nd Edition

Richard F. Chambers

SPONSORED BY

The Institute of
Internal Auditors
Chicago Chapter

Paul J. Sobel,
CIA, QIAL, CRMA

Published by the Internal Audit Foundation
1035 Greenwood Blvd., Suite 401
Lake Mary, Florida 32746, USA

Limit of Liability: The Internal Audit Foundation publishes this document for informational and educational purposes and is not a substitute for legal or accounting advice. The Foundation does not provide such advice and makes no warranty as to any legal or accounting results through its publication of this document. When legal or accounting issues arise, professional assistance should be sought and retained.

The IIA's International Professional Practices Framework (IPPF) comprises the full range of existing and developing practice guidance for the profession. The IPPF provides guidance to internal auditors globally and paves the way to world-class internal auditing.

The IIA and the Foundation work in partnership with researchers from around the globe who conduct valuable studies on critical issues affecting today's business world. Much of the content presented in their final reports is a result of Foundation-funded research and prepared as a service to the Foundation and the internal audit profession. Expressed opinions, interpretations, or points of view represent a consensus of the researchers and do not necessarily reflect or represent the official position or policies of The IIA or the Foundation.

Hard Cover ISBN-13: 978-1-63454-058-2
Soft Cover ISBN-13: 978-1-63454-059-9
23 22 21 20 19 1 2 3 4 5 6

Printed in Canada

To the men and women around the world
who have made internal auditing their careers,
and who continue to inspire us with their
personal journeys on the audit trail.

CONTENTS

FOREWORD

I was greatly honored when Richard Chambers asked me to write the Foreword to his latest book, *The Speed of Risk: Lessons Learned on the Audit Trail,* 2nd Edition. His previous two books have been great successes, helping the internal audit profession learn from the vast wisdom he's gained throughout his illustrious career. After he explained the focus of this updated edition, I was excited that he was willing to put in the effort I know it takes to author a book. Our profession is very much in need of his updated insights.

I don't recall when I first met Richard, but it was during his first stint with The IIA back in 2001–2004. I didn't have the opportunity to work directly with him until he served as the national practice leader for Pricewaterhouse-Coopers in 2004–2008. I was the chief audit executive for an energy company in Atlanta, Georgia, and we had decided to bid out our internal audit co-sourcing contract. We selected PwC, due in no small part to the advisory role Richard was committed to play during the first year of our contract. It was extremely valuable to have access to an experienced thought leader such as Richard. His knowledge of the energy industry from his time with Tennessee Valley Authority enabled him to help me think through key business risks facing our industry. Also, his deep understanding of The IIA's *Standards* allowed him to provide valuable advice as I conducted a quality self-assessment before our initial external quality assessment.

During his time at PwC, Richard and I started working more closely on IIA volunteer activities. He chaired the International Conference Committee when The IIA's Atlanta Chapter was awarded the 2010 International Conference (I should note that he recused himself from the vote because he didn't want his prior connections to the city of Atlanta to influence the committee's selection in any way). We then worked together on the North American Board before I moved on to The IIA's Executive Committee.

During my first year on the Executive Committee, Richard rejoined The IIA as its president and CEO. I had the good fortune of watching him navigate some very difficult financial times when he first took that office, and then working with him as he shepherded The IIA through some of the most prosperous years in its history. My year as IIA chairman of the board in 2013–2014 gave me the opportunity to work side by side with him and gain a great appreciation for his exceptional leadership skills and business acumen. It also helped me develop a deep respect for him as a person. He's a good listener and communicator and has proven adept at surrounding himself with talented people. He and his wife, Kim, go to great lengths to show how much they appreciate the contributions of The IIA's many volunteers. I'm proud to call him colleague and friend.

So what does that have to do with writing a book? Well, I believe the better you know someone the greater the understanding and appreciation you have for their commitment to writing a book of this nature. In addition to his full-time job as IIA president and CEO, Richard finds time to write blogs and have an active presence on social media. These are just some of the many ways he gives back to the profession, and the business world in general. The recognition he's received in *Accounting Today* and by the National Association of Corporate Directors (NACD) for his influence in accounting and corporate governance are richly deserved. But he doesn't do all of this for the recognition; rather, he genuinely cares about advancing the profession. I don't know how he finds the time to have such an active social media presence, but I follow him closely, knowing that he will provide insights on current events affecting the profession. I try to read all of his blogs and look at every post, because I know I can never stop learning in life and he is a great teacher. This book shows his continuing commitment to educate the profession.

I was very pleased when Richard told me the title of this updated edition started with *The Speed of Risk* because that's such a relevant thought for the rapidly changing, disruptive times in which we live. He's always had his finger on the pulse of risk, having created The IIA's first comprehensive risk assessment and initiating the annual Pulse of Internal Audit surveys that have helped to inform the profession. While the internal audit profession has been risk-based for some time, Richard has helped all of us better understand what that really means.

Which brings me to the contents of this book. Richard's extensive and diverse experience make him uniquely positioned to share the valuable lessons gleaned from his career. Having read both of his previous books, I knew how valuable those lessons were to a growing profession in an increasingly complex world. I believe this book better reflects the timeless nature of those lessons and reinforces the trusted advisor attributes. However, it also demonstrates how timeless insights still must be customized to meet the needs of an ever-changing world. This book's focus on stakeholder expectations, relationship acumen, the nature and pace of risk, disruption, and culture creates messages that are relevant not only today but for the foreseeable future as well.

I highly recommend *The Speed of Risk: Lessons Learned on the Audit Trail*, 2nd Edition. It should be on every internal auditor's reading list in 2019 and beyond. The new lessons, and application of the old lessons, apply to internal audit leaders as well as those just starting their career. They apply to both public and private sector organizations, in any industry and any country throughout the world. I commend Richard and thank him for taking the time to share his wisdom with the profession.

Paul J. Sobel, CIA, QIAL, CRMA
Chairman of the Committee of Sponsoring Organizations
of the Treadway Commission (COSO)
Chief Risk Officer and former Chief Audit Executive,
Georgia-Pacific, LLC

ACKNOWLEDGMENTS

As I noted at the time when crafting the first edition of *Lessons Learned on the Audit Trail*, writing the book was one of the most rewarding experiences of my life. Revisiting and updating lessons learned for this edition has been equally rewarding and also inspiring. Once again, however, it would not have been possible without the encouragement and support of so many family members, friends, and colleagues.

My wife, Kim, has been a vital partner on the audit trail I discuss in this book. She is a source of encouragement and support each time I write a book. Her words of advice, reassurance, patience, and understanding were vital to undertaking such demanding projects. My father, Linville Chambers, was a lifelong source of inspiration personally and professionally. His death in 2013 was a catalyst for my own self-reflection and the decision to write the original book. Thanks, Dad, for all you taught me about life, the pursuit of excellence, and perseverance. My mother, Mildred Chambers, has always been a pillar of strength. Without her loving support throughout my academic years and the early years of my career, there would likely have been no audit trail. My talented and beautiful daughters, Natalie McElwee, Christina Morton, and Allison Chambers, have always been unwavering in their affection and support. No matter how many times the new chapters in my professional journey disrupted their lives, their love and resilience always shined through.

Thank you to Paul J. Sobel and The IIA's Chicago Chapter for sponsoring this 2nd edition of *Lessons Learned on the Audit Trail* and to The IIA's Dallas Chapter for sponsoring the first edition. Thanks to Lillian McAnally, my editor on the original manuscript, who graciously agreed to come back and reprise her role with this edition. Lillian's expertise and time in organizing the 2nd edition and polishing the manuscript were invaluable. Thanks to

Robert Perez, Jane Seago, and Mike Gowell for their contributions to new content in this edition. I remain indebted to Barbara Dycus, Jodi Swauger, Edward Popkins Jr., and John Babinchak for their contributions to the manuscript of the first edition, and thanks to John Babinchak for returning for round two. Thanks to Erika Beard and Lee Ann Campbell for their contributions in managing this project and putting the finishing touches on the manuscript. Thank you to Jim Kinder and Monica Griffin for their extraordinary work on the cover design of the book. Thanks also to Paul Sobel for the kind words he shared in the Foreword to this edition.

Finally, I would be remiss if I didn't thank the countless men and women whom I had the privilege of calling my colleagues in the Trust Company of Georgia, the U.S. Government Accountability Office, the U.S. Army, the U.S. Department of Health and Human Services, the U.S. Postal Service, Tennessee Valley Authority (TVA), PwC, and The IIA. The opportunity to work with such extraordinary professionals over the course of more than 40 years has been the highest honor of my life. Without them, my audit trail would have been a lonely and unfulfilling path.

ABOUT THE AUTHOR

Richard F. Chambers, CIA, QIAL, CGAP, CCSA, CRMA, is president and CEO of The Institute of Internal Auditors (IIA), the global professional association for internal auditors. He has spent more than 40 years in internal auditing, serving as inspector general of Tennessee Valley Authority, deputy inspector general of the U.S. Postal Service, and director of the U.S. Army Internal Review at the Pentagon. Before joining The IIA, he was national practice leader in Internal Audit Advisory Services at Pricewaterhouse-Coopers (PwC).

Richard is a prolific blogger and speaker and has been featured in numerous major media outlets, including *The Wall Street Journal*, *The New York Times*, Bloomberg Radio, and CNBC. *Accounting Today* selected him as one of the 100 Most Influential People in Accounting, and the National Association of Corporate Directors (NACD) named him one of the most influential leaders in corporate governance. Richard and his wife, Kim, reside in the Orlando, Florida, area and have three grown daughters, Natalie, Christina, and Allison.

CHAPTER 1
There Are No Speed Limits on the Audit Trail

When I "put my pencil down" and submitted the final manuscript of *Lessons Learned on the Audit Trail* for publication five years ago, I assumed it was my last word on the subject. Yet, I was ignoring a key message from the book: We must never stop learning from the lessons that life teaches us. Since the first edition of this book was published, I feel I have almost lived another professional lifetime. I have shared numerous new lessons across various content media—blogs, presentations, and social media. In fact, the speed at which life is teaching us new lessons is a lesson unto itself. For that reason, I am compelled to update *Lessons Learned on the Audit Trail* to share new perspectives on the lessons in the first edition and to impart new lessons learned during these last few years.

As we travel down life's path, each of us experiences things in both our personal and professional lives that prepare us for what lies ahead. In that regard, my journey is not unique. What sets it apart, however, is that I have invested more than four decades serving the same profession—internal auditing. During that time, I have learned many important lessons, some early in my career and some recent. The paradox of encountering lessons later in life is that you have less time to apply them, which is a motivating factor for me in writing my books. If I can help just one internal auditor to be better prepared for the challenges and opportunities that await in his or her career, then the effort will have been worth it.

A Bird's-Eye View of My Audit Trail

I suspect that you, as the reader, might want to have some idea of where I gathered these lessons before you dive headlong into reading about them.

After all, there are many useful books in the marketplace written by highly experienced authors. Why should you read this one? To answer that, I have listed below a brief chronological review of my career. I have been fortunate to have the opportunity to work with many talented experts in numerous fields with significant levels of responsibility. The experiences and milestones I have accrued combine to forge the insights discussed in this book.

- 1975–1976: Internal audit associate with Trust Company of Georgia, a large regional bank in Atlanta, Georgia, USA
- 1976: Auditor, U.S. General Accounting Office, Washington, DC, USA
- 1976–1980: Internal auditor at levels of increasing responsibility at a major U.S. Army command in Atlanta, Georgia, USA
- 1980–1981: Accountant with the U.S. Department of Health and Human Services Bureau of Medicare, Atlanta, Georgia, USA
- 1981–1984: Returned to the position of internal auditor at the major U.S. Army command in Atlanta, Georgia, USA
- 1984–1988: Operations research analyst with the major U.S. Army command in Atlanta, Georgia, USA
- 1988–1991: Chief audit executive of the internal audit department of the major U.S. Army command in Atlanta, Georgia, USA
- 1991–1992: Student at the U.S. Army War College resident program, Carlisle, Pennsylvania, USA
- 1992–1993: Resumed the role of chief audit executive with the major U.S. Army command in Atlanta, Georgia, USA
- 1993–1998: Chief audit executive (chief of Internal Review) for the U.S. Army, the Pentagon, Washington, DC, USA
- 1998–2000: Deputy assistant inspector general; assistant inspector general; and deputy inspector general of the U.S. Postal Service, Washington, DC, USA
- 2000–2001: Inspector general, Tennessee Valley Authority (TVA), Knoxville, Tennessee, USA
- 2001–2004: Vice president, the Learning Center, The Institute of Internal Auditors (IIA), Altamonte Springs, Florida, USA
- 2004–2008: National practice leader, PricewaterhouseCoopers, USA

- 2009–date: President and CEO, The Institute of Internal Auditors (IIA), Lake Mary, Florida, USA

Over the course of these assignments, I have come to believe that internal auditing can be an extraordinarily rewarding profession, fostering a sense of accomplishment unlike any other. It has been so for me, and I believe that as we explore the lessons discussed in this book, you will discover principles that can make your personal internal audit journey equally rewarding.

The *Merriam-Webster Dictionary* defines an audit trail as "a record of a sequence of events from which a history may be reconstructed."[1] As I reflect on my own career in internal auditing, I often contemplate the sequence of events that brought me to where I am today—my own personal audit trail. As the chronology above reflects, there were periods in my career in which I advanced very rapidly. We should never hold ourselves captive to artificial timelines. There are no speed limits on the audit trail. More important than the events themselves, however, are what they taught me.

In this book, I share the most impactful of the lessons I have learned about our profession and those we serve. More than ever, I believe that—far from being a monotonous, black-and-white job—internal auditing holds exciting potential for those seeking a vibrant profession that provides real value to the enterprises they serve.

What's New on the Audit Trail

In 2014, I shared what I believed were the most critical lessons from almost 40 years as an internal audit professional in the first edition of this book, *Lessons Learned on the Audit Trail*. The response to the book was quite remarkable. It was swiftly translated into Spanish, French, Traditional Chinese, and Simplified Chinese, and internal auditors scooped up more than 15,000 copies worldwide.

The lessons we learn over the course of a career will serve us well if we remember and apply them. And we will need every one of those lessons to surmount the ever-increasing challenges and opportunities internal auditors face today. This edition has been updated to include perspectives on recent developments that pose critical implications for the profession.

I have written more than 200 blogs and articles since the first edition was published. The research and conversations with global experts I used to prepare those writings have afforded me insights I share in this book on topics of concern to the profession today:

- Perspectives that management and audit committees are reluctant to share
- How marketing internal audit can enhance awareness about its value
- Frequent sources of tension between management and internal audit
- The idea that internal auditors can audit anything—but not everything
- The importance of tact and the art of bringing about positive change
- How poor audit planning can cause "the wheels to come off" the engagement
- How smart internal auditors ask smart questions
- The need for ethical internal auditors to be courageous

These topics are of increasing concern to the internal audit profession, which is called on to excel in an environment that is shaped by challenging trends, including the following:

1. The Speed of Risk

Businesses worldwide frequently focus on managing risks, both internal and external, whether related to finance, operations, strategy, technology, regulations, or reputation. While organizations are raising the bar on effective risk management, executives face extraordinary headwinds spawned by a turbulent environment in which risks materialize virtually overnight. In the past five years, global financial and business markets have been rocked by spectacular cybersecurity breaches, corporate failures induced by toxic cultures, the #MeToo movement highlighting sexual assault and harassment in the workplace, and more.

Internal auditors are finding that rigid, risk-based annual audit plans are increasingly relics of the past that position them to addressing yesterday's challenges. This reinforces my long-held belief that internal audit must take a more continuous approach to risk assessment—auditing at the speed of risk—which is a recurring theme in this updated edition.

2. The Implications of Auditing Organizational Culture

Our profession has long recognized that tone at the top is critical to the overall effectiveness of an organization's system of internal controls. When the first edition of this book was published, auditing culture was not a frequent topic of conversation for many of us. In the last few years, however, there has been virtually an epidemic of corporate failures induced, at least in part, by a toxic culture.

Regulators, stakeholders, and the public have looked to internal audit as a source of assurance or insight on organizational culture. Organizational culture reflects "how we do things around here," so when the culture becomes toxic, it impacts the workplace environment and generates a ripple effect on the entire organization, ultimately impacting the bottom line. In this edition, a new chapter has been added to cover the concept of auditing organizational culture and potential roles internal audit can play in its assessment.

3. Technological Innovation

The speed at which technological changes have advanced since the first edition of this book affects how innovation drives greatness in internal audit departments. In chapter 8, I explore how new and emerging technologies such as robotics process automation and artificial intelligence will impact internal audit, and the imperative to embrace them.

4. Becoming a Trusted Advisor

Near the end of the first edition, I introduced what I believed were the essential skills that internal auditors needed to build and sustain trust with those they serve. In this edition, I update the definition and attributes of trusted advisors and incorporate these concepts throughout the book to align with those outlined in my second book, *Trusted Advisors: Key Attributes of Outstanding Internal Auditors*.

We are well positioned as a profession to tackle the challenges now before us. New regulations are imposed with increasing frequency, causing audit plans to undergo regular adjustments to encompass compliance activities. But not all changes are challenges; opportunities are emerging as well. Internal audit departments continue to receive added resources, reflecting stakeholders' expanding recognition of the value they provide. And internal audit is increasingly offered a more engaged role in addressing strategic business risks.

When Reading This Book

A few words before you begin reading this book. While I believe firmly that the content within this revised edition is valuable, useful, and helpful, it does not constitute professional guidance from The IIA, although you will find that these lessons clearly align with the current version of The IIA's International Professional Practices Framework (IPPF). I am not endeavoring to give you direction or guidance as you manage an internal audit department or undertake internal audit engagements. Every internal audit department is different, and every set of circumstances is different. This book is a composite view of organizations I have worked in, led, or dealt with throughout my career, and these are my personal views about how best to address some of the challenges we face in this critical profession.

In sharing my experiences and exploring how the lessons I learned apply to internal auditing today, I frequently draw on my time spent in government. Because government operations are generally more transparent than those in the corporate sector, I am able to talk more candidly about the details, referring to real people, dates, and locations. Having spent portions of my career in government, the corporate world, and the not-for-profit sector, I find the similarities far outweigh the differences. As you proceed through the book, I strongly suspect you will agree.

While I do not yet know if The IIA will be the last stop on my audit trail, it has certainly enabled me to pull together and draw upon all of the lessons learned during my other stops along the way. In the pages ahead, I share many of those lessons and the circumstances that enabled me to get the most from them. My hope is that, as you read this, you will find the journey worthwhile and be inspired to harness your personal passion for the profession.

CHAPTER 2
Attributes Outstanding Internal Auditors Share

If you are going to succeed in the internal audit profession, not only must you pursue excellence on an ongoing basis, you must also exemplify certain core attributes. Developing these attributes must be at the forefront of your mind, because it's a process that takes time—but one that is well worth the effort. Ultimately, pursuing excellence will position you to exceed even your own expectations.

Early in my career, I learned this lesson after returning to my old internal audit department, following a one-year assignment at a different agency. I was surprised to learn that I was not the only new employee joining the department that week. The chief audit executive (CAE) had also recruited a young, certified public accountant (CPA) to join the staff—quite a coup for the unit.

It didn't take me long to realize that my boss was quite smitten by my new colleague's CPA qualifications. A few months after we had both joined the staff, a huge opportunity arose to be part of an audit team on an important engagement in Southern California. During my first stint in internal audit, I would have certainly been on the engagement team; but this time, the CAE selected my colleague instead. When I expressed disappointment, my boss said he needed my colleague's CPA credential to enhance the team's stature.

I thought the CAE's reasoning was flawed—the audit in question was focused mainly on operational, not financial, risks—and while I was disappointed, I wasn't defeated. I held my head high and supported the engagement team in every way I could from almost 2,000 miles away at headquarters. I redoubled my efforts and took every opportunity to demonstrate the characteristics that had served me well thus far in my career—hard work, passion, courage, dependability, and so on. It didn't take the CAE long to realize I was the one he really needed on the team. Within a few months, my colleague and I switched roles, and I spent the next several months on the engagement.

While certifications, credentials, and qualifications are important for demonstrating proficiency, they're no substitute for the attributes truly successful internal auditors share. The lesson I learned was that committing yourself to absolute excellence is essential. Don't settle for simply being good enough; pursue greatness in everything you do.

Characteristics of Success for Internal Auditors

Over the course of my career, I've invested a lot of personal resources to researching what attributes make an internal auditor valuable to an organization. I've spoken on the topic, written blogs about it, and collaborated with colleagues on research reports. In the first edition of this book, I offered my list of the attributes of outstanding internal auditors. Three years after the first edition was published, I wrote my second book, *Trusted Advisors*. One of my objectives for writing it was selfish: I wanted to create a definitive list of what CAEs around the world believe it takes to be an outstanding internal auditor.

To find out what other leaders in the profession thought, colleagues and I surveyed members of The IIA's Audit Executive Center (AEC). I was delighted with the feedback from hundreds of global CAEs who took the time to respond. Their insights confirmed my previous conclusions and broadened my perspectives on the topic. According to survey respondents, nine attributes in three categories are critical to success as an internal auditor.

Personal Attributes
1. Ethical resilience
2. Results-focused
3. Intellectually curious
4. Open-mindedness

Relational Attributes

    5. Dynamic communicators

    6. Insightful relationships

    7. Inspirational leaders

Professional Attributes

    8. Critical thinkers

    9. Technical expertise

The following sections highlight these nine attributes to give you a glimpse into what it takes to become an outstanding internal auditor. I also strongly encourage you to read *Trusted Advisors* for more depth and detail.

1. Ethical Resilience

In my view, ethics play a significant role in internal audit performance. I believe ethical resilience is core to an internal auditor's long-term success, enhancing performance when it is abundant and limiting performance when it is lacking. Evidently, the CAE respondents to the survey agreed, with more than 50 percent placing it at the top of the list.

Outstanding internal auditors do more than just commit to ethics; they model ethical conduct in everything they do, even when it is not a popular stance. They may be challenged ethically, but they withstand those tests and come back stronger than ever.

No one is saying that exercising ethical behavior is easy; but maybe half the challenge is in agreeing exactly what constitutes ethical resilience. In the *Trusted Advisors* survey, we used the following terms to elaborate on what we meant by "ethical commitment":

- Integrity: Being known for strict adherence to high moral principles
- Courage: Being brave enough, even in the face of professional or personal danger, to do the right thing
- Honesty: Displaying unwavering commitment to dealing in truth

- Accountability: Taking responsibility for our actions and the resulting perceptions
- Trustworthiness: Building a history of ethical behavior that forms a foundation upon which people can place their trust

It's hard to argue with that list. For me, integrity and courage are equally important for any internal auditor. If you are not honest and fair with people, or not willing to go to bat for someone when honesty and fairness are at stake, you'll have a very difficult time getting others to listen to you or accept your work. Not everyone who has served in the internal audit profession has unfailingly behaved ethically (as I discuss later in the book), but in my experience, the vast majority of those in the profession are people of integrity.

For internal auditors, courage sometimes comes at significant cost. One of my personal heroes in our profession is Heidi Lloce Mendoza, currently undersecretary general for the United Nations Office of Internal Oversight Services. Prior to this role, she was commissioner and officer-in-charge of the Commission on Audit (COA) of the Philippines. While at the COA, Mendoza's audit team performed an audit that revealed broadscale bid rigging by a former mayor of Makati City. Mendoza underwent tremendous personal harassment, including physical threats, for her "badge of courage." You can read the full account in *Trusted Advisors*. I first met her in 2016 when she delivered opening remarks to The IIA's Global Council in New York. She spoke about the importance of ethics and the need for internal audit professionals to stand together to support each other when doing the right thing sparks adversity in response. Her messages that "internal auditors should never be alone when they have to stand and tell the truth" and that the profession must "work together to become the conscience of society" resonated with the audience. Most internal auditors may never have to face a situation similar to Mendoza's in which their ethical resilience incites threats of bodily harm. However, she provides us with a role model of holding strong to our beliefs even under extreme pressure.

The higher you go during a career in internal auditing, the more important it becomes to have a reputation for unflinching integrity and ethical behavior. The CAE has to be willing to go out on a limb as part of an organization's collective conscience. I recall instances in my own career when, as the chief auditor, I had to call out others because of their actions or behavior. For me, ethical resilience means being proactive and standing up for what you believe is right.

2. Results-Focused

During my years at the U.S. Postal Service (USPS), I had the opportunity to help build a large audit function from scratch. The new inspector general (IG)—a position that did not exist within the USPS until the late 1990s— asked me to help her put together an audit team capable of auditing one of the largest and most complex organizations in the world. We set about acquiring hundreds of auditors—many of them quite experienced in identifying fraud, waste, abuse, and mismanagement—a hiring spree that was completed in less than three years.

The influx of so much new talent in such a short time provided certain unique challenges. As with any new hire, it wasn't always evident how they would perform until they started doing the job. Those who were results-focused adapted quickly to the new organization and environment and made believers of certain skeptical managers within the USPS. Those who were content to just "get by" in their new audit roles did not adapt as quickly or easily; in some cases, they not only didn't contribute to our success, they actually undermined the progress we needed to make.

As I reflect back on this experience, I recognize that those professionals who were results-focused were obsessed with learning about their new organization, immersing themselves in the operational risks and challenges in the areas they audited. They were quick to establish credibility with management, and the audit reports and recommendations they delivered were embraced and implemented. Bottom line: They were trusted.

As internal auditors in the twenty-first century, we must possess a strong, unwavering focus on results and an unwillingness to let go of a project or problem until we know that the desired results have been fully achieved. Without it, there is no way to accomplish all we are responsible for achieving.

3. Intellectually Curious

Intellectually curious internal auditors are not satisfied until they know why something happened. They won't relent until they fully understand the root cause of the issue.

The critical elements of an audit's findings typically include criteria, condition, cause, and effect. Cause is the element that depends on asking "why" as often and in as many different ways as needed to get the answer. In fact, positive change cannot come about until the "why" question is answered. Without the answer, internal auditors can't confidently make recommendations to mitigate risk or prevent a recurrence of an issue. Trusted advisors stop asking "why" only when they have the final answer—the root cause.

Early in my career as an internal auditor for the Army, I was auditing an area dedicated to providing training with a budget assigned from higher up the command structure. The training area had run through its annual budget midway through the year, which meant that all remaining training exercises had to be cancelled. I was sent to investigate how the shortfall occurred and recommend ways to keep it from happening again.

After two weeks of interviews and reviews of the paper trail, I was still not sure I understood how they exhausted their budget. I remember sitting in my hotel room, replaying the interviews in my mind, when it suddenly became clear. Traditionally, the higher command gave the training area its budget with the understanding that the funds had to last the entire year. However, when the higher command itself got more money partway through the year, it would send some of the additional funds to the training function. It was a classic case of conditioning: Every year, the commander in the training unit was given an annual budget, then given a half-year's funding more. He assumed the scenario would repeat itself, so the unit spent the budget within the first six months. It was quite a shock to learn that no additional funding would arrive.

To test the hypothesis, I conducted the interviews again with the idea that the current year's shortfall was based on the expectation of additional funds, and both the commander and other staff confirmed the assumption. (By the way, this illustrates another facet of intellectual curiosity—a complete lack of fear even in an uncomfortable situation. It wasn't easy going back to the commander and interviewing him yet again, especially since I was zeroing in on something he had not previously admitted.) By applying intellectual curiosity (with its partners—skepticism and intuition), I was able to solve the mystery.

Outstanding internal auditors must be willing to ask a question again (and again and again), even if they've already asked it. In essence, they are not doing their job if they don't know why something happened.

4. Open-Mindedness

Today's environment requires internal auditors to maintain an open, creative approach to their work and accept the inevitability of change. Trusted advisors are receptive to new information, new ideas, new techniques, new tools, and new solutions, regardless of their source. I have already mentioned the need to audit at the speed of risk; we cannot afford to fear the risk of speed.

There are many benefits to being perceived as open-minded. It connotes flexibility, which positions internal auditors as being reasonable—an attribute much in favor among internal audit's stakeholders. Open-mindedness, flexibility, and reasonableness build on each other, culminating in credibility. And, after all, we will never be seen as incredible unless we are first credible.

In my career, I have seen internal auditors exhibit certain behaviors that tend to undermine any effort to be open-minded. Trusted advisors don't practice the following; make sure you don't either:

- Don't dwell on the past; instead, focus on the future.
- Don't shrink from getting to the bottom of issues.
- Don't take a myopic view of potential solutions.
- Don't neglect to seek input from those you are auditing.
- Don't view the world in black and white.

5. Dynamic Communicators

I was not surprised to see that CAEs identified being a dynamic communicator as one of the attributes of outstanding internal auditors, in response to the *Trusted Advisors* survey. After all, an entire chapter of this book is dedicated to the importance of communication. Consequently, I will keep my comments brief here and expand on lessons related to communication at the appropriate time.

Back in the era when internal auditors were known as "bean counters," communication was not such a pressing issue. That is not the case today. When operational auditing arose late in the twentieth century, it wasn't enough to simply communicate numbers. We had to become articulate in describing enterprise risks and controls. This posed challenges for some internal auditors, while offering those with extraordinary communication skills the opportunity to rise to the role of "crown jewel" in their internal audit departments. Today, communication skills are expected, even demanded, by most CAEs.

What makes a particular type or style of communication "effective"? According to IIA Standard 2420: Quality of Communications, communication should be accurate, objective, clear, concise, constructive, complete, and timely. I might add a couple of additional adjectives—continuous and conversational. Good communication takes into account the audience's priorities and expectations; it uses effective questioning; it leverages body language and eye contact; it starts with the "headline" and follows with the details; and, if at all possible and appropriate, it focuses on the positive.

6. Insightful Relationships

Those surveyed for *Trusted Advisors* were often adamant about the importance of relationships in building and sustaining trust. I observed the same phenomenon in writing the first edition of this book, resulting in my devoting a full chapter to lessons related to building and sustaining effective relationships. That chapter is updated for this edition.

Fostering strong relationships is hardly a skill that applies solely to internal auditors. Most of us prefer to interact with or do business with people and companies we know. We trust them because, based on our experience with them, we feel sure they will do a good job for us and treat us courteously and fairly. We even forgive their mistakes; we believe they are doing the best they can and we expect that they will fix any issues. The relationship we have built with them over time results in our trust and our loyalty. Well-developed relationships are perhaps especially helpful for internal auditors because they can help to overcome the negative perceptions and apprehension that sometimes accompany "audit time," making people feel more comfortable about discussing challenges and concerns. When we perform our jobs well, we strengthen our relationships with our stakeholders. In turn, they will spread the word about the favorable experience they had in dealing with the internal audit team, which makes our jobs easier in the future.

I firmly believe that honesty, empathy, and sincerity are key to building relationships, which, in turn, generate trust. Those who place a priority on building and sustaining strong relationships, and are willing to put effort into that activity, are likely to achieve their own goals and inspire others to do the same.

7. Inspirational Leaders

When I became a CAE, I had the good fortune to work for General Colin Powell, who was extremely supportive of me and my internal audit team. As a function of his genuine interest in my career, he inspired me to pursue a strategic studies program at the U.S. Army War College—a career changer for me.

My first boss at the Pentagon, Ernie Gregory, was an incredible orator. Watching and listening to him inspired me to enhance my own leadership and speaking skills, pursuits that proved highly beneficial as I guided the Army's internal review community through the most tumultuous period in its history.

Bill Bishop, The IIA's CEO from 1992 to 2004, inspired me to join him in a leadership role at IIA headquarters. This was a complete departure from the plans I had already made for my post-government career.

Each of these leaders had a profound influence on me and on the thousands of other men and women around the world who were fortunate enough to interact with them. Because I so firmly believe that organizations and professions need leaders who inspire others to achieve greatness, I have plumbed my research and experience to identify behaviors that such leaders exhibit.

In *Trusted Advisors*, I share several behaviors that I believe to be especially pertinent for leaders who are also internal auditors. They:

- **Share their experience.** They save others from experiencing some of the same challenges they have faced by sharing what they've learned, how they learned it, and why it matters.
- **Let others lead.** They provide help when needed, but they also focus on creating opportunities for others to experience leadership.
- **Coach and train their people to greatness.** They look for talent, provide opportunities for them to expand their skills, and then celebrate their success. By doing so, they contribute to the continued strength, credibility, and relevance of the profession.
- **Build teams and promote teamwork.** Inspirational leaders make connections across geographic and organizational boundaries and then leverage those connections to accomplish meaningful objectives.
- **Employ purposeful emotion.** They experience honest emotions and express those feelings sincerely and impactfully at appropriate times.
- **Lead through culture.** Inspirational leaders build a values-based culture that embraces transparency and recognizes accomplishments. We will explore culture in greater detail later in the book.
- **Face challenges.** They know that challenges are best dealt with openly and honestly, so they consistently keep their employees informed, whether the news is good or bad. When the news is bad, they do not waste time complaining; instead, they focus on what can be done to improve the situation and build a plan to implement the solution.

- **Earn and extend trust.** It is no surprise that this behavior would be exercised by trusted advisors, who not only are trusted but also trust others. They understand that when employees feel trusted, they will be inspired to do their best work.

8. Critical Thinkers

As an audit executive, nothing frustrated me more than watching internal auditors or audit teams generate vast amounts of data and audit evidence without being able to identify and connect the critical issues hidden in the material. They were not bad auditors; they developed excellent risk-based audit plans and gathered information thoroughly and effectively. They simply failed to use critical thinking skills to convert raw information to a well-reasoned, nuanced understanding of the situation and subsequently make appropriate recommendations.

Patty Miller, retired partner at Deloitte & Touche LLP and now owner of PKMiller Risk Consulting, LLC, contributed to the development of the joint Deloitte/IIA course on critical thinking for internal auditors. She defines critical thinking as "using reasoning and logic, not emotion, to evaluate information and consider alternatives." She further points out that this must be done with objectivity and an open mind to ensure a reasonable conclusion.

In any profession, thinking critically requires conscious thought and discipline. For most of us, it requires practice and an ability to avoid bias and familiarity. Miller notes, "Good internal auditors always realize there could be an issue, there could be a problem. We can't afford to rely solely on prior experience and disregard or dismiss signs and symptoms of a problem."

We have discussed the benefits of building strong relationships. However, internal auditors cannot allow such relationships to engender a preconceived notion about an upcoming audit's outcome or be less than rigorous in finding or reporting discrediting information about an organization, department, or individual. Nothing must interfere with our ability to think critically about what we see.

There are many challenges that can block critical thinking, some of which may be out of our control. However, we can, and should, focus on those things we can control. We can't let such hindrances as intellectual arrogance ("I already know the answer") or intellectual laziness ("Good enough is good enough") get in the way of our efforts to think carefully, objectively, and critically.

9. Technical Expertise

Without a doubt, outstanding internal auditors who possess technical expertise are a breed apart from their peers. After all, good relationships and effective communication are not particularly useful if we don't know what we are talking about. Business acumen, industry expertise, and technological insight are distinct skillsets, but they intertwine to create technical expertise.

When I was at the USPS, I had the extraordinary opportunity to hire professionals with technical expertise to build the audit arm of the new IG function. We recruited hundreds of auditors from government and corporate backgrounds, which enabled me to observe—almost in a laboratory setting—a wide spectrum of skills and characteristics. It didn't take long to identify the attributes that distinguished the most successful new recruits. They were the ones with knowledge of the business, industry expertise, and technology skills. Some possessed these skills from the start; others were sharp enough to know they needed to acquire them quickly. They earned the respect of their clients and their peers.

I hope you use the lessons discussed in the remainder of this book to build upon these nine attributes of outstanding internal auditors. While both the lessons and the attributes will serve you well in many ways, they are likely to be especially helpful in dealing with one of the most constant facets of stakeholder expectations—their predilection for changing course.

CHAPTER 3
Stakeholder Expectations Can Change Swiftly

Early in my career, I took for granted that internal auditing existed simply because it was necessary. Very rarely did anyone use terms like *customers* or *stakeholders;* I don't remember ever hearing those terms during my first decade in the business. I knew that U.S. Army regulations at the time required that every activity have an internal review (internal audit) function, so I assumed we were there because we had to be. Resources were plentiful and no one was really scrutinizing the value we delivered, which isn't surprising. People generally don't begin to question the value of something until it no longer meets their needs or becomes unaffordable.

By the end of the 1980s, all of that changed swiftly for those of us in the military. The Berlin Wall came down, the Cold War ended, and the U.S. Department of Defense—for the first time in more than five decades—faced the prospect of significantly downsizing as other government programs began clamoring for a piece of what was called the *peace dividend.*[1]

Military budgets started shrinking dramatically. Leaders in the Army and throughout the Defense Department began to scrutinize the value they were receiving for the money they were spending on internal auditing. Resources in my area, the Army's internal audit organization, were in free fall. In just three years, more than 400 staff positions were eliminated from various internal audit departments around the world. The speed at which change was occurring and risk was accruing was palpable.

When I moved to the Pentagon as the Army's director of Internal Review (internal audit) in the fall of 1993, one of my first conversations was with the principal deputy assistant secretary of the Army. He sat down with me that first week on the job to remind me of the dramatic reductions underway in internal audit.

"As you know, Richard, the Army's internal audit resources are being decimated," he said. (By that time, two years after the initial staff reductions, 300 more positions had been eliminated, slashing internal audit's worldwide head count from 2,100 to 1,400.) "I need you to figure out how to put a stop to it!"

I responded by saying, "I agree with you. It's a big concern. But before I can help figure out *how to stop it*, I have to understand *why it's happening.*" The Army overall wasn't shrinking that fast. Yet, in some internal audit offices, resources were down 75 percent in less than four years.

So, I set off on a six-week tour of internal audit operations, with stops at about 24 offices, including sites in Japan, Hawaii, and all over the United States. At each location, I sat down with the commander, the chief of staff, or the controller; by regulation, internal audit had to report to the commander or chief of staff. In most cases, those I interviewed told me, "I like the internal audit team. They are nice guys and they do good work."

"But why did you downsize them?" I asked. "Why did you cut internal audit by 75 percent last year, when you had only about a 10 percent cut in your overall budget?"

Their responses were eye-opening. "You know, those guys come in and tell me what I already know," some of them said. Others responded, "They tell me things are broken, but I already know they are broken. *I need somebody who can tell me how to fix them.*" Conversely, more than once I heard, "Sometimes I only need to know 'what time it is,' but the internal audit guys insist on giving me voluminous reports that tell me 'how to build the watch.'"

In preparing for this book, I reviewed some of my notes from that period and concluded that the root cause of the sharp reductions in internal audit was the speed of change that had engulfed the Army. The swift change manifested itself in three ways:

1. The Army was rapidly downsizing and cutting back drastically on spending throughout its operations.
2. Our products and services were not what stakeholders needed and expected.
3. Our performance wasn't up to stakeholder expectations.

Downsizing

There was really nothing we could do about the Army's downsizing. That was a macro issue of strategic significance far bigger than what any of us in internal audit could hope to influence. It was the current reality and the impetus for the change in our stakeholders' expectations. It would be natural to expect that, if the organization we served was getting smaller, we would need to absorb our share of budget reductions.

Products and Services

There were clearly some things we could do about the products and services we offered our stakeholders. Stakeholders were telling us that the full-scope audits we historically had performed—evaluating an entire department or system or activity—were not really what they wanted. They considered them laborious, cumbersome, and time-consuming.

I also traced some of our difficulties to rigid planning cycles and inflexible policies that dictated what had to be documented in our reports and workpapers and when. I discovered that stakeholders often considered our audit reports to be too focused on compliance issues and not focused enough on ways to help them improve the efficiency and effectiveness of their operations.

Finally, I noted that a lot of our audits were irrelevant. It's not that they lacked all merit, but they weren't focusing on the rapidly emerging risks that were suddenly engulfing the Army—they didn't relate to the key issues being discussed and debated throughout the organization. Of course, few internal auditors anywhere were talking a lot about risk-based auditing in 1993, and the Army was no different. In military terms, we in internal audit hadn't learned how to *pick our battles*, so we were missing out on some of our biggest opportunities to add value to our organization.

Weak Performance

As I looked back at my notes, I realized our performance was considered weak because our stakeholders viewed us as not being focused on the real risks to our organization. Our commanders had a mission: To ensure our armed forces were trained, equipped, and ready for deployment when needed for our national defense. Shrinking resources created new risks toward achieving our organizations' missions. But internal audit didn't necessarily view the risks to commands' missions as the areas where we needed to concentrate in our audit programs. We had well-established audit cycles that had been the traditional focus of coverage for years. Change wasn't one of our strengths.

I also heard complaints that we were not very *customer-oriented*. Excessive overhead had become a problem and the quality of our work had suffered. I noted that some internal audit offices had been downsized in such a way that they were top-heavy with management and administration. I remember a department that at one time had five staff members—a CAE, a secretary, and three audit staff. Two positions were eliminated—a 40 percent reduction—but the cuts had been allowed to occur through attrition, so when two of the three audit staffers departed, the department was left with a CAE, a secretary, and an internal auditor. In effect, the department had absorbed a 66 percent reduction in internal audit capability, rather than 40 percent.

One commander noted that he had spent almost $1 million on the department the previous year, yet had received only five reports. Although the number of reports really shouldn't be used to determine the value received, clearly in his mind there was a correlation.

"Look, they are good guys and ladies," more than one commander said of their internal audit staff during my six-week tour. "I really appreciate what they do, and they are professionals. But at the end of the day, if I've got to take a cut in spending, and I have to choose between [keeping] the internal audit function and support for family housing for soldiers, I'm going to choose the family housing, and we are going to cut down on our audit capability."

Such comments were particularly unfortunate because I considered that a false dilemma. If we had truly been effective as internal auditors, we would have addressed the problem and identified sufficient savings, allowing a commander to fund both the internal audit office and the family housing budgets.

Somehow, I had to convince these commanders that we were all in this together and needed to work as a team. I formed a steering group comprising the chiefs of internal audit from all the major Army commands. The resulting strategic plan for the Army's internal audit organization included five key steps:

1. Defining our stakeholders and their needs
2. Defining our mission
3. Articulating assumptions and our values
4. Forging an internal audit vision, correlating goals, and supporting actions
5. Assessing our progress

Our strategy worked. Army-wide, internal audit's return on investment (the cost of operations versus identified, agreed-to savings) jumped from 3-to-1 in 1992 to an astounding 24-to-1 by 1996. The number of audit engagements completed worldwide doubled over the same period, from about 2,200 in 1993 to more than 4,400 in 1996. Although downsizing continued throughout the Army, internal audit no longer shrank at a disproportionate rate. That was the first time I realized that internal auditors have stakeholders, and disenchanted stakeholders are hazardous to an internal audit operation's health. In the years since then, I have seen similar problems crop up in the corporate sector; while not as widespread as in the military, in some instances, the stakeholders' dissatisfaction with a corporate internal audit function led to the operation's complete outsourcing—or, worse yet, its abolishment.

Who Are Our Stakeholders?

A stakeholder is any party with a direct or indirect interest in an organization's activities and outcomes. Internal auditors typically have several groups of stakeholders within a company or an organization, and all of their needs should be considered.

1. Primary Stakeholders

You cannot effectively serve your stakeholders if you do not know who they are. So, the first step in serving them is to identify them. I generally consider primary stakeholders to include:

- The organization's audit committee and board (and elected officials, in the case of government agencies)
- The CEO or overall head of the enterprise (hopefully the one to whom internal audit reports administratively)
- The chief financial officer (CFO) (or other individual to whom the CAE reports administratively)
- The other chief officers of the enterprise (in some cases)

When we speak about internal audit stakeholders in the twenty-first century, it's often in terms of the various groups with an interest in the operation. The most important group for an internal audit department in the corporate setting is the board of directors. The board has critical oversight responsibilities, and its members are the pinnacle of governance within the corporation. Senior executives are also critical stakeholders for internal audit. The CAE typically reports administratively to the CEO or CFO of an organization and functionally to the audit committee or the board of directors. As I discovered when leading the Army's internal audit organization, it is vital for the CAE to maintain a continuous dialogue with stakeholders to ensure that expectations are understood and internal audit is delivering on those expectations.

In 2016, the Internal Audit Foundation undertook the most comprehensive assessment of internal audit stakeholder expectations worldwide. The Foundation documented the results of its research in *Voice of the Customer: Stakeholders' Messages for Internal Audit*.[2]

More than 1,100 internal audit stakeholders (board members and C-suite members) were surveyed as part of the Common Body of Knowledge (CBOK) study, and more than 100 were interviewed. The stakeholders' key messages to internal auditors were:[3]

- **Internal auditors should know their organization's mission, strategy, objectives, and risks.** The research was clear that the effectiveness of internal audit continually comes back around to this imperative.
- **Assurance work is highly valued.** While other tasks and projects performed by internal auditors may be value adding, they should not be done at the expense of assurance work.
- **Conformance with The IIA's *International Standards for the Professional Practice of Internal Auditing* is expected.** Stakeholders expect a level of professionalism from internal auditors, and professionals follow standards.
- **Assurance work is most valuable when it is aligned with the strategic risks of the organization.** Internal auditors are expected to use the organization's strategy to drive risk assessment and the selection of assurance work.
- **Advisory work is highly desired, with areas related to risk requested most frequently.** Stakeholders made it clear that internal audit should be risk-centric in all of its work—whether assurance or advisory.
- **Internal audit should coordinate with functions in the second line of defense.** Stakeholders expect internal audit to rely on the assurance work of these functions once they have been proven to be objective and reliable.

These are key takeaways internal auditors should bear in mind when providing assurance to primary stakeholders.

2. Secondary Stakeholders

Internal audit's secondary stakeholders include business-unit executives and other leaders not identified as primary stakeholders. These executives are the ones who typically head up the business units and operations on which our audits are focused. They are what we used to call *auditees*; in the twenty-first century, we need to think of them as *clients*. We should try to focus our work in such a way that it not only addresses the needs of our primary stakeholders but also adds value for these business-unit executives. Much like the Army commanders I dealt with in the early 1990s, these executives often already know they have problems—they are looking for solutions. They need our help designing and implementing effective internal controls to mitigate the most critical risks.

They also view us as business partners. They would like us to focus more on areas they consider to be high risk or of particular significance to them. They, too, are looking for insight, and increasingly they consider us a source of talent for their business units.

3. Tertiary Stakeholders

Internal audit's other stakeholders may include:

- Employees (and, in some cases, retirees) of the enterprise
- Investment analysts and others with an interest in the performance of the enterprise and the effectiveness of risk management and internal controls
- Shareholders
- External auditors and regulators
- The general public (including news media) for government auditors

Regulators are an increasingly important stakeholder group. They are very interested in making sure internal auditors are independent and can provide assurance on risks and controls. They are seeking assurance that the organization is in compliance with government laws, regulations, and policies and is not likely to fall victim to a significant scandal or calamity.

Internal audit's stakeholders and their expectations can vary dramatically from one organization to the next. Every CAE must continuously review current and potential stakeholder groups and reassess their needs and expectations. I discovered with Army internal audit stakeholders that it is important to recognize that stakeholders' needs and expectations are not static—they can change dramatically in a short period of time. In the mid-2000s, for example, corporate internal audit stakeholders were mainly seeking assurance on the adequacy of internal controls over financial reporting because of the newly enacted U.S. Sarbanes-Oxley Act of 2002. By the end of the decade, however, expectations had shifted within many companies, and their internal auditors were looked to for assurance on the adequacy of the operation's risk management and internal controls, and insight into cost-reduction and cost-containment opportunities. Today, as the global economy has improved, internal audit's stakeholders are once again seeking risk-centric assurance from risks such as cybersecurity, data privacy and protection, and other operational and compliance risks.

As swiftly as stakeholder expectations can change based on the risks to the organization, there are also telltale signs that internal auditors may not be getting the full picture when it comes to reconciling expectations among different stakeholders. Over the course of my career, I have learned that there are some things management may not be willing to share and there are some things the audit committee may not wish to share with you. Each group comes to that conclusion based on its own perspectives and expectations.

Five Things Management May Be Reluctant to Tell You

Ask management executives about fraud management or internal controls and they will not mince words in letting internal audit know what's on their minds. But on other topics, they may be less forthcoming for any number of reasons, from a lack of familiarity to an attempt to be tactful. Whatever the reason, any hindrances to open and honest communication with management are barriers that we need to break down if we are to do our jobs well. Here are a few things they may be thinking—and keeping to themselves.

1. "We don't believe you fully understand the business."

If you have ever made a suggestion that is met with a roll of the eyes or a heartfelt sigh, the reason could be management's lack of confidence in your knowledge of the business. Not all responses are so blatant, however. They may discount your recommendations or avoid asking you for help. Even worse, they may disagree with your draft audit report—a disagreement for which you are completely unprepared because they have not challenged your findings or suggestions to date. As with many problems, the best solution is communication. In this case, it could be one-on-one (a candid conversation with the manager) or communal (group meetings with the business unit's staff and the internal audit department to ensure both parties are up to speed on the pertinent issues of the other).

2. "You provide us more value when you talk about the future than when you limit your view to the past."

Risk-based auditing should look to the future in keeping with management's focus on what's happening now and, more important, what's coming up. We cannot drive change if we're constantly looking behind us. Worse, we risk making ourselves irrelevant and out of touch.

3. "You are too often duplicating the work of others, and vice versa."

Duplication between internal audit and other monitoring and control activities (often referred to as the second line of defense) is frustrating and inefficient in the eyes of management. Worse yet, it can often create new risks— the potential for serious gaps in coverage. Internal audit departments that are perceived to be simply duplicating the work of others are unlikely to receive management's support or sufficient funding. Admittedly, the division of responsibilities between internal audit and other assurance providers can sometimes be unclear, so duplication is a constant risk. The Three Lines of Defense model can rectify this, but it is not clearly and consistently applied in many organizations.

4. "It would be nice if you occasionally point out things we do well."

When I was a CAE, I had my staff include a "management accomplishments" section at the beginning of every audit report. This enabled us to provide some balance to the report and support our claim to unbiased observation. This means auditors must discipline themselves to change their view and look for positive outcomes whenever possible—a good habit to develop.

5. "Sometimes, we agree just so you will go away."

This sentiment is hard to accept, but I am guessing that more of us than we know have been on the receiving end of it. Let's face it, not all of our recommendations are accepted with whole-hearted enthusiasm. Still, we should avoid the temptation to continue arguing the issue just to prove the point. Chances are you may win a "concession," but at what cost? You have not changed management's mind and you have certainly not improved their perception of the internal audit function. If your recommendation receives a lukewarm response, it's time to ask more questions and listen carefully to the answers. You may learn something.

Five Things the Audit Committee May Be Reluctant to Tell You

Most CAEs work hard to develop open relationships with their audit committee members, and generally the effort pays off. However, regardless of how hard CAEs work at it, some audit committee members may not be comfortable telling us everything that's on their minds. Sometimes they simply may not know enough about internal audit to know what we are capable of; sometimes they are simply trying to spare our feelings. But often these are the things we need to hear most—the very things that can help us improve our internal audit departments.

Over the years, I have worked with quite a few audit committee members in an advisory capacity, and they have told me many things they are reluctant to say to their internal auditors. Here are five:

1. "Your information is not as valuable as the information external auditors provide us."

I realize this statement will be a major disappointment to many of you, especially as you mentally pore over the extraordinary value you and your team have contributed to your organization and the list of internal audit accomplishments that would rival the impact of even the most outstanding external auditors. Yet, look at the typical audit committee charter. The description of the audit committee's responsibility for the external auditor often dwarfs that for the internal auditor. I have seen many audit committee charters for large companies that included exhaustive discussion on the responsibility for the oversight of external auditors, but very limited reference to the oversight of internal audit.

I saw one sample audit committee charter that was based on a review of select Fortune 1,000 companies' audit committee charters. Its content was even more revealing, containing nine paragraphs on the external auditor; nine paragraphs on oversight of financial reporting processes, accounting policies, and internal control structure; and only five paragraphs on oversight of internal audit. Many audit committees are populated with retired partners of public accounting firms, and their emphasis is often on what they know—external audit. But internal audit should be every bit as important, so it's up to each of us to keep ourselves trained, expert, up to date, and ready to excel.

2. "You send us too much information."

Unfortunately, this one is not always a misconception. I have seen well-intentioned CAEs send as many as *40 internal audit reports a year* to their overwhelmed audit committee members. I've seen reports that numbered more than 200 pages and were distributed, unabridged, to their audit committee members. Is it any wonder that audit committees think we inundate them?

People drowning with "information overload" struggle to find the critical issues that merit their attention. Audit committees are no different. They may not want to admit they can't keep up, but the reality is that they are usually busy people with multiple responsibilities and limited time. We must exercise professionalism and courtesy by being as succinct as possible and making it easy for them to identify the issues on which their focus is needed.

3. "We wish you would 'connect the dots.'"

It's easy to miss the forest for the trees. Sometimes we are so busy communicating the details that we neglect to focus on answering the essential question, "So what?" Yes, culling through all the facts and making judgment calls on what needs to rise to the top are not always easy tasks, but internal auditors demonstrate their value when they do exactly that. They offer educated, reasoned assessments and evaluations, articulating why the information is important, why the committee needs to hear it, and what the consequences might be. They do the hard work of making a clear picture out of a mass of pixels.

4. "We want you to focus on more than just financial controls, but we are not sure you have the skills."

Most internal auditors pride themselves and their teams on being able to address the full portfolio of risks facing their organizations. We believe strongly in internal audit's capacity to maximize its value to the organization by focusing on key areas of risk and the adequacy of the company's risk management processes generally.

According to KPMG's 2017 Global Audit Committee Pulse Survey, most audit committee members agree. The survey results showed that the majority of audit committees are looking to internal audit to focus on the critical risks to the business, including key operational risks (e.g., cybersecurity and technology risks) and related controls—not just compliance and financial reporting risks. They also want the audit plan to be flexible and adjust to changing business and risk conditions. So far, so good; we agree. But, while that is good news, there is another statistic that should cause us some concern: 42 percent of the respondents indicated a need for the talent and expertise in the internal audit organization to be improved. Clearly, we have work to do to ensure that we maintain our skills and expertise at levels that shore up audit committee members' confidence in our ability to perform the work they seek from us.[4]

5. "Be more than just a mouthpiece for management; step up and speak up."

Audit committee members are an astute group of individuals. They can usually discern when we're being genuine and when we're just giving them the "party line." A united front with management might look good, but we need to remember that our primary strength is that we are organizationally independent.

Does that mean we should go out of our way to contradict management? By no means. But when we talk to the audit committee, some of us need to concentrate more on presenting the results of our audit work and less on reflecting management's point of view. Management is usually capable of speaking for itself. Our value resides in our transparency and candor.

Obviously, every audit committee member is different. Perhaps you are fortunate to have a committee that speaks openly and candidly and shares an overwhelmingly positive view of internal audit's contribution. For the rest of us, we need to make an effort to learn what's on their minds. The more we understand our audit committee members, the better equipped we are to do our jobs.

Signs That Stakeholder Support Is Waning

If your internal audit department is unfortunate enough to struggle with the issues discussed in the previous two sections—lack of transparency from both management and the audit committee—it's a safe bet that stakeholder support is declining as well. Here are some signs that might indicate a falling-away of stakeholder enthusiasm.

1. Lackluster response to the risk assessments.

If you're having trouble getting stakeholders to respond during the annual risk assessment, that's a problem. Virtually all executives and board members have things that keep them awake at night, so if they aren't sharing their concerns with you, it could mean they don't trust you to act on them or don't think your team has the ability to address them.

As an internal auditor, you go through this process at least annually (though I hope much more often). If your stakeholders don't appear interested in the risk assessment, offering you little or no food for thought, that's not a good sign. It may mean they view your risk assessment as irrelevant; perhaps they have gone through the process with you before but concluded that nothing had come of it.

2. The phone never rings.

Yes, this is a throwback to an earlier time (not that long ago) when we used phones a lot more than we do now. Email or instant messaging may be your main form of business communication these days. Regardless of method used, if no one is reaching out to internal audit to ask that you address a rapidly emerging risk or evaluate a developing situation, it's likely your stakeholders don't see you as responsive or a resource.

Delivering value is the key to long-term success for any internal audit operation. If top executives and business unit leaders don't think internal audit adds value to the organization, they won't seek you out when a problem arises.

3. Breakaway republics.

When business units start creating their own audit teams (or elements within a unit that duplicate the capabilities of internal audit), chances are you're not living up to their expectations. When different business groups within an organization come to the conclusion that internal audit isn't serving their needs, they may start to set up review functions of their own. They may not call them internal audit, but they do the same kind of work. That's a sign those stakeholders don't see the value of internal audit or don't think it can be trusted.

4. Reduced resources.

There are times when financial pressures mandate cutbacks throughout a company. When resources are reduced across an organization, it's only natural to expect reductions in internal audit's resources, too. But if your unit's budget is slashed disproportionately compared with other departments, that's a clear indicator that your stakeholders don't see enough value in your work. Organizations invest in what they value, and if their investment in internal audit is shrinking when overall budgets are stable or expanding, it's a sign that an expectations gap may have developed.

5. The external quality assessment is not your idea.

IIA Standard 1312: External Assessments states: External assessments must be conducted at least once every five years by a qualified, independent assessor or assessment team from outside the organization. The chief audit executive must discuss with the board:

- The form and frequency of external assessment.
- The qualifications and independence of the external assessor or assessment team, including any potential conflict of interest.

The internal audit department should always be the one proactively pushing for that assessment; if your stakeholders independently initiate a quality assessment, then it is likely they have concerns about your department and are looking for validation. If you haven't had an external quality assessment for a few years and you get a call from the CEO, the CFO, or even the audit committee, and they say, "We'd like you to get a quality assessment"—or, worse yet, they take the lead in identifying who is going to come and do the assessment—that may be the clearest sign possible that something is seriously wrong between your unit and its stakeholders.

Enhancing Stakeholder Awareness Sometimes Takes Marketing

Why do people buy a certain product? First, they know about it. They know what it's made of, how to use it, and what it will accomplish. They have realistic expectations of what will happen once they buy and use the product. Second, they have been the recipient of marketing messages about it. I'm sure all of us have heard the old saying that marketing doesn't sell the steak, it sells the sizzle. That's a fairly "marketing-centric" way of explaining that, while education describes the features of the product, marketing elaborates on the benefits.

When faced with enhancing stakeholder awareness of the internal audit function, we can make effective use of both approaches. For instance, CAEs can educate management and the audit committee on what internal audit really does or can do—setting realistic expectations up front and addressing any confusion. Marketing can then pave the way to clarifying the important role internal auditors play within the organization—the value they provide.

Not long ago, I heard a colleague express his frustration when called on to explain internal auditing to non-auditors. "When I have to 'sell' people on the internal audit function," he said, "it feels too much like what a used-car salesman does. It just doesn't feel professional to me."

While his comments didn't come as a surprise, they still concerned me. "Promoting" our profession doesn't come naturally to many of us. When I first became a CAE, I worked with my leadership team to develop new strategies and an expanded portfolio of internal audit services for our clients. I soon discovered, however, that simply having these new services wasn't enough. For our transition to a new type of internal audit function to be successful, we needed our clients to understand the strategy and appreciate the benefits of the new "menu" of services.

To get there, we developed a deliberate strategy for improving awareness of our capabilities and the value we would deliver. In a word, we needed marketing. There was no other way to change our clients' expectations so they would know what to expect and feel comfortable calling us in.

No one on the project team felt they had the appropriate skills to take on the marketing role. So, we called in the entire audit team, with similar results. After convincing the team of the criticality of marketing to our success, everyone knuckled down and began to hone their skills, becoming increasingly comfortable with the concept of marketing our services.

Despite the enthusiasm, rigor needed to be applied. To deliver our messages effectively, we need to equip our team with tools, techniques, and consistent information. If you are going through a similar process at your organization, here are some tactics we used that I believe you'll find useful, regardless of what messages you are trying to promote.

Hold one-on-one conversations with key stakeholders.

Some people feel comfortable meeting with key stakeholders for the specific purpose of enhancing their understanding of the internal audit function. Others prefer a less-direct approach. In those cases, you can include marketing activities in other types of meetings. For example, during an enterprise-wide risk assessment, ask the client about his perceptions of the internal audit function. The answers will not only provide useful information, they may also spark a constructive conversation.

Develop a professional presentation.

Formal presentations and marketing collateral can be useful in kickoff meetings, new-employee orientation, lunch-and-learns, and various other ways. The materials reinforce the information you share and help people remember the key points long after the presentation is over. Creating an up-to-date, professional-looking presentation that explains what internal audit does, why it is important, and what management's responsibilities are should be a high priority. But the presentation is not the end game. Effective marketing is a two-way street, so the presenter needs to watch for opportunities to elicit comment and discussion from the audience.

Build marketing messages into periodic reports on internal audit's performance.

Another type of indirect marketing is providing information. I believe every internal audit department should issue periodic reports about accomplishments, strategies, clarifications, and announcements. While these reports may not be directly promotional, they do reinforce useful (and favorable) messages.

Develop and distribute an internal audit brochure.

A digital (or paper) brochure or flier can be a simple first step for raising awareness about internal auditing, but they should never be considered the entire marketing campaign. They can be extremely effective in reaching individuals who learn best through the written word, but those who prefer to hear information or who respond well to graphic representations may be left out in the cold. Nor should brochures be sent out for no particular purpose or without supporting material; an effective use of brochures is to include them in announcements about upcoming audits. Clients are likely to be "all ears" then.

Create an intranet site for access by your company's executives and employees.

Intranet sites can communicate much more than what might be included in traditional marketing collateral. They can constitute a convenient, central "gathering place" for important messages about internal audit, but they are only as effective as the information they contain. If the content is outdated, people will stay away in droves. A regular schedule of updating the site and issuing consistent messages to clients to call their attention to the site are critical to the site's success.

I mentioned earlier in this chapter that audit committees are looking to internal audit to focus on the critical risks to the business and maintain enough flexibility in our audit plans that we can adjust as business and risk conditions change. They clearly understand the need for a highly and diversely skilled audit function. But not all stakeholders are as well informed as the audit committee members, and, regrettably, ignorance or misunderstanding of our role could have wide-ranging implications for our enterprises. We all need to add a few marketing skills to our portfolios—even a little can go a long way toward ensuring stakeholder buy-in and support.

Stakeholder Expectations Lifecycle

We've talked a lot in this chapter about what stakeholders may expect and how those expectations may stack up against what internal audit can and should do. For the most part, I believe expectations and outcomes match up fairly closely, but in some cases, a gap may exist between what stakeholders want and what we can provide. If you sense an expectations gap exists, what can you do to close it? I think the best way to start is to acknowledge the elephant in the room and simply say, "I understand that we may not be meeting your needs and expectations, and we are recommitting ourselves to doing a better job."

The rehabilitation process can be difficult, but recognizing that there is a problem is half the battle. This entire process constitutes a *lifecycle* for aligning, maintaining, and meeting expectations. This four-phase "stakeholder expectation lifecycle" forms a necessary part of the internal audit department's ongoing operations.

1. Understanding the Current Expectations of Key Stakeholders

Most CAEs are keenly aware of the benefits of identifying the specific expectations of their key stakeholders and articulating them in a short list of specific actions that stakeholders believe add value to the organization. Having a clear understanding of what is *on their mind* is critical. To accomplish this, it's imperative for CAEs to invest the necessary time and resources in understanding the key challenges, issues, and opportunities that are relevant to these stakeholders.

Once the list is created, it needs to be validated with the key stakeholders to ensure their support. It should also be communicated to other stakeholders and to internal audit personnel. Finally, the CAE should ensure that the internal audit charter reflects the specific expectations of the key stakeholders.

2. Building and Maintaining the Capabilities to Deliver on the Expectations

Knowing stakeholders' expectations is not enough to guarantee the long-term success of the internal audit function; internal auditors must deliver on them as well. To do so, CAEs need to perform a robust gap assessment that matches internal audit's current capabilities and skills to each expectation. CAEs should then draft or update a strategic plan that builds or enhances internal audit's capabilities as needed to fill the gaps. CAEs also can use expectations as filters to identify the best practices for meeting stakeholders' needs.

3. Creating a Process to Measure and Report on the Achievement of Specific Expectations

A stakeholder management strategy can be a powerful way to assimilate the many insights gained by members of the internal audit team from the multitude of planned and unplanned interactions with key stakeholders. This big-picture approach should provide a collective, integrated view of all stakeholders. With such a strategy, tactics for interacting with each stakeholder can be developed.

Three main activities CAEs can undertake to measure the efficiency and effectiveness of internal audit's efforts to meet stakeholder expectations include: 1) developing appropriate objectives, 2) creating appropriate measures to gauge performance, and 3) developing and deploying reporting mechanisms such as a balanced scorecard. CAEs should view this as their opportunity to demonstrate specifically and tangibly how they performed relative to their stakeholder expectations and added-value goals.

4. Establishing Processes to Reassess Stakeholder Expectations Periodically

Finally, CAEs need to establish a time frame and a process for reassessing stakeholders' expectations at least annually. CAEs should identify events, such as the addition of new audit committee members, that will trigger such reassessments. Because communication is key to understanding stakeholder expectations and raising those expectations to the next level, it is important for CAEs to communicate with stakeholders as opportunities and issues arise and to deliver what they said they were going to deliver.

One of the most pivotal aspects of a stakeholder management strategy is setting up the right communication protocol for each target audience. Formal protocols for communication encourage the exchange of information with stakeholders and help CAEs during audit planning and execution.

Ensuring Continued Alignment

The "speed of risk" is a huge disruptor when it comes to internal audit stakeholder expectations. CAEs must recognize how swiftly the alignment with stakeholder expectations can become obsolete. Although stakeholder expectations do not typically change dramatically from year to year, when they do change, the shift can often take internal auditors by surprise.

CAEs should watch for events that may trigger a change in stakeholder expectations. For example, a new audit committee chair, CEO, or even CFO can signal a shift in stakeholder expectations as new people often bring new views with them. Also, outside influences such as new compliance requirements or the current renewed focus on risk management may cause many stakeholders to shift expectations regarding internal audit's involvement and coverage. Finally, internal events, including changes in business strategy and emerging risks that follow, may alter stakeholder expectations pertaining to the focus of internal audit's work.

The internal audit departments that have the most noticeable stature with executive management are those whose CAEs and staff understand their stakeholders and never forget that stakeholder expectations are a moving target. The audit departments that were successful at one time but later failed often didn't make the adjustment when their stakeholders' expectations changed.

If we continuously realign the delivery of our services to meet the evolving expectations of our stakeholders, then we are more likely to deliver the value they are seeking.

CHAPTER 4
Stakeholders Have the Last Word on Value

I once had the opportunity to lead an external quality assessment for the internal audit department of a large U.S. health-care provider. As I interviewed the company's key executives and board members, one word came up over and over: *Value*.

The CEO noted that internal audit provided *extraordinary value* for the company as a "trusted source of assurance on compliance, risk management, and internal controls." The CFO said internal audit provided *value* by ensuring the effectiveness of the business's financial controls. Other executives saw the *value* in the internal audit department's annual enterprise risk assessment, which many said they used as a road map for managing risks within the company. And, according to the chairman of the company's audit committee, board members saw *value* in internal audit because it enabled them to "sleep better" knowing that such "a strong and effective oversight function was keeping a watchful eye on risks, controls, and compliance in the company."

From my experience in leading external quality assessments, use of the word *value* by internal audit stakeholders is common. What made the interviews with the health-care executives noteworthy was the extraordinary degree to which the stakeholders appreciated the value they received from the company's internal audits. As I discovered during the course of the assessment, this was no accident. Delivering value to stakeholders was part of that internal audit department's culture, from the CAE down to the least-senior member of the 100-person staff.

That experience also reinforced a lesson I learned early in my career—delivering value is a continuous imperative for internal auditors.

The Essence of Value for Internal Auditing

I sometimes think *value* is the least appreciated word in The IIA's definition of internal auditing. If an internal audit department does not add value to the organization it serves, then it really isn't fulfilling its reason for being. Every element of an organization should be adding value to the operation, and internal audit is no different. When internal audit fails to generate value for the organization, then it is simply another cost center—a drain on company resources.

The question then is, "Where is the value?" The answer, as I have preached for many years, is, "In the eye of the beholder." We can't objectively define our value to others, though I've seen it tried many times. Internal auditors often say, "We measure it by the number of reports we issue. We measure it by the number of individuals in our department who have their certification. We measure it by the number of recommendations in our reports." But our stakeholders aren't likely to cite those measurements in assessing our value. And, ultimately, it is internal audit's stakeholders who have the last word on the value provided.

"We don't think you are of any value to us because you have yet to help us fix a problem we're having," management might say. "Besides, we don't get any value from internal audit because you cost us more money than you save us." There are increasing grumbles among stakeholders who perceive that internal audit is simply duplicating the roles played by second-line-of-defense functions (i.e., corporate compliance or risk management). In such cases, stakeholders fail to see the incremental value internal audit delivers beyond the company's monitoring and oversight functions.

Just as consumers decide whether there is value in the products they purchase, it is for others to decide whether we are valuable. If they say we aren't, the problem may be one of quantity (we simply aren't adding enough value to the operation) or perception (we haven't helped our stakeholders to appreciate the value we add). Either way, we must address the problem.

The Value Proposition

Some time ago, The IIA formed a task force to explore stakeholders' expectations and determine what internal auditors should deliver in the way of value. The task force submitted its report and recommendations to The IIA's Board of Directors. The "value proposition" illustration below sums up its work.

INTERNAL AUDITING = ASSURANCE, INSIGHT, AND OBJECTIVITY[1]

The task force's value proposition for internal audit rested on three core concepts: assurance, insight, and objectivity. In 2015, The IIA completed a refresh of the International Professional Practices Framework (IPPF). One of the most significant changes to the IPPF was the adoption of a set of Core Principles for the Professional Practice of Internal Auditing. Among the Core Principles is the requirement that internal audit be "insightful, proactive, and future-focused." As a result, I would now add *foresight* to *insight* in defining internal audit's value proposition. Internal auditors ignore these components of the value proposition—**INTERNAL AUDITING = ASSURANCE, INSIGHT AND FORESIGHT, AND OBJECTIVITY**—at their own risk.

As a CAE in one of the Army's largest commands, I learned the lesson of having insight *and* foresight as part of the value proposition. It came to me after I had completed a quality assessment of one of the command's biggest internal audit offices.

As with all our quality assurance reviews, I undertook a comprehensive assessment of the department, evaluated its conformance with applicable standards, and had extensive discussions with the local CAE. I came away thinking this might be one of the best internal audit departments I had ever seen. It was led by a bright CAE who appeared to have a firm grasp on the department's role. The team's work was impeccable and in accordance with the Yellow Book (Government Accountability Office Government Audit Standards). I gave them high marks.

Imagine my surprise less than two years later when I learned that very same internal audit department had been abolished and the CAE reassigned to another area.

I couldn't believe it. I even suspected the department might have fallen victim to a conspiracy of some sort—its work had been that good. But as I asked around to find out what had happened, I learned that the commander, the chief of staff, and the controller had concluded they weren't getting any value from the internal audit department—at a time when the downsizing of the Army was underway—and one more internal audit casualty had just been claimed. So, regardless of its impeccable leadership, processes, conformance, and procedures, the internal audit department had failed to deliver assurance, insight and foresight, and objectivity. It was a classic case of doing something exceedingly well that added very little value.

To help internal auditors understand the value proposition's three core elements, each element can be further defined:

1. *Assurance* = **Governance, Risk, and Control:** Internal auditing provides assurance on the organization's governance, risk management, and control processes to help the organization achieve its strategic, operational, financial, and compliance objectives.

2. *Insight and foresight* = **Catalyst, Analyses, and Assessments:** Internal auditing is a catalyst for improving an organization's efficiency by providing insight and recommendations based on analyses and assessments of data and business process. Foresight illuminates potential

future threats, or risks, if critical actions are not taken, and is a critical—if not *the* critical—element of value. Successful organizations are able to navigate tomorrow's often rapidly emerging risks, not simply relive yesterday's.

3. *Objectivity* = **Integrity, Accountability, and Independence:** With commitment to integrity and accountability, internal auditing provides value to governing bodies and senior management as an objective source of independent advice.[2]

Articulating Internal Audit's Value

Internal auditors often don't have a clear sense of how to articulate the value of their services. You may think internal audit's value is obvious, but sometimes stakeholders need help to see how our work relates to the value it generates. Since moving from the government to the corporate sector, I have been privileged to work with some outstanding internal audit departments whose CAEs clearly understand how to demonstrate value.

Some time ago I worked with an internal audit department in the energy sector that produced an annual report on the department's accomplishments. The report not only summarized the unit's annual assessment of the company's risks, it included the results of key audits and highlighted some of the more proactive assistance that it had given management and the board of directors, such as helping managers with their own self-assessments and risk assessments. The report noted some of the risks that had been exposed during the past year because of its activities and reiterated the savings realized by implementing its more significant audit recommendations. In an effort to provide foresight, it also looked ahead, outlining key risks facing the industry and the company going forward. In addition, the entire package was visually compelling and impeccably produced.

Such a document by itself doesn't demonstrate internal audit's value to an organization. But it does help certain stakeholders to see clearly the important role internal audit plays in ensuring the effectiveness of an organization's risk management and internal controls.

Delivering Value to Our Stakeholders

The value proposition is critical to understanding the core of what our stakeholders today expect from internal audit. But the value proposition alone cannot ensure that we deliver the services that best fulfill our stakeholders' needs and expectations.

Sometimes stakeholders are looking for assurance, sometimes they are looking for insight and foresight, and sometimes they are looking for an assessment. Every internal audit operation today must develop a strategy for delivering on those specific expectations. Unless internal audit can do this, it faces the risk of an emerging gap between stakeholder expectations of value and internal audit's delivery.

"Can the profession seize its rightful role in risk management, governance, and compliance?" asks Rick Telberg, former editor at large and editorial director at the American Institute of Certified Public Accountants (AICPA). "Maybe, but it'll take vision and guts. Do you have what it takes in the post-meltdown world of the new normal?"[3]

In an online editorial about governance, risk, and compliance, Telberg cites responses to this question from others in the profession, including this:

> Researchers at PwC report that internal auditors are being challenged "to remain relevant and meet stakeholder demands" in ways like never before.[4]

> Brian Brown, PwC principal and Internal Audit Advisory Services leader, says, "What's required today is a whole new, and somewhat unnerving, concept of the internal auditor . . . . More than simply checking accounts, internal auditors need to adopt a new way of thinking about their job that goes beyond audit as we've known it and embraces the fast-developing body of knowledge in governance, risk, and compliance." Or else, Brown says, "They run the risk of becoming marginalized and obsolete as new risk-management professionals take over."[5]

Internal auditors have been told in the past that they need to develop "soft" skills, create a "client-service culture," "leverage technology," and "promote improvement and innovation." That all may still be true, but internal auditors are not limiting themselves to a focus on soft skills. Instead, PwC researchers note that today's internal auditors increasingly find the focus of their conversations to be "critical risks," "aligning internal audit's value position with its stakeholder's expectations," and "matching the staffing model with that value proposition."[6]

The Internal Audit Strategy

The IIA's Practice Guide, Developing the Internal Audit Strategic Plan, is an excellent resource for an internal audit team creating a strategic plan for meeting its stakeholders' expectations. This section highlights some of the information from that practice guide and provides important information for development of your plan.[7]

The strategy is fundamental to internal audit remaining relevant within its organization. With it, internal auditors can adapt to stakeholders' changing expectations and realign themselves with the organization's changing objectives.

A systematic and structured process, similar to the one I used when I first became the IG at TVA, should be used to develop the internal audit strategic plan. The following steps are offered for consideration in the practice guide:

1. Understand the organization's objectives, as well as those of the industry in which it resides.
2. Identify all of your stakeholders.
3. Learn all you can about your stakeholders' expectations, particularly those of your primary stakeholders.
4. Undertake a comprehensive assessment of current and emerging risks facing the organization (this step is not actually in the practice guide, but I believe it is critical to undertake in dynamic organizations).
5. Perform a strengths, weaknesses, opportunities, and threats (SWOT) analysis for internal auditing.
6. Update the internal audit department's vision and mission.

7. Define the critical success factors for internal audit to achieve its vision.
8. Identify the key initiatives needed to bridge the gaps that exist between where internal audit is versus where it should be.

It is important that CAEs vet their strategic plans with key stakeholders and obtain endorsement from the organization's board (or its audit committee); this is part of the CAE's obligation to report periodically to senior management and the board on internal audit's purpose, authority, responsibility, and performance (Standard 2060: Reporting to Senior Management and the Board).

Once a strategic plan for meeting stakeholders' expectations exists, it must be reviewed periodically. Factors influencing the frequency of these reviews include:

- Change in the organization's strategy
- The organization's rate of growth and degree of maturity
- The degree to which the organization and its senior management rely on internal audit for independent assessment of, or help managing, organizational risks
- Significant change in internal audit resources
- Significant change in relevant laws or significant change to organizational policies and procedures
- Significant changes in the risks the organization is facing, including emerging risks and the speed at which they are likely to materialize
- The degree of change in the organization's control environment
- Key changes in an organization's leadership team or the composition of its board of directors
- Evaluations of how internal audit has qualitatively or quantitatively delivered on its strategic plan
- Results of other internal/external assessments of internal audit

While there is no way to mitigate all risk, an internal audit team can proactively manage its risks with a strategic plan. Each time I have assumed the role of CAE somewhere, I have taken my internal audit or inspector general team through a strategic planning initiative.

Strategic Planning and Value

I have emphasized strategic planning in this chapter because it is an excellent way for internal audit to identify, produce, and assess the value it should be delivering to its stakeholders. As noted earlier, however, stakeholder expectations continuously shift and so must our search for the appropriate value proposition for internal audit.

Leaders of the high-performing internal audit teams I've become familiar with during my career were not content to merely meet stakeholder expectations as they delivered value, they were always looking for ways to exceed them. Identifying and monitoring stakeholders' needs, however, also requires the ability to develop and sustain strong relationships, a subject we will explore next.

CHAPTER 5
Relationship Acumen Is Essential to Success

When I reflect on the experiences I have enjoyed as a CAE, I realize I might have missed out entirely on the opportunity to become one if not for my ability to cultivate and sustain relationships.

When my long-time CAE decided to retire as chief of Internal Review for the Army command where I worked, I was astounded to learn that the CFO had recommended me to the chief of staff as a candidate to replace the CAE. At first glance, I was an improbable choice. Although I had worked twice in the internal audit department, I had also left twice to pursue opportunities elsewhere. Now I was a senior cost analyst in another part of the command with little day-to-day interaction with the CFO, who was a brigadier general.

But I also was president of the local chapter of the American Society of Military Comptrollers (ASMC), and in that capacity I had established a relationship with the CFO and other senior officials in the organization. The CFO had been able to observe the relationships I had developed with others throughout that organization and had apparently concluded it was a much-needed skill I could bring to the command's internal audit department.

My Army experience would repeat itself 12 years later at the U.S. Postal Service (USPS). As the USPS deputy IG, I had supported the IG in building and sustaining a relationship with the USPS audit committee. Following a routine committee meeting in early 2000, the audit chairman pulled me aside and asked if I would be interested in taking over as interim IG of TVA in his home state of Tennessee. TVA needed an IG who could forge a solid working relationship with the federal authority's board and senior management; it was in the midst of a very public feud at the time, with the board chairman having improperly accused the IG of ethical misconduct. When I acknowledged interest in the job, the USPS audit committee chairman told TVA's board members that I would be a strong choice. The rest, as they say, is history.

I share these stories not to toot my own horn but to illustrate how vital building and maintaining relationships can be in leading a successful internal audit operation and advancing one's career.

Internal auditors must juggle a variety of often-conflicting relationships with various stakeholders as they work to meet their responsibilities to the organizations they serve. Typically, the internal audit function is accountable to the organization's audit committee and one of its senior executives—often the CEO. But to fulfill all the responsibilities outlined in their charters, internal auditors must also develop and maintain strong, constructive relationships with other managers and business-unit personnel within the organization and collaborate with external auditors, compliance experts, and others. Each of these stakeholder relationships requires a conscious, ongoing effort to ensure the organization's risks are being appropriately identified and evaluated.[1]

You can't start too early in your career learning how to forge and sustain positive, fruitful relationships with your peers and stakeholders. If you truly expect to contribute meaningfully to an organization, you have to cultivate relationships based on genuineness of character so others are confident that you are truly trying to help them—not just yourself.

The Relationship Advantage

As CAEs find themselves in an ever more visible, pressure-packed role, many have come to realize that business and financial acumen are not enough. In my book, *Trusted Advisors*, I note that relationship acumen is among an internal auditor's most essential skills for success—particularly for a CAE.

Given many internal auditors' background in accounting, the profession isn't exactly known for its interpersonal savvy. As corporations increasingly view the CAE role as critical, some are looking beyond the walls of internal audit when filling the job, often making it a short-term, rotational post for executive development. These non-traditional CAEs, armed with broader organizational experience, often exhibit impressive relationship-building skills to complement their deep knowledge of the business.

CAEs certainly need strong relationship skills. As previously noted, most have dual reporting structures—to the CEO, CFO, or another C-level officer (administratively) and to the audit committee (functionally)—so they must craft effective relationships with both. That can mean navigating complex and competing agendas for key stakeholders as well as the needs of external auditors, regulators, and others. If management wants its CAE to serve as a business partner or advisor—which is increasingly the case—but the board is looking for the CAE to be its eyes and ears as a source of assurance on the overall effectiveness of risk management and internal controls, then the CAE must somehow fulfill these seemingly conflicting roles while maintaining strong working relationships with all concerned.

Successful CAEs acknowledge that these competing expectations can be uncomfortable and stress-inducing. On one hand, the CAE must be a keen observer and assessor of organizational risks, which requires the kind of access that comes only from a close working relationship with management. On the other hand, this same CAE must remain objective and guard the organizational independence of the internal audit function—a task that inevitably results in occasional unflattering, if not damaging, reports about the performance of business units under the direction of senior executives. Such conflicts can easily erode relationships. Nearly everyone associated with internal audit knows of a highly respected CAE whose career was upended by conflicts with senior members of corporate management.

During my journey on the audit trail, I have made relationship building a priority in every position I have held, whether the relationships were with members of the organization's audit committee, its top executives, or other staff, including those in internal audit. I have seen both the rewards of strong relationships and the severe consequences of ineffective relationships.

No matter how strong your relationship acumen is (or how strong you think it is), you are likely to encounter situations that require you to step back and reexamine your approach. In 1998, I joined the USPS as deputy assistant inspector general for audit. After 10 years as a CAE, I suddenly found myself as a mid-level manager in a much bigger pond. In early meetings with staff members, I was unconsciously providing one-on-one coaching and direction, using the same tone and approach that I had employed in my prior role as a CAE in the military. Word quickly got back to the IG, who was determined to cultivate a team-based culture in the USPS void of individual egos. She quickly signaled her concern about the feedback she was getting.

The next few months were a challenge for me, as I sought to fit into this new and very different culture. I even considered going back to the Pentagon, where I had built and sustained relationships for years. But a light came on eventually; I realized that I could not begin adding real value to the Postal Service or the IG's office if I did not adapt my relationship-building approach to my new environment.

I started by leveraging the USPS team report-editing process (more on this later) to get to know and better understand the staff, managers, and peer executives in this non-military culture. As a result, I succeeded in winning the respect and trust of many who had been skeptical when I first arrived. And as I succeeded in building stronger relationships within the organization, the IG took note. She became much more supportive and began to make use of my knowledge, skills, and abilities on an ongoing basis. Within a year, she had promoted me to the assistant IG for audit, and within two years, I was the organization's deputy inspector general. Although I didn't see it at the time, my initial struggles were the result of my taking relationship acumen for granted. No matter how strong you think your relationship skills are, you must be prepared to learn new ones.

The Relationship Triangle

One of the most important relationships within our profession is the one connecting internal audit, executive management, and an organization's audit committee—a relationship Deloitte characterizes as a triangle. In a report titled *The Broken Triangle*, Deloitte noted, "The disconnect between internal audit, executive management, and the audit committee is nothing new. The broken triangle has existed for decades at many organizations, with varying degrees of severity."[2]

Dysfunction that was deemed tolerable in the 1980s, 1990s, and early 2000s is unacceptable today. The stakes—both personal and corporate—have ratcheted upward to new levels. Regulators, analysts, stakeholders, and even litigators all have a keen interest in how well this corporate trio, so essential to good governance and effective risk management, works together to protect and propel their organization.

What are the symptoms of a broken triangle? The Deloitte report[3] calls out:

- Financial restatements
- Material weaknesses
- Regulatory noncompliance
- Contentious or ineffectual board meetings
- Voluntary and involuntary turnover
- Missed earnings
- Excessive litigation
- Failed partnerships and alliances
- Unmitigated risk

Deloitte maintains that the first move to mend the triangle should be taken by the CAE, which may require adopting a more assertive role than in the past. The CAE should ensure that management and the audit committee have a clear view of internal audit's activities and are full partners in development of the unit's objectives, audit plan, and related activities.

The Deloitte report also offers 11 practical steps for restoring harmony to the triangle:

1. Communicate: Be open about the relationships among internal audit, the audit committee, and executive management.
2. Check your reporting lines: Determine whether your current reporting structure for the CAE is optimal.
3. Rebrand: Consider renaming your internal audit group to "audit services" or another, more descriptive and appropriate name.
4. Align expectations: Ensure that internal audit's audit plan and areas of strategic focus are understood and agreed upon by all parties.
5. Manage expectations: There's no such thing as perfect assurance.

6. Embrace risk: Expand your attention to risks that can impede your growth and profitability objectives.
7. Define internal audit's identity: Cop, detective, or counsel?
8. Expand your audit scope: Address emerging issues and trends.
9. Take control of your budget: Can you do more with less?
10. Adopt a workable model: Determine what fits best for your organization: In-house? Co-source? Outsource?
11. Make the CAE an officer: Bestow a title that helps garner the respect accorded to those in leadership positions.[4]

All internal auditors should strive to build strong relationships with the people they audit. It takes time, but our ability to have candid discussions with managers on difficult subjects can make all the difference if a manager is faced with the choice of sharing important information with us—or covering up the problem until the internal auditor leaves town. While there certainly are exceptions—fraud examinations and other specialized engagements, for instance—your audit results will almost always benefit from you having already established candid, effective working relationships with the individuals you are auditing.

Five Frequent Sources of Tension with Management

In an ideal world—and, indeed, I think in most organizations around the world—management and internal audit have a strong relationship that unites them in a common pursuit to strengthen their organization's risk management, internal controls, and governance processes. Of course, this does not mean that perfect harmony between the two always reigns. Disagreements can vary in intensity and solutions can range from the simple and obvious to the complex and potentially disruptive.

In my long career as an internal auditor, I had to navigate my own disputes with management and, as an IIA leader, I have heard similar stories from CAEs and others about their own disagreements. Each disagreement differs in its own way, but I believe there are five frequent sources of tension that characterize conflicts between management and internal audit.

1. Internal Audit Resources

While management, particularly the CEO and CFO, and internal audit should always be directed toward the same enterprise mission, sometimes the way they approach it is different. Management is focused on achieving organizational objectives, within which the delivery of profitable results features prominently. They may decide to address that goal through cost reductions, perhaps achieved via streamlined operations. A CAE's contribution to the enterprise mission is different and constant—enhancing and protecting organizational value by providing risk-based and objective assurance, advice, and insight.

Management may see internal audit as an ideal target for budget or staff reductions, placing CAEs in a tough spot. Because CAEs serve two masters, they are faced with alienating their administrative boss (typically the CEO or CFO) by protesting the resource reductions, or they may engender in their functional boss (the audit committee) a false sense of confidence that they can still perform as expected, even though they are operating with fewer people or less funding.

If only there were a scientific formula or international standard for calculating the precise level of staffing or budget for internal audit departments. That would eliminate that particular source of tension. But, until that formula is created, I often advise CAEs and audit committees to take a risk-based view of the subjective topic of resources. Identifying the top five risks that internal audit will not be able to address with current resources is a good way to gauge the committee members' level of comfort with the assurance they will receive. If their "comfort quotient" remains high, chances are good the resource discussion is at an end—at least for a while.

2. Risk Assessment

The fact that The IIA's *Standards* mandate the assessment of risks at both the enterprise and engagement levels should eliminate this as a source of contention. But nothing is ever quite so clear-cut. As long as the Committee of Sponsoring Organizations of the Treadway Commission (COSO) considers risk management "both an art and a science," there will be arguments about whether the resulting portrait should be flattering or a "warts and all" representation.

As one way to demonstrate internal audit's coverage, the CAE should be sharing with the audit committee the results of the (preferably continuous) enterprise risk assessment—unaltered, unedited, and transparent. Disagreements between management and the CAE over the accuracy of the risk assessments should be presented to the audit committee.

3. Results of an Internal Audit

Disagreement between management and internal auditors over the results of an audit is a source of tension that is both frequent and occasionally heated (especially when operating management is involved). This occurs even despite internal auditors' objective and systemic evaluation of operations and management's agreement with internal audit's findings and recommendations. However, that momentary sense of harmony can change when the audit report is issued.

If discussions and negotiations cannot be resolved by the parties involved, the issue must be elevated through the ranks of management, including to the CEO, if necessary. If the CEO sustains a disagreement, then the CAE should report that to the audit committee. While management has the prerogative of accepting one or more risks identified in an internal audit report, the board has ultimate oversight of the risks.

It is no secret that companies can find themselves mired in scandal as a result of a risk management or control failure that had been on internal audit's radar, sometimes for years. No one comes out of such instances unscathed. It should be a lesson to us that, despite how uncomfortable a disagreement with management may be, we serve our enterprises best when we do our work well and stand up for our findings.

4. Ratings and Opinions

Let's say we manage to work our way past management's ill feelings or lack of enthusiasm for unflattering internal audit results. We are still not out of the woods. The ratings exercise is still to come, and that can be when tempers flare. A "satisfactory" rating is, of course, met with a smile; even "needs improvement" is generally accepted, if a bit grudgingly. But an "unsatisfactory" rating is likely to cause a distinct tension among operating management, especially if the rating results in punitive actions, such as impacting management's performance assessment or incentive compensation.

Not everyone is averse to ratings. I have noted that, unlike operating management, executive management and the audit committee seem to have no particular issue with them. Still, they are a sensitive topic, and internal auditors have an obligation to take all opinions into account. When I was a CAE, I discouraged the use of such ratings as a sole basis for reducing management's incentive compensation. That's a practice that is tailor-made to place internal auditors in an adversarial position relative to those we audit.

5. Relationship with the Audit Committee

According to a recent IIA Global Pulse of Internal Audit survey, more than 85 percent of internal audit leaders worldwide report functionally to a board or its audit committee.[5] This marks a significant degree of progress in our reporting relationships. My experience indicates that, over time, management typically becomes comfortable with internal audit's dual reporting relationship. They appreciate that strong audit committees exercise oversight of internal audit, and they understand that internal audit's access to or reporting relationship with the committee is unlikely to be impeded by the CEO and other executives in most organizations.

This does not mean tension does not exist. I often hear from CAEs that they feel smothered by their CEO or CFO relative to their relationships with the audit committee, especially in terms of the content or nature of their communications with the committee. This is yet another tough spot for the CAE. I often urge audit committee chairs to be firm in communicating their expectations on internal audit access and to speak up to the CAE if they have reason to believe management is interfering with communication.

While I don't often recommend leaving an organization as a solution to a problem, this is one area where I feel strongly that if a CAE cannot overcome the organization's cultural bias against open communication with the audit committee, it is time to leave. It is difficult to escape the suspicion that management's interference with internal audit's access to the committee may hint at other, more nefarious cultural issues within the organization. Of course, before marching out the door, CAEs should examine themselves to ensure their own relationship-building efforts are up to par.

Attributes that Add Up for CAEs

A few years ago, I co-authored a report, *The Relationship Advantage: Maximizing Chief Audit Executive Success*, with Charles Eldridge, Paula Park, and Ellen Williams, senior executives in the research arm of the global talent management firm Korn/Ferry International. We spoke to more than a dozen executives from the field as well as some audit committee chairs. It goes without saying that strong technical audit skills and business acumen remain essential for today's CAEs. But the attributes and skills that collectively we termed *relationship acumen* benefit CAEs in specific ways:

1. **Positive intent:** A fair, independent, and objective approach to the job that projects that the CAE has everyone's best interests at heart. Makes clear that he or she isn't set on being right, but is set on finding the right answer.

2. **Diplomacy:** Direct, forthright communication (including listening) skills, political astuteness, and sensitivity to the organization's culture and how things get done. CAEs need to be intuitive about people and have the ability to read an audience. The best can be skillfully contrarian without being confrontational.

3. **Prescience:** Spotting the risks ahead to provide foresight requires curiosity, an ability to see matters with fresh eyes, and a willingness to question assumptions. Top CAEs can "see around corners"—that is, they anticipate needs before they are felt by others and identify issues before they arise.

4. **Trustworthiness:** A CAE must always walk the talk, keep confidences, operate with integrity, and be mindful of maintaining credibility with

those he or she advises. While consistency and predictability may sound boring, they're desirable qualities in this job.

5. **Leadership:** A CAE must set the tone for the entire internal audit staff, to be sure. But he or she must also be able to steer others toward consensus, manage conflict, and gain alignment on issues.

6. **Empathy:** A CAE must be able to understand and focus on each stakeholder's point of view and be sensitive to those needs and feelings. He or she must listen. A genuine caring about others amplifies all the other qualities on this list.[6]

Applying Relationship Acumen

Our professional standards require that we be objective, but that doesn't mean we can't be human. Some people are already predisposed to seeing internal auditors as cold and impersonal. We know this is not the case, and I believe we can do much to change this stereotype by:

1. Acknowledging that it exists, and
2. Actively working to change it by honing our people skills.

The importance of placing our humanity ahead of our credentials when building professional relationships was best demonstrated for me during my first encounter with Gen. Colin Powell in the late 1980s, just prior to his appointment as chairman of the Joint Chiefs of Staff.

As the CAE of one of the Army's largest commands, I always briefed the commanding generals when they came on board. When one of these four-star generals—the highest-ranking officers in the U.S. military—assumed the helm of my command, his staff would place me on his calendar. On the appointed day, at the appointed hour, I would report to the general's office and brief him on the command's internal audit program and the operations of the internal audit department.

But when Gen. Powell arrived, his staff did not schedule me for a meeting in his office. "He will come to you," they said. The day of my briefing, the general came all the way over to meet with me in the dinghy, the 50-year-old wooden structure that held our offices. It was one of many relationship-building lessons I learned from Gen. Powell.

The four-star general, who would go on to become the U.S. Secretary of State, sat at my desk while I briefed him on what the internal audit department did for the command. Later during that briefing or a subsequent one (I'm not sure which), I brought up the staff reductions that were occurring throughout the command.

The Cold War was ending, military spending was being reined in, and Army commanders were cutting budgets, including those of their internal audit departments. At our command, the cuts were beginning to hurt internal audit's ability to carry out its mission.

Gen. Powell looked at me and said, "All right, Dick." (He was one of the only people to ever call me Dick.) "What do we need to be concerned about?" he continued. "Tell me what I *really* need to be concerned about in this situation."

The general was giving me permission to level with him, to explain what kind of real risks the budget cuts might pose to his command.

Despite the stereotypes, internal auditors—*and the people we audit*—are first and foremost a part of humanity. It's just that, as we strive for objectivity in our work, we may sometimes accidentally flip off our *personality switches* to our detriment. It is possible to be collegial and objective at the same time—to "trust but verify," as the old expression goes. We need to learn from Gen. Powell and give people permission to feel comfortable sharing candid perspectives with us.

It may help if we remember that our audit clients face exactly the same issues and challenges in their work as we do in ours. They are under the same pressures and constraints. The only difference is that, in this instance, we are not the ones being audited.

What I'm really talking about here is empathy. Submitting to an audit is an exercise in vulnerability. A little human understanding can go a long way toward changing the way people view the process and the auditors responsible for it. Remember, the goal is to improve the organization, and that's usually easier to do when everyone works together.

Establishing Rapport with Skeptical Clients

I engaged more than a few skeptical or adversarial internal audit clients in my time, so I developed five simple strategies for disarming them or winning them over:

1. **Promise achievable results and over-deliver.** Good relationships grow when people keep their promises to each other. We can avoid adding to the rolls of disappointed audit clients by not promising results we're not sure we can deliver. If you're not sure when the audit report will be approved, for example, don't promise a report "next month." If you're not sure how long the audit will continue, say so. If you promise to limit your team's on-site presence to a specific time frame, make every effort to keep that promise. Of course, if your team discovers significant problems or potential fraud, all bets are off.

2. **Practice the fine art of appreciation.** Thanking clients for their time at the beginning and end of an audit is obligatory—but if you are not showing appreciation for your clients throughout the process, you are missing opportunities to turn adversaries into supporters. It's particularly important to show your appreciation when you are not in agreement. If a client questions your findings or criticizes your audit, for example, start by saying, "Thank you so much for sharing your perspectives. How would you recommend we word that instead?"

3. **Don't dwell on the past.** Clients can't undo the past, so it helps to keep conversations forward-looking. How? Limit the use of phrases like "should have" and "failed" in your client meetings and audit reports. Instead, use phrases like "from now on" or "in the future." By doing so, you are repositioning internal audits—often perceived as "fault finders" focused on past mistakes—as forward-looking reports focused on future improvements.

4. **Lend an ear.** We all know that listening is an important component of communication, but auditors too often forget that just because we now understand our client's point of view doesn't mean the client is finished

talking about it. Internal audits often dredge up troublesome issues, and when clients push back, it's often because they don't think we have heard them out or truly understand their position.

5. **Try to conclude with consensus.** The best way to transform a skeptical client is to consistently strive for consensus. A few simple words such as, "Let's see if we can't find some common ground!" can diffuse a confrontational discussion and demonstrate your collaborative attitude. If, after extensive discussion, your client still vehemently disagrees with your conclusions, you should probably offer to reevaluate your conclusions to allow for a "cooling-off period." Ultimately, the two sides may agree to disagree, but clients almost always appreciate an effort to reach consensus on an audit's results.

Client relationships, though often based on trust built over a period of time, are still very delicate. Skeptical clients often had a bad experience with internal auditors in a past life. Unfortunately, the best we can do in such cases is work tirelessly to erase the memories of those bad encounters and replace them with a new relationship built on trust. We don't always agree with those we are auditing, but we should always demonstrate through what we say and what we do that they have been heard and their words considered.

Forging a Bond with the Audit Committee Chair

Many CAEs will tell you that their regularly scheduled annual, quarterly, or monthly meetings with the chair of their board's audit committee are simply a starting point for their relationship with that key stakeholder. CAEs and chairs who establish stronger bonds tend to reap the benefits of their relationship.

Our professional standards require the CAE to communicate and interact directly with the board.[7] The CAE's regular attendance at board meetings that relate to audit activities facilitates an ongoing exchange of information that enables the CAE to be apprised of strategic and operational developments and, in turn, inform board members of business risks and control issues at an early stage.

But forging bonds with the chair of the audit committee should extend beyond interactions at formal meetings. Between those meetings, the CAE should remain in close, transparent, and informal communication with audit committee members—particularly the committee's chair—so that any questions or issues that arise can be addressed in timely fashion. This is particularly true given the challenges that the speed of risk can present to the organizations we serve.

In my experience leading external quality assessments over the years, CAEs of high-performing internal audit departments often have a strong relationship with their audit committee chairs. These relationships often extend beyond the formal audit committee meetings. These CAEs frequently reach out between meetings to touch base on the department's performance or the risks its staff is addressing. Strong CEOs and CFOs are typically comfortable with this type of interaction, because they understand that internal audit has responsibilities that extend beyond reporting directly to them.

Audit committees can be very dynamic in terms of membership turnover. The same can be true of the chair's role. CAEs must continuously cultivate new relationships as committee members or chairs come and go. That means adapting to new styles and expectations on a continuous basis. My advice to CAEs preparing for the arrival of a new audit committee member or chair: Do your homework. Make sure you research a new member's background and experience; it will help you better anticipate his or her frame of reference. If the incoming member serves on the audit committee of other companies, reach out to the CAEs in those companies for insights and perspectives on the new member. I frequently see CAEs from two or more companies develop strong relationships with each other because they share a common audit committee member or chair.

Developing Your Own Relationship Acumen

The abilities that got you the CAE job—observing, absorbing, probing, listening—should also be applied to your own development, including the development of your relationship-building skills.

Behavioral scientists have made strides in the past decade decoding the personal attributes that lead to strong professional relationships. Daniel Coleman's seminal work, *Emotional Intelligence*, brought these types of "EQ" skills into stark relief alongside the more "technical" skills prized within many corporate functions.[8] Korn/Ferry has articulated a development plan, called the "70-20-10" rule, for ensuring an individual's next-level readiness: "The formula for developing successful executives is quite clear: 70 percent of development comes from experience, 20 percent from feedback and people, and 10 percent from courses or training events."[9]

Following almost 10 years as an internal auditor, I ventured away from the profession and accepted a post as an operations research analyst. Because of the educational qualifications generally required in operations research, I found myself suddenly surrounded by professionals with degrees in mathematics who possessed skillsets that were completely different from mine. To say I was intimidated was an understatement. For the next three years, I found myself constantly challenged to measure up to their extraordinary background and training.

To ensure my success in this new role, I scheduled myself for extensive professional and academic training. I suspect that I overcompensated out of a fear of failure. In the end, I was promoted within the field and ended up leading several important projects.

Some years earlier, I had finished my MBA and wanted to do something with my graduate degree, so I began to teach accounting and economics courses at a local college. When I walked into class my first night, I was mortified. I had never done anything like this before, and as I stood at the front of the class with my notes, I was gripping the podium very tightly. A lot of older students were pursuing degrees in higher education in evening classes, and I was by far the youngest person in the room. It was all just a little bit overwhelming for a 25-year-old. But I quickly learned to build relationships with my students by being myself and getting to know them as people. I quickly discovered how much I loved teaching. I taught for eight years, and those classroom experiences made me much more comfortable when getting to know new people or speaking in front of large groups. I've had a passion for training and education ever since.

Long-Term Care

Successful CAEs understand that, even in the best of circumstances, the process of building and sustaining relationships is a never-ending task. Senior executives come and go or change hats, and the audit committee roster changes. The CAE must reach out early and often when personnel change. Tending to long-standing relationships is also imperative. Picking up the phone or extending a lunch invitation to talk through a touchy issue pays enormous dividends to the CAE and the entire internal audit staff.

Building trust and understanding in others requires an investment of the CAE's time and energy, in part because the needs and expectations of key stakeholders are constantly evolving. Successful CAEs recognize the signs of change and recalibrate as necessary.

The exercise of establishing and maintaining important allegiances changes the entire CAE experience. Having the audit chair as an ally gains the CAE credibility with the whole committee and inspires respect from management.

In the long run, success depends on a balanced mix of relationship acumen and the ability to identify risks—and then using the results as a basis for audit planning and internal audit value creation.

CHAPTER 6
When in Doubt, Follow the Risk

Early in my career, the word *risk* rarely came up during my internal audit activities. In deciding what to do, we typically developed an "audit universe," consisting of all of the operating units, business entities, organizational processes, and controls that were our responsibility. We then used that universe as our "audit register" to ensure that each area was assessed on a predetermined schedule. For example, the Army's officers' clubs had to be audited every three years by regulation, whether they needed it or not. By the time I became a CAE, those cyclical requirements were gone, though they were still very much a force of habit.

By the late 1990s, however, internal auditors had begun to focus on risk as an important determining factor when developing their audit plans and allocating resources. We began experimenting with risk assessments as part of the audit-planning process when I was the assistant inspector general for audit at the USPS. We informally documented our view of the USPS's risks on the back of a napkin en route to an international postal conference in China in 1999. Preparing risk assessments and using the results to develop a comprehensive audit plan was still generally viewed as a leading practice at the time, so we were proud of our preliminary efforts.

By the time I moved to TVA as inspector general in the summer of 2000, the Postal Service Office of Inspector General (OIG) had completed its second risk assessment, and I thought of myself as a fast-developing expert on risk-based audit planning. So, when I showed up at TVA headquarters in Knoxville, Tennessee, I was confident I already knew the key risks facing the giant power authority—and was certain the first audit plan under my direction would focus extensively on the risks posed by TVA's nuclear power plants.

Imagine my surprise when, after several days of meetings with my audit team, the risk assessment identified the authority's contracting processes for acquiring coal as the biggest risk. Buying coal is riskier than operating nuclear power plants? No way. But what I hadn't realized was that TVA's OIG staff had been using risk-based planning for its audits prior to my arrival and had a much better understanding of TVA's risks than I did.

I began to appreciate that risk has at least two dimensions—likelihood and impact. While even a single accident at a nuclear power plant could be catastrophic in terms of its effect on the organization, the environment, and the surrounding community, the likelihood of such an accident was relatively remote given the oversight track record of the U.S. Nuclear Regulatory Commission and other regulatory bodies, coupled with the extraordinary safety, security, and operating controls that were in place.

Meanwhile, TVA spent billions of dollars annually buying coal, the fuel responsible for generating most of the electrical power used by its customers. Not only did wasteful, ineffective, or even fraudulent coal-acquisition practices have the potential to cost TVA and its ratepayers lots of money, but the likelihood of those things occurring in the coal-contracting processes was high as well.

High impact combined with high likelihood trumped high impact with low likelihood. I also learned that this risk-based approach can add real value to an organization. During my tenure at TVA, we identified more deficiencies, cost recoveries, and cost savings from our coal-contract audits and investigations than from all the other audits combined!

The Fundamentals of Risk

In 2002, The IIA adopted its first standards mandating that risk assessments serve as the basis for audit planning. During my years at PwC, I worked with the internal audit departments of several Fortune 500 companies to enhance their risk assessment and audit planning processes. Other organizations were dipping their toes into the risk waters as well. Springing forth from multiple sources was one overarching principle that was taking hold in the profession—make sure internal audit follows the risks.

Of course, risk and risk management are not new to the world of commerce. In his book, *Against the Gods: The Remarkable Story of Risk,* Peter L. Bernstein writes that systematically understanding the risk factors affecting business has been a goal for millennia. Among his examples:

- Advancement of the theory of probability, in use since the mid-seventeenth century to explain outcomes in games of chance.
- Risk transfer and distribution practices that Chinese and Babylonian traders used as early as the third and second centuries BCE.
- Historical records of financial loans in Babylon dating back to the eighteenth century BCE.[1]

Fast-forward to the twenty-first century, and business risk is defined in multiple ways. COSO, for example, defines risk as "…the possibility that events will occur and affect the achievement of strategy and business objectives."[2] Other definitions take a more holistic view of risk and recognize that there can be a positive dimension as well. Still, it is safe to say that most internal auditors today focus on the potential bad consequences when assessing risk.

The Importance of Risk Assessment

Not long ago, annual risk assessments were considered a leading practice but were not required under The IIA's IPPF. Today, Implementation Guide 2010: Planning provides the following guidance when undertaking a risk assessment:

> To ensure that the audit universe covers all of the organization's key risks (to the extent possible), the internal audit activity typically independently reviews and corroborates the key risks that were identified by senior management. According to Standard 2010.A1, the internal audit plan must be based on a documented risk assessment, undertaken at least annually, that considers the input of senior management and the board…(R)isks are measured in terms of impact and likelihood.[3]

Given the speed of risk that organizations face in today's world, performing an annual risk assessment is unlikely to serve organizations well. So, internal audit will need to deploy a continuous risk assessment component to its risk assessment methodology in order to provide assurance.

In working with different internal audit departments over the years, I have observed that, even if internal auditors vary their approach, certain features are common to the development of their risk-based plans. These include:

- The establishment and maintenance of a risk register or inventory for the organization, linked to key business objectives
- The assignment of an inherent rating for risks in the inventory
- A process for scoring or rating risks on an annual basis
- A process for gathering and analyzing data, management perspectives, and other evidence on the current level of risk for each element in the inventory
- A scoring or rating methodology that is assigned based on the data, perspective, and evidence gathered
- A ranking or prioritization of risks based on the scoring methodology
- A determination of the most highly rated risks to be included in the proposed internal audit plan
- A review of the proposed annual internal audit plan with key management officials
- Submission of the proposed annual internal audit plan to the audit committee for approval

I have seen the use of elaborate, time-consuming methodologies, including formulas, to score individual risks. Sometimes these formulas seemed better suited for a rocket launch than calculating a single risk in an audit plan. As I often coach internal auditors, simplified formulas can be just as effective as complicated ones. After all, if risk assessment is as much art as science, as COSO characterizes risk management, professional judgment will invariably be a factor no matter how complex the process.

The Value of Risk Assessment to Stakeholders

While the primary purpose of most internal audit departments' risk assessment process is to generate a basis for the annual audit plan, its value to internal audit's stakeholders cannot be overstated. In the early years of risk-based planning by internal audit, managements tended to find the assessment process and outcome useful, but audit committees typically received little exposure to it. However, in recent years, audit committees have taken more direct oversight of internal audit in many organizations. Before approving internal audit's annual plan, audit committee members naturally want to know the basis for prioritization of key internal audits for the year ahead. Often, the more they see, the more they want to be involved. Today, many internal audit departments include interviews with audit committee members as an integral part of the risk assessment process.

Internal auditors spend a great deal of time and resources to undertake an annual risk assessment. For large internal audit departments of sizable organizations, the effort can represent hundreds of staff hours. Often, the risk assessment itself is then filed away as evidence of the planning process for possible review during a subsequent external quality assessment of the department. However, I believe internal auditors miss a significant opportunity to deliver value by not sharing the risk assessment with management. In fact, I have received favorable responses from management and audit committee members by packaging the risk assessment results as an engagement deliverable—similar to an internal audit report. When internal audit is seen as the enterprise expert in risk management, its annual risk assessment can serve as an important reference document for the entire organization.

Internal audit pioneered enterprise risk assessments at many companies. As managements and boards placed greater importance on enterprise risk management (ERM), beginning about 15 years ago, many turned to internal audit to leverage its expertise. In some companies, internal audit departments were asked to champion or implement ERM, and the CAE was asked to wear a second hat—that of chief risk officer (CRO). While such moves reflect stakeholders' growing confidence in internal audit, the long-term consequences of internal audit retaining responsibility for ERM are not without risk, because its ability to serve as an objective source of assurance on the effectiveness of risk management for the organization could be compromised. After all, internal auditors should never audit their own work. IIA Standards and Implementation Guide 1112 provide guidance for CAEs who have or are expected to have roles and responsibilities that fall outside of internal auditing.

Where Is the Risk Taking Us?

The IIA's Audit Executive Center conducts an annual survey to assess key trends in the profession. Since 2012, the survey has added a dimension—documenting the categories of risk on which internal audit spends most of its risk-coverage resources. An average of the recent survey results provides interesting insights as to which risks are getting the most attention and which are getting the least.[4]

First, the results reveal that internal audit is looking at a broad portfolio of risks, one that arguably contains many of the risks organizations face today. Of course, that should not be surprising given the risk-based approach that most internal audit functions pursue in developing their annual audit plans.

Risk Category	Average time spent per risk category[5]
Operational (not included elsewhere)	17%
Compliance/regulatory (not related to financial reporting)	16%
Financial reporting (including Sarbanes-Oxley testing)	14%
IT (not covered in other choices)	9%
Financial areas other than financial reporting	8%
Cyber (prevention and/or recovery)	7%
Enterprise risk management programs and related processes	6%
Fraud identification and investigation (not covered in other audits)	5%
Governance and culture	4%
Other risk category not listed	2%

The survey results help dispel the myth that internal audit is primarily concerned with financial risks. Only 22 percent of internal audit's risk-coverage resources are dedicated to financial risks (the "Financial reporting" and "Financial areas other than financial reporting" categories combined). And the results reflect that, when combined, more than 43 percent of internal audit's risk-related resources were dedicated to operational, compliance and regulatory, and IT risks.

Assurance on the Effectiveness of Risk Management

For some time, I have urged the internal audit profession to provide assurance on risk management's effectiveness. I consider it the most significant opportunity for our profession in a generation, yet internal auditors seem reluctant to make such assurances an integral part of their portfolios. What are we waiting for?

There is widespread agreement that failures of risk management in the late 2000s, particularly in the financial services sector, were a major contributor to the global economic crisis. Among the legacies of that crisis are the many new regulations and laws worldwide designed to pressure corporate executives into more effectively managing their companies' risks and corporate boards into more effectively exercising their oversight responsibilities. To whom should these boards turn for assurance? Surely they cannot rely strictly on management, for management cannot be fully objective about its own performance.

The IIA is convinced that assurance on risk management is a very important issue for our profession in the decade ahead. In late 2011, The IIA launched the Certification for Risk Management Assurance (CRMA) as a way for internal auditors to demonstrate their proficiency in providing assurance of risk management's effectiveness. The response was amazing! Since the certification's launch, more than 15,000 internal auditors and risk management professionals worldwide have added CRMA to their résumés. Currently, it is The IIA's second-most widely held certification, behind the Certified Internal Auditor (CIA) designation.

Despite the potential value of risk management assurance to companies and other organizations, internal audit departments dedicate very few of their resources to this emerging priority.[6] Why aren't CAEs, who play a major role in setting internal audit priorities, embracing the change? I think it is a matter of not wanting to leave one's *comfort zone*. Assurance on risk management was simply not a priority for the profession in the past, and many CAEs still don't feel comfortable taking on such a role. Meanwhile, because we do not have a history of providing assurance on the *effectiveness* of risk management, boards and management are not yet clamoring for internal audit to assume this new, broader role either.

It's ironic that all of this is occurring at a time when audit executives are appealing for a "seat at the table." Such a seat, it is argued, would afford CAEs a better understanding of their organization's key strategic and business risks. Perhaps it was a bit harsh, yet when noted thought leader Norman Marks observed on Twitter that "internal auditors who don't provide assurance on risk management deserve a seat at the 'children's table,'" I couldn't help but smile.

Internal auditors should remember that, for many internal audit functions, access to the audit committee and its chairman is still a relatively recent development. The need for assurance on financial controls' effectiveness—which was a key priority for audit committees during the past decade—opened doors for internal audit within many organizations and raised the profile of CAEs with many audit committees and management teams. But internal auditors cannot take that for granted. If, having realigned their audit coverage, they compensate by spending less time on issues of importance to the audit committee or management, there is a risk that committee members (or those in the executive suites) will start to think that internal audit's work is no longer relevant or adding value.

Expanding Our Risk Horizon

For generations, accountants and auditors have disparagingly been referred to as "bean counters." If we have been guilty of counting beans, it's time to demonstrate our true capabilities and the value we bring to our organizations. It's time to move beyond *bean counting* and begin to fully comprehend *how the beans are grown,* which is often where crucial risks to an organization lie.

But many new internal auditors have little or no experience with operational auditing, having spent most of their time focused on financial controls. How do they develop their business acumen generally and their understanding of the risks specific to the businesses and industries in which they operate? I suggest the following:

- **Become a "sponge" for information about the business.**
  Read and learn everything you can about your organization and
  the industry in which it operates. While a typical U.S. Securi-
  ties and Exchange Commission (SEC) 10-K report for a publicly
  traded company can be dry reading, it is a treasure chest of information about your company and the strategic risks it faces.
- **Seek variety in your assignments.** While it is great to become
  an expert in a specific area of a business's operations, you will be
  even more valuable as a resource if your expertise spans multiple
  areas.
- **Be passionate about every assignment.** During my years in
  the Postal Service's OIG, I came to realize that the new auditors
  who truly impressed management were the ones with the enthusiasm and drive to quickly become conversant enough in business
  risks and controls to talk with 20-year veterans.
- **Rotate into other areas of the business.** As much as we
  would like to think we can learn everything we need to know
  about a business while wearing our internal audit hat, there is
  no substitute for hands-on experience. My foray into operations
  research and cost analysis earlier in my career made me a much
  better internal auditor when I returned to the profession.
- **Seek training or other professional development to fill
  gaps in your knowledge.** I frequently share the story about
  how, as the newly appointed inspector general of TVA, I enrolled
  in a basic utilities course so I could better understand the fun-
  damentals of generating and distributing electric power. No one
  ordered me to do it, but I realized I needed to know more about
  the business if I was to succeed as the newly appointed CAE.
- **Be patient.** Learning all you should about a business and sharp-
  ening your business acumen overall take time.

Auditing the Circus

While internal auditors often declare they can address the full portfolio of
an organization's risks, skeptics still abound. I have heard many executives
complain that "internal auditors just don't understand the business." My
sense is that some of these complaints are legitimate, while others originate

with unit managers who simply don't want internal auditors poking around in their business.

Many internal auditors hired by their organizations in recent years were brought on to help with enhanced coverage of risks related to financial controls. Many of the auditors in this new generation had little knowledge of their company or its industry; they were proficient in supporting activities related to Sarbanes-Oxley, but they had little, if any, experience in auditing operational risks. So, it's understandable that internal audit's efforts to cover a broader portfolio of risks have exposed some internal auditors' limited knowledge of their particular business.

The IIA's Audit Executive Center survey suggests some strategies for internal auditors seeking to improve their business acumen. Almost 90 percent of those responding to the survey indicated that a good way to improve a unit's collective knowledge of the business is "internal development of existing personnel," such as:

- Subscribing to industry periodicals or other literature— 75 percent
- Training focused on industry risks or issues—69 percent
- Pairing inexperienced staff with more experienced staff— 69 percent
- Sending the CAE to industry-focused CAE groups or events— 55 percent
- Networking frequently and informally with other CAEs— 49 percent[7]

I am confident that, as professionals, we can always close any gaps in knowledge we may have about our businesses. But there will always be executives and managers who think their business units are too complex or sophisticated for mere auditors to understand. They will push back when our risk assessments indicate that their areas of responsibility warrant internal audit coverage. If the internal auditors prevail and complete the audits, then the managers will often dispute the findings on the basis that the auditors don't have the proper expertise and don't know what they're talking about.

During my career, I have debated with more than a few disgruntled managers who wanted to keep my staff out of their areas on the basis of perceived lack of expertise. With very few exceptions, I was successful in refuting their assertions. On those occasions where there was some validity to their concerns, I typically secured the necessary expertise by co-sourcing the engagement with a third party. My advice to any CAE faced with such circumstances is to stand firm. As one of my colleagues once cleverly responded to a business-unit manager who doubted internal audit's ability to assess his operations, "You don't have to be a clown to audit the circus."

We Can Audit Anything—But Not Everything

When we consider that internal auditors function as analysts, controls experts, consultants, teachers, business partners, watchdogs, financial advisors, compliance experts, and more, it is not surprising that confusion and unrealistic expectations about our profession abound. While the range of our abilities may be quite broad, some risks clearly require additional expertise to audit. I like to think we can audit anything, but we can't audit *everything*.

I'm sure I'm not alone in hearing the question, "Where were the internal auditors?" every time a major control breakdown makes headlines. We are human and may occasionally overlook a risk, sometimes with catastrophic consequences. But, more often, the internal auditors were engaged, vigorously waving red flags, but their warnings were not properly heeded. And many organizations today are so large and so complex, they encompass a massive portfolio of risks—more than the typically staffed and funded internal audit can cover. Even if we have all the resources, training, and talent we need, we cannot be everywhere at once.

I've talked a lot about the gap between expectations and the reality of what internal audit can do. Unfortunately, our stakeholders sometimes want more assurance than we may be able to provide. Take, for example, information security, where we see a dramatic annual increase in the number of cybersecurity breaches worldwide. Obviously, while internal auditors can provide important assurances, we cannot give absolute assurance about our organizations' cybersecurity controls, despite stakeholders' expectations.

We have to be careful about what we say and do—or don't say or do—to avoid suggesting anything that might raise unrealistic expectations among our clients. We already have to deal with their "selective hearing"; let's not give them more to work with.

I am sure most of us regularly explain what we can do for our organizations and how we can add value. These messages—in our charters, our announcement memos, our opening meetings at the outset of engagements, and other communications—help stakeholders understand the benefits of internal auditing. It would also be a useful practice to balance the discussion of what we *can* do with some explanation of potential limitations in what we can provide. And when we deliver more than we promised, we have built a short, straight route to client satisfaction.

No one can eliminate risk entirely. Management and the board will always turn to internal audit following a risk or control failure for explanation of causes and consequences. Of course, we can and should try to assess key risks before they become failures. But even when we audit at the speed of risk, we can't audit *everything*—a message that bears emphasis in setting key stakeholder expectations.

CHAPTER 7
We Must Audit at the Speed of Risk

When Iraqi military forces under the command of Saddam Hussein invaded neighboring Kuwait on August 2, 1990, it was one of the more geopolitically destabilizing events in decades. Little did I realize, however, how much the invasion—unfolding more than 7,000 miles from the U.S. Army base where I was a relatively new CAE—would teach me about the speed of risk and its dynamic impact on stakeholder expectations.

We had compiled the 1990 internal audit plan for our giant, Atlanta-based military command during the summer of 1989; the Berlin Wall had yet to fall and the world was a relatively peaceful place. As a result, the organization's internal audit priorities were much the same as they had been in previous years. I was enjoying the support of my boss, the organization's two-star general chief of staff, and I had coordinated closely with him to ensure that his expectations were reflected in our plan.

But in the ensuing months, the chief of staff would depart and be replaced by a new general. My new boss seemed to have little interest in internal audit or our annual audit plan. He made it clear to me when he arrived in the organization that he was no fan of auditors and he thought there were too many auditors conducting too many audits in his command. (Considering that, during the heart of the subsequent Gulf War our command was the subject of as many as 140 audits by *outside* audit agencies alone, I could understand his point of view.) Yet, once we started addressing the risks emerging from the unanticipated Gulf War, and demonstrating real value to him, he seemed to soften his views.

I was determined to prove to my new boss that internal audit added value to his command, and it was the Gulf War that provided me with my best opportunity. Shortly after Iraq's invasion of Kuwait, another large command nearby was deployed to Saudi Arabia at the invitation of the Saudi government. The deployment was so swift and sudden that the soldiers had to leave their personal belongings behind, unattended, in their barracks. Turns out that situation was one of many organizational risks that were probably keeping my new boss awake at night.

When I sat down with the general for my monthly update, I asked him point-blank if there was anything internal audit could do to address the command's war-related risks. He thought for a moment, then asked if our auditors could review security provisions for the barracks of those soldiers sent suddenly to the Mideast, to provide him some assurance that their personal effects were adequately secured. We immediately undertook the audit, and it was a transformational event in internal audit's relationship with the new chief of staff. It was also a pivotal event for me, for it deepened my understanding of how rapidly new risks can emerge in an otherwise stable organization.

He didn't stay at that command for long. When he was promoted to three-star general and made one of the Army's prestigious corps commanders, a large farewell dinner was organized for him and, as a senior member of his staff, I attended. When he stood to give his farewell speech, he began going around the room directing personal comments to individuals with whom he had worked. He eventually pointed at me and said, "Chambers, you back there. I still don't like auditors, but you are welcome at my command any time." That was a capstone moment for me, and it demonstrated the value I had provided him once I recognized that we must audit at the speed of risk. In the years since that important lesson, the world has become incredibly more complex, and enterprise risk management has become essential to long-term organizational survival.

Deciding how much risk should be tolerated for the sake of growth, identifying which risks must be mitigated, and uncovering hidden risks with the potential to devastate an organization can be a daunting assignment. Yet, the opportunities are enormous. And who within an organization has the independent and objective perspective, the skills, and the experience to identify these risks and provide assurance that they are well managed? In most organizations, the answer to that question is the internal auditors.

In the months following Iraq's invasion of Kuwait, new risks seemed to emerge weekly in my organization. After internal audit demonstrated its agility in addressing the security of those deployed soldiers' personal effects, we took on a series of new challenges, from auditing the logistics contracts that moved thousands of soldiers halfway around the world and back, to assessing processes for activating and deploying reserve soldiers, to studying how personal mail was being delivered within the theater of operations. We eventually identified and deployed to the Middle East a team of military internal auditors—the first U.S. soldier-auditors to serve in combat conditions since the Vietnam War.

The point is, not one of those audits or actions was envisioned in the annual internal audit plan that we had so painstakingly assembled a few short months before. I learned that, in a highly dynamic environment, a good CAE has to continuously be on the lookout for new risks that might warrant internal audit coverage.

The Speed of Risk Requires a Continuous Focus

As new potential risks surface and require assessment, audit plans and coverage must evolve at a commensurate pace. We are unlikely to avoid surprises if we apply traditional methods and painstakingly follow a plan that was built six months earlier. We need to base our efforts on continuous assessment of risk and fresh information.

Of course, this is not the easiest approach. In fact, I often hear internal auditors point to the difficult and time-consuming nature of continuous risk-assessment processes. And I have some sympathy with that perspective, knowing that many departments struggle to find time for even one enterprisewide risk assessment annually, much less several. But here are some logical techniques that can be deployed to keep your risk assessment current:

1. **Formal methods.** In the Common Body of Knowledge (CBOK) Study, IIA's Internal Audit Foundation noted that the idea that "an internal audit activity can update its audit plan only once a year and still remain timely, responsive, and effective needs to be challenged strongly." One way to continuously monitor risk is to identify key risk indicators (KRIs)

at the outset of the year and monitor them periodically or continuously throughout the year. These KRIs can be linked to the results of the annual risk assessment or to risks that are notoriously volatile. When anomalies appear, internal audit should assess whether the organization's risks are shifting, and internal audit's coverage should adapt accordingly.

2. **Shoe-leather assessments.** Another way to keep your risk assessment and audit plan up to date is what I like to call "risk assessment by walking around." This method is exactly as the phrase implies and relies on developing strong working relationships with key members of senior management. This way, you know about new risks as soon as they do. Risk assessment by "walking around" may lack the discipline and structure of more formal assessments, but it's a powerful strategy for keeping in touch with what's happening in your organization and may reveal new risks that your formal risk indicators do not. Given the number of business units and executives in large companies, risk assessment by walking around cannot be the responsibility of only the CAE; the entire internal audit department must be organized and deployed.

3. **Bird's-eye view.** A third approach is simply to set your antenna as high as possible to detect industry-wide changes, economic trends, and other external factors. Industry publications, seminars, and professional association meetings can be valuable sources for acquiring crucial intelligence that might impact your risk assessment. This, too, must be a team effort.

So, what's the best type of continuous risk-assessment program for keeping up with the speed of doing business? Any one of the methods I've outlined is a far better option than merely establishing an audit plan once a year, then following it regardless of changing circumstances. Unfortunately, none of these methods is truly complete by itself.

My advice is to use a combination of approaches. Formal methods are best for staying on top of previously identified risks; risk assessment by walking around helps identify new internal risks; and taking a bird's-eye view by setting our antenna high allows us to address new external risks as they emerge within our industry or within the overall economy.

This is evidenced in a recent CBOK study, which included among its "Imperatives for Change" the need to "Conduct a More Responsive and Flexible Risk-based Audit Plan."[1] The study followed up this recommendation with some key action steps for CAEs:

- Assess the maturity of your risk assessment process and develop plans to extend its application across the enterprise.
- Develop processes within internal auditing to identify and report on emerging risks:
    - Make the identification of emerging issues a key performance responsibility of your direct reports.
    - Coordinate with your organization's other risk and control units to share information and views on emerging issues.
    - Identify and use external sources of relevant data, knowledge, and business issues to help uncover additional emerging issues.
- Assess your process for making periodic updates and revisions to your annual audit plan. Develop steps to enable internal auditing to move faster and make more frequent changes to the audit plan as the organization's risks evolve.
- Talk to your key stakeholders (executive management and the audit committee) about the need to make more frequent updates to the audit plan. Seek agreement on an appropriate balance between the need for internal audit to "complete the annual plan" and the desire for internal audit to make changes in response to emerging and changing risks:
    - Consider implementation of a "rolling" audit plan—for example, a plan that is rolled forward to cover the next six months.
    - Conduct regular and frank discussions with both senior management and the audit committee about the nature, scope, and severity of the organization's risk profile.
- Develop or refine your audit reporting to demonstrate a more direct link between changes to the organization's risk profile and associated changes to the audit plan.

Risks today are more dynamic than ever. For this reason, we must adapt our approach to planning our work so that we can audit at the speed of risk.

No Surprises

Having had opportunities to speak with the audit committee chairs of many leading U.S. and European corporations during the past decade, I like to ask them during our conversation, "What is your foremost expectation from internal audit?" With amazing regularity, the most common response is, "No surprises."

In other words, these audit chairs, reflecting their personal views and those of their committees, want internal auditors to identify issues *before* they become problems for the company and appear on the front page of *The Wall Street Journal* or the *Financial Times*.

If you stop to think about it, you realize that "no surprises" is an extraordinary expectation. It suggests internal auditors must be omniscient. Is the eradication of unwelcome surprises what audit committees really expect from our profession? I seriously doubt it. Instead, I think they are urging internal audit to anticipate risks that could present a problem down the road, rather than dwelling only on what has already gone wrong. To do that, internal auditors need to recognize that risk is a moving target—and a volatile one at that.

Monitoring Dangerous Storms

We internal auditors are accustomed to the confusion that often follows our attempts to explain our profession to those unfamiliar with it. So, it was a delightful surprise for me when my most recent explanation, to a doctor, was met with a succinct description of our value to the organization: "You guys are the thunder before the storm."

As much as I am taken with that phrase, it is only the beginning. Yes, we use our eyes and ears to scan the horizon for the dark clouds of ineffective risk management, defective controls design or implementation, or other risk-increasing issues. But those of us who want to provide a deeper level of foresight need to rely on more sophisticated tools and techniques, just as meteorologists have moved from thermometers and weather balloons to Doppler radar and satellites.

And, like meteorologists, we deal with extremely complex variables and seek ways to monitor related risks and mitigate negative outcomes. But, while our tools have become more sophisticated over time, no one has yet invented a satellite that can detect the potential of fraud, noncompliance, or weak cybersecurity controls. But we are not entirely unarmed; data analytics, continuous auditing, and, increasingly, artificial intelligence help us better understand current conditions and warn us of future dangers that require the swift and immediate intervention of management or the board.

However, we cannot be complacent and rely solely on technology to solve our problems. Here are a few techniques and best practices that supplement technology tools and help us broaden our perspective on risk:

- Integrated thinking and enterprise risk management. These practices can help internal auditors from within the organization by breaking down barriers that may conceal risks or weaken mitigation efforts. Internal audit contributes by providing assurance on their effectiveness.
- Strong business acumen and expertise within the business sectors where our organizations operate. When internal auditors acquire or enhance these skills, they improve their insight and foresight. They become better able see the secondary or tertiary effects of risk on the organization.
- Supportive relationships with risk managers, including chief risk officers, chief information security officers, and chief information officers. Comfortable, open, honest, and transparent relationships with these executives enable internal auditors to keep current on what they are seeing and locate potential gaps in risk management.

Technological advancement has eliminated hours of tedious record reviews, streamlined processes, improved our accuracy, and enabled us to expand our scope of services to organizations. Its importance cannot be overstated.

However, we must always keep in mind that technology is not a turnkey solution. It is a tool that can help us focus on problem areas with greater accuracy and efficiency.

We have an opportunity to increase internal audit's value as stakeholders turn to us to provide insight on risks that threaten the organization. Our success will depend on our ability to find and deploy innovative methods—including technology—to identify and monitor risk.

Moving from Hilltops to Desktops

While we must be skilled in monitoring the risks that are clearly visible to our organizations, that is not enough. We must also become more adept at identifying risks that may not be as evident. Just as today's risks may not have been evident last year, next year's risks may not be obvious today.

As a profession, internal auditors have become very good at one of our least valuable skills—hindsight. I suspect all of us can do a bang-up job of looking at last year's data and telling management exactly where the mistakes were made. I am not saying that hindsight has no value in internal auditing; I am just saying we are usually telling clients what they already know.

Then operational auditing came along and, with it, the introduction of consulting/advice into our portfolio of services. With this evolution, we broadened our expertise and became purveyors of insight. This gave us a bit more credibility with our stakeholders, but when risks are unfolding at lightning speed, knowing what is going on today is valuable for only 24 hours. By tomorrow, it is hindsight.

Hindsight and insight are not going away, but foresight is where internal auditors should be staking their claim. Stakeholders want guidance on what to expect in the future; they find minimal value in revisiting the past or dwelling in the present. Auditing at the speed of risk requires us to concentrate on the risks of tomorrow if we are to protect and enhance value for our organizations.

So far, we are not amazing our stakeholders with our ability to detect emerging risks. A 2016 KPMG survey of CFOs and audit committee chairs revealed that only 10 percent agreed that their internal audit function adequately identified and responded to emerging risks that threatened their companies. We clearly have room to grow.

I spoke earlier about the similarities between meteorologists and internal auditors, noting that professionals in both fields have enhanced their skills through the use of increasingly sophisticated tools. Those seeking to know the weather used to go stand on a hilltop and peer at the sky; now they gaze at computer screens to monitor the output of satellites. We too must climb down from the hilltop and instead turn to our desktops, laptops, and expertise. These are the tools that will help us identify and analyze emerging risks—from the impact of shifting economic trends or natural disasters to financial and compliance issues. That calls for shifting our focus beyond the immediate future and creating our own virtual radar.

KPMG Partner Michael Hill has noted, "Emerging risks can arise from many sources—economic or demographic shifts, changes in the competitor landscape, technology advances, or customer preferences."[2] Clearly, the scope of potential emerging risks is too vast for it to be assigned to the CAE alone. It will take the entire audit team, given specific assignments based on expertise.

Fred Stuckel, vice president of ERM and audit at Express Scripts, shared the process his company uses to identify emerging risks in a video posted by North Carolina State Poole College of Management's Enterprise Risk Management Initiative.[3] Among the Express Script tactics, he and his team "spend a lot of time on the internet and on social media" perusing international newspapers that are translated from the native language to English "to get different perspectives of what the impact of any kind of change might be to the United States or to the global market."

There is no 100 percent right or wrong way to identify emerging risks, but we have to give ourselves a fighting chance by at least looking in the right direction. A profound understanding of your industry and your business can probably suggest certain conditions that are rife for creating potential risks, and you should familiarize yourself with sources you can reference for greater insight, such as:

- Economic forecasts (macroeconomic and industry-specific)
- Known strategic business risks facing your company
- New corporate initiatives in the planning phases
- Legislative and regulatory outlook specific to your industry
- Geopolitical developments and political risks in areas where your company operates
- Disruptive threats or opportunities pertaining to your industry
- Performance of your leading competitors
- Risks emerging as headlines via traditional or social media

Management is likely to have already identified many emerging risks that threaten the organization, so internal auditors should work in collaboration with them as a partner, not a competitor. After we compile and cull an inventory of emerging risks, we should share the list and explain our reasoning, evidence, and perspectives with the audit committee. Our conversation with the committee is not complete until we, as the organization's trusted internal auditors, describe our plans for monitoring and responding to these risks.

It seems that a new crisis occurs almost daily, and I have already pointed out management's common reaction of wondering where the internal auditors were before the disaster occurred. If we are to be a world-class audit function, we must be fully prepared to address that question. Hindsight is never the answer. We need to make a 180-degree turn and focus on the future. Only then can we respond to the "Where were the internal auditors?" question with "Way ahead of the risk."

The Ever-Present Storm of Cybersecurity

Cybersecurity. The word alone is enough to keep management and internal auditors awake at night in today's interconnected society. This is not a novel thought, but something I frequently hear from CAEs wherever I travel may be new to you: "Cybersecurity risks are just too complex for internal audit."

What? I'm not sure where this opinion arose, but apparently there is a widespread view that cybersecurity issues should abide in the domain of IT and security experts, with internal audit providing little more than support. Not only could this troubling perspective imperil the internal auditors who espouse it, it could also endanger the organizations they serve. I am convinced that there is no contemporary battlefield more suited for internal auditors to engage than cybersecurity.

We need to ensure that we and our stakeholders understand that cybersecurity is as much a business risk as it is a security risk. Based on this understanding, it becomes eminently clear that internal audit should be called on to provide the necessary assurance and governance guidance in this critical area.

I'll grant you that charging to the front of the pack to lead the fight against cybercrime is a daunting consideration. Any breach could involve high stakes and/or negative publicity. What seem to be small, internal compromises can become front-page news in no time. Despite the hazards, we must be ready to do our jobs. Shrinking from complex risks or hard tasks is not a characteristic of the internal audit profession.

But, if you still feel reticent, here's something that should shore up your confidence. Cybercriminals would prefer we didn't know this, but it is true and it is powerful: We have home-field advantage.

Think about a criminal breaking into your house. He or she has to find a way in, locate whatever you may have of value, then deal with whatever protections you have in place—perhaps a camera and a security alarm. Cybercriminals entering your organization face the same challenges. There are many things they don't know that will affect the success of their planned caper, but we do know them. If we have planned properly, we can force them to play by our rules. This gives us a marked advantage, and knowing this should inform our approach to creating the protocols that secure and protect our data.

A good first step in protecting data is to identify the information that is most important to the organization. There are many approaches to this process of segmentation, but a simple and effective one is to assign data to any one of three categories based on its value to the organization:

> **Don't care.** This is information that would have no appreciable impact on the organization or its clients if it is accessed by hackers. A good

example might be information that is readily accessible on the organization's website.

Reputational risk. This is information that would not kill the organization, but it could generate negative publicity or embarrassment to the organization if it fell into the wrong hands. An example is employee disciplinary reports.

Real harm. These are the crown jewels of data that must be protected at all costs. It consists of information (say, financial data or strategic business plans) that could create major problems for a company or its clients if it is hacked.

Information in the "real harm" category must be separated from the other two categories, isolated and protected, so resources can be concentrated where they are most useful. When it comes to data protection, one size does not fit all. Once protection is in place, internal audit can swing into action and do what it does best—test for effectiveness and efficiency of controls and protocols and provide assurance to management, the board, and other stakeholders that the processes in place to protect the data are effective and efficient.

Daimon Geopfert is the national leader for RSM's Security and Privacy Services practice and strongly encourages internal audit to engage more actively on cybersecurity matters. A popular speaker who has appeared at several IIA conferences, he offers straightforward insights that help put cybersecurity issues squarely in the internal audit camp:

- Internal audit can and should conduct data mapping and classification exercises to test protections. It is important to know where the data comes from, where it resides, who uses it and how, and how long it is kept in the system—in essence, following its lifecycle.
- These exercises may uncover instances where protected data is exported from its protected environment for local use. This exportation significantly raises the data's vulnerability to being hacked.

- Performing these exercises and sharing the results enable internal audit to take the lead during discussions on what data is most vulnerable and recommend appropriate controls throughout its lifecycle, no matter where it travels.
- Internal auditors cannot effect positive change until they learn to ask the right questions regarding data protection. Acquiring or enhancing this knowledge will enable them to focus on what actually is happening in the field and not just what is written in policy statements.
- Taking a more active role in cybersecurity may have its sacrifices. For example, internal audit must be prepared to let go of some long-held business practices, especially behaviors that may make operations easier but increase vulnerability and, therefore, the likelihood of data breaches.
- As with everything, setting stakeholder expectations is key, including expectations relative to data protection. Gaining commitment, especially at a high level, to protecting certain data will make it easier to manage behavior that places convenience before risk.

Geopfert also shares a statistic rarely reported in media coverage of cybersecurity issues. Basic data protections through sound practices and policies is likely to discourage 60 to 70 percent of hackers, many of whom are not highly skilled, significantly reducing cybersecurity risks. Some of these practices include limiting access to sensitive information, maintaining up-to-date patches, encrypting data on mobile devices and media, and conducting security reviews of third-party vendors. These are basic, widely known best practices, and I suspect they are already on internal audit's radar.

Technology and innovation provide massive benefits to businesses. But they also disrupt the status quo and result in a constant cycle of change—making evident the need for us to audit at the speed of risk.

CHAPTER 8
Disruption Drives Innovation

I have seen many examples of innovation during my career, but I could never have anticipated the speed at which change occurs in today's business and internal audit environments. While we used to have months, even years, to prepare ourselves for the "next big thing," we are now flooded with new tools that allow us to do more, work smarter, and generate more impact with fewer resources and in less time than ever before. It's an exhilarating environment in which to work, but it also poses challenges. Not everyone thrives in such a climate, and perhaps it is that ability to embrace and master innovation that separates successful internal auditors from the rest of the pack.

I experienced an early example of the impact of innovation during my tenure at the Postal Service. The USPS OIG's office received a request from a U.S. senator concerned about the integrity of a relatively new postal money order that offered USPS customers an affordable and convenient way to transfer limited amounts of money to another country. The senator was concerned these money orders might be used to launder drug money by enabling criminals to break large amounts of drug money into smaller, transferable amounts to keep the dollar amount below the threshold that would normally trigger added scrutiny.

The senator wanted to know if these money orders were being used for such illegal purposes—*and he wanted an answer in one week!* Given the number of transactions and the geographic dispersion of the facilities issuing these money orders, I was convinced that producing a comprehensive report in a week was virtually impossible. But telling the senator that might only heighten suspicions about the program and embarrass the USPS and the OIG.

I gathered the internal audit staff and explained the situation, asking them to do their best to collect the data and put together a report by the deadline. Completely surpassing my expectation, the team examined all 200,000 money orders and issued a well-written report—*in three days.*

How did they do that? They used a software program called ACL that enabled them to electronically review every one of those money-order transactions and analyze them based on specific criteria.

Today, of course, the use of data analytics software is business as usual, but back then it was a massive—almost unimaginable—leap forward in productivity. Such is the power of innovation.

Innovation in Internal Auditing

A major source of value generated by internal audit departments is the promotion of positive change within an organization—yet, paradoxically, as a profession we seem to struggle with innovation when it comes to doing our own jobs. Despite the fact that almost all the processes we audit, regardless of the industry, have been transformed in recent decades, some internal auditors perform their work today in much the same way they did when I set out on my personal audit trail more than 40 years ago.

Even as internal auditors enthusiastically talk up the benefits of positive change for their clients, they typically go about their business as creatures of habit, focused more on controls than on innovation. Controls are important, but a singularly controls-focused strategy does not add the most value to a company.

Internal audit currently operates in a global business environment of increasing competition, technological advances, and downsizing. As a result, demand for internal audit's services is growing much more quickly than its capacity. Given these conditions, the profession's traditional practices may not be adequate. To stay relevant, internal audit needs to at least match the speed of the organizations it serves.

Because the demands on internal audit grow faster than its resources, I am convinced one of the best opportunities for improvement is adding to internal audit's capacity and ability to deliver value without busting the budget. I like to think of strategies in these areas as *capacity multipliers* that can elevate the level of value we deliver and enable us to exceed our stakeholders' expectations.

Leading internal audit departments have been leveraging capacity multipliers in three main areas: 1) strategic staffing solutions, 2) transformed processes, and 3) technology applications. Let's take a closer look at each of these.

Strategic Staffing Solutions

Strategic staffing solutions often start by identifying capacity and capability gaps within the internal audit department. When a capability gap exists, functional and subject matter experts (SMEs) can provide additional insight in highly complex or specialized subject areas, allowing engagement teams to "leap the learning curve." But few internal audit departments are large enough to have SMEs for every topic, so other, more affordable alternatives must be considered.

Leading internal audit departments address such staffing needs by leveraging SMEs from other business units within the company. In many situations, this practice may ease short-term staffing constraints, enable the department to undertake unique audit projects, or enable streamlining of engagements in remote locations. It's important to remember that this approach requires appropriate supervision and assurance that the temporary help is qualified and objective.

Many companies have a "guest auditor" program, typically for the duration of a single engagement or a series of shorter ones. Guest auditors can provide functional expertise and institutional knowledge while serving as "goodwill ambassadors" for internal audit, returning to their regular jobs with a deeper understanding of internal audit's processes, risks, and controls.

If you like the idea of a guest auditor program, remember that turnabout is fair play. Internal auditors can gain valuable operational experience through staff rotation programs that enable them to work temporarily in other divisions. These kinds of programs place extra demands on internal audit's management, but in the long run, they enhance people's knowledge of risks and controls throughout the organization.

When gaps in staffing can be filled by less-experienced help, consider internships. Vigilant supervision is required when working with interns, but ongoing supervision and quality control should be integral to every internal audit program, and internships serve a dual purpose by also fostering talent for the future.

When the budget allows, third-party internal audit providers are a flexible form of augmenting staff. Third-party services are commonly used to acquire foreign-language or other specialized skills, expand geographic coverage, provide a quick response to fast-changing conditions, or otherwise add flexibility to a department's operations.

In most cases, if your audit committee sees a need for third-party resources to address significant risks, money will be made available. But even with limited budgets, internal audit departments can take advantage of resources outside the company. For example, some audit departments "borrow" internal auditors with specialized skills from other organizations such as companies in their geographic area or industry. (Borrowed internal auditors can be especially helpful after a natural disaster or other major emergency.) Confidentiality issues can be a challenge, especially if industry-specific skills are needed, but imagine the knowledge that can be gained. And while such exchange programs seem to occur more often among large companies, there's no reason smaller companies can't benefit by swapping internal auditors with hard-to-find skills.

Keep in mind that, if an internal audit department wants to take advantage of one or more innovative staffing solutions, its success depends on three things:

- Ensuring participants' qualifications and credentials
- Ensuring their objectivity as internal auditors
- Deploying the resources during the most critical phases of the audit—typically planning and reporting

Transformed Processes

As mentioned previously, too many internal audit processes are not cost effective. Many internal audit departments are dealing with excessive cycle times, outdated results, and a resulting diminished value that leads to stakeholder dissatisfaction. This gives us plenty of room for improvement. Here are the internal audit processes that I consider the best candidates for reengineering.

1. **Risk assessment.** Key features of a streamlined risk-assessment process include an efficient, documented methodology and integration of stakeholders' views and expectations. The most effective risk-assessment methods are continuous in nature (rather than annual or semiannual events), and continuous-monitoring metrics can streamline the process considerably. Collaborating with other elements within the enterprise that also conduct risk assessments can also prove valuable. Management quickly develops "interview fatigue" if a stream of professionals shows up to ask them over and over, "What keeps you awake at night?"

2. **Audit planning.** The key features of an efficient and effective engagement-planning process include:
   - Ensuring that risk assessment is the primary basis for determining objectives, scope, and specific tests
   - Using a sound and consistent methodology
   - Leveraging expertise from SMEs
   - Incorporating advice from management and operating personnel
   - Designing the engagement for efficiency, keeping the budget in mind

3. **Documentation and review.** These processes should follow a sound and documented methodology. It's important to keep in mind that internal audit, like any other process, can lose efficiency if it's over-controlled; more is not always better. Leading internal audit departments do not mandate incorporation of all documentation into the workpapers; they make use of digital-age technology in their documentation and review processes.

4. **Reporting.** Innovative internal audit groups experiment with a variety of ways to enhance the timeliness of their reporting.

5. **Monitoring and follow-up.** Follow-up is too often neglected. If internal auditors report significant risks to the audit committee but do not ensure that management addresses the risks appropriately, then they are actually raising the audit committee's risks rather than lowering them. Consider, for example, those companies that had compliance problems with the U.S. Foreign Corrupt Practices Act. The consequences were invariably more severe if senior management and the audit committee knew about the problem but took no action. We must design efficient, timely follow-up systems that conform to professional standards and leverage management assertions on the status of corrective actions in decisions about the timing and methodology for follow-up.

Deploying Technology

As much as staffing and processes offer room for innovation, I think most of us would agree that technology is where the major breakthroughs occur, which makes The IIA's 2018 North American Pulse of Internal Audit data in the report, *The Internal Audit Transformation Imperative*, even more alarming. Surveying more than 600 North American CAEs, directors, and senior managers, less than one-third of CAE respondents strongly agreed their internal audit functions challenge their own status quos. Only 13 percent of survey respondents strongly agreed that they adopt new technologies or processes.

The Pulse survey also disclosed that a majority of internal auditors have embraced technology such as electronic workpapers (77 percent) and data analytics technology (62 percent). Yet, internal auditors are slow, or reluctant, to use new or emerging technologies such as robotics process automation (18 percent) or automation of analysis of evidence (i.e., artificial intelligence) (13 percent). We live in a time of revolutionary advances in technology, yet we are apparently failing to capitalize on them.

I realize that any technological advances I discuss in this edition will be "old news" within a year. However, I still want to touch on four areas of innovation I believe will have—and are already having—a significant impact on internal audit.

Artificial Intelligence

Of the many technological advances that hold the promise of being transformative, artificial intelligence (AI) could have the greatest potential impact, not only to the organization but also to internal audit itself. In fact, I would even go so far as to suggest that AI poses a threat to the profession, or at least the profession as some practice it.

In this book I speak about internal auditors offering hindsight, insight, and foresight. Trusted advisors focus on the third element; other internal auditors are content with just providing hindsight and insight. I believe those internal auditors run the risk of being replaced by AI. AI's computational power and advanced algorithms, which enable it to act with purpose and perform autonomously, can provide information on what has happened and *why*. As yet, however, it cannot combine data, information, trends, rumors, breaking news, competitors' actions, and even hallway gossip to formulate reasoned and rational suggestions of future developments and their associated risks and opportunities. Expert internal auditors, however, can.

Not long ago, I was quoted in a *Forbes* magazine article on whether AI could one day replace the internal audit profession. I responded that the growing ability of sophisticated technology to monitor large and complex systems won't replace internal auditors, but it will enable them to become more efficient and effective in helping organizations solve problems and meet goals.

What wasn't addressed in the article is how AI, along with other digital and technological breakthroughs, will fundamentally change how business is done and, in turn, how that will change the demands internal audit must begin to prepare for now, especially in these areas:

- **Governance of AI.** This is a matter of establishing policies and procedures to ensure accountability and oversight. Is it clear who in the enterprise is accountable? Does that individual have the needed skills and expertise? Are the organization's values and ethics reflected in its AI policies and practices?

- **Data quality.** AI is only as good as the data it is analyzing; yet, most organizations fail to define a coherent structure for their data. When systems do not communicate effectively, it is likely that the appropriate data is not brought together for analysis. Internal auditors' traditional focus on completeness, accuracy, and reliability can be especially helpful in this area.

- **Human factors.** So much focus is placed on the purported correctness, objectivity, and consistency of the algorithms that drive AI that it is easy to forget that humans create those algorithms. Whenever humans are involved, there is a possibility for bias and error. Internal auditors' focus on testing, transparency, and the maintenance of privacy and security can ameliorate the impact of unintended human failings.

- **Performance measurement.** The need to know if a process, system, or procedure is achieving its objectives is fundamental to every area of business. AI is no exception, although its complexity may make measurement harder. How are performance metrics established? Do they indicate how well the goal is being attained?

- **Cybersecurity.** AI is performed by networked systems whose connectivity gives them both strength and vulnerability. As with all automated processes, maintaining security over AI is critical.

- **Creating understanding.** Few internal audit teams, audit committees, executive management, and boards begin the AI journey with a universal and consistent understanding of what AI is, how it works, what its benefits are, and how it presents risks to the organization. Internal audit must first master that understanding and the necessary skills; then it can help boards and audit committees be prepared to discuss AI-related risks and make good decisions based on the right information.

Enterprises don't set up AI systems and walk away, assuming they are operating correctly. Malfunctions can result in lost revenue, reputational damage, and even loss of human life depending on the type of system. Enterprises want assurance that the systems are performing as planned, and they will look to internal audit to provide that assurance.

I'm convinced that internal auditors are more prepared for the challenge than many may realize. We have accommodated new technologies before. Remember all the hand-wringing about the risk associated with cloud computing? Ultimately, new technologies offer unique characteristics and challenges, but the basic issues—determining the performance of processes and the existence of effective governance, understanding and assessing risks, and testing the effectiveness of controls—remain.

These issues call for internal auditors to apply the skills they have learned and refined over their careers. They must ask good questions—Are there backup systems? Have they been tested? Are the algorithms reliable? Is the data accurate?—then think critically about the answers. They should include AI in their risk assessments and consider whether to include it in their risk-based audit plan. And, as with most significant enterprise programs, they should seek to be actively involved in AI projects as early as possible, providing advice and insight that will contribute to successful implementation (without sacrificing objectivity).

Of course, we will not just be auditing AI; we will likely be using it to support our audits as well. CAEs must develop a keen understanding of how AI can assist the audit function and how the use of AI influences risks, risk mitigation, and the internal audit plan. On a day-to-day basis, some of the more manual tasks will become automated. However, analysis and judgment will remain the unique and valuable contribution of internal auditors.

Robotic Process Automation

Robotic process automation (RPA) promises a fast, cost-efficient, and easy-to-implement way to accomplish repetitive and time-consuming processes by using a technology-agnostic virtual workforce (bots). Bots can work 24/7, are less expensive than human capital resources, and make fewer errors, while meshing well with the existing infrastructure that is already controlled and governed by IT. Employees who are freed of mind-numbing repetitive work can become more engaged and productive because they have time to focus on more rewarding activities. And, music to internal auditors' ears, RPA provides a complete and compliance-aligned audit trail of activities and tasks performed.

With such a rosy description, it hardly seems there is any downside to RPA. But, of course, as with any technology, there are risks. Is access to the bots controlled? Are change management procedures implemented within bot activities? Are policies and procedures in place? Is performance measured?

These questions are familiar to internal auditors because they address the same issues that apply to non-RPA processes. However, there are some facets that are specific to RPA as a new technology. For example, it is still evolving, which means that vendors will come and go, and skilled staff may be scarce. Regulations will evolve as well, so it is important to keep an eye on compliance risk in a shifting landscape. RPA is disruptive, so it can cause issues in governance, information security, performance, availability, data integrity, and change management.

Internal auditors can help their enterprises use RPA safely and securely by identifying the risks involved with its implementation and recommending controls that are well suited for automation (and assessing the impact of automating them). They can provide guidance around the design of new controls or enhancements to existing controls and suggest an approach to testing them. They can help evaluate the return on the RPA investment and efficiencies that may be gained.

In addition to enterprise uses of RPA, internal auditors should not overlook the benefits of using it in the performance of their own audit activities. RPA can perform certain manual activities, enabling internal auditors to focus their limited resources on more valuable contributions to the enterprise, such as quality assurance reviews and exception management. RPA's speed and lower error rate may support a move from statistical sampling to full population testing performed more frequently, perhaps resulting in a continuous auditing model.

Blockchain

It is a rare week that blockchain is not in the news. At heart, it is a trans-action ledger executed on a distributed, rather than centralized, basis and shared across a peer-to-peer network in which members contribute and journal transactions. Participation may be open to the public (per-missionless) or restricted to approved membership only (permissioned). Secured via cryptographic keys, blockchain's claims to fame are the integrity of transactions and the immutability of records. Not everyone is completely convinced of these claims, however, citing the cryptographic key, which can be stolen, as a weak link. Still, blockchain shows no sign of slowing down, expanding from cryptocurrency to health-care applica-tions to smart contracts.

As we have seen with the other emerging technologies discussed in this chapter, blockchain is not immune to risks associated with new and rela-tively untested products. Its limitations and effectiveness are still being explored, regulatory response is still in development, its scalability is in question, the cost per transaction seems to vary widely, and its base code is evolving rapidly—perhaps too rapidly to be entirely secure and supportable. Other concerns relate to access control, the strength of the algorithms and nodes in the network, and the impact of a successful denial-of-service attack. Already, counterfeiters have made their mark, and Ponzi schemes are cropping up.

Some may think that blockchain's inherent benefits (integrity and immuta-bility) render internal audits irrelevant. This is, of course, untrue, as indi-cated by the risks I've mentioned already. Auditors will still be needed to ensure that transactions are authorized and legal, are executed between approved parties, reflect actual costs, are "whole" within the chain, and are correctly classified in the financial statements.

Internal auditors must get involved early in the blockchain process, when it is easier to build in governance, risk management, and controls, as opposed to tacking them on after the fact—often in the wake of a failure. Many block-chain initiatives occur outside the traditional walls of the IT organization, so internal auditors should look beyond the traditional IT function in assessing the use of blockchain in their organization. Internal audit teams that have been involved in systems development know the importance of auditing at the speed of risk and are prepared to perform a detailed analysis of the technical blockchain architecture. Beyond that, internal auditors must develop strategies for maintaining a sufficient level of transparency and verifying that the blockchain and related applications are performing as intended.

After deployment, internal auditors must do their usual work of assessing the existence and effectiveness of controls to validate transactions before they are executed. We can also make an effective contribution in evaluating disaster recovery and loss mitigation procedures should the unexpected occur.

DevOps

DevOps is a process rather than a technology, and it has been around longer than the other innovations discussed in this chapter. Internal audit has had more time to understand the process and include it in audit plans. Because of that, I just want to focus on a few points.

But first, a definition. DevOps entails integrating the activities of business software development and operations teams to minimize conflicts, spark inspiration, reduce development time, and increase efficiencies. It is truly a technological breakthrough, but it is not without risk, which is, of course, a topic of interest to those of us focused on assurance, security, and governance.

It's the very nature of DevOps—the fast turnaround among integrated teams with much of the testing left until the end—that gives us cause for concern. It treads on some of our most sacred tenets. What about segregation of duties? Where is the audit trail? When do internal control reports get done?

These problems aren't insurmountable; many internal audit departments have already tackled them successfully. The trick is that implementing internal controls the old-fashioned way doesn't always work in a DevOps environment. Other approaches more specific to DevOps can be taken, such as automating many audit, compliance, and security controls to ensure that testing is done on every build; using only software with no known vulnerabilities; and relying on the automatic generation of the audit trail in the process.

The best results come when the audit and the DevOps teams share information. Internal audit can help the DevOps teams understand the critical business risks, so they take those into account as they progress through the process. On the flip side, the DevOps team can educate internal audit on how the DevOps procedures proactively minimize risk. If the two sides can be integrated, and both remain willing to accept feedback from the other, the enterprise is likely to benefit from applications that are quickly developed, more inclusive, compliant, and secure.

Innovation and the Human Factor

Innovation does not automatically bloom where it is planted. We have all seen examples of organizations that set up systems and processes designed to achieve certain things, only to fail because the corporate culture did not allow them to succeed. This can happen anywhere in an organization, including within internal audit.

When focusing on culture, the leadership, the team, and the interaction between them are of paramount importance. "Tone from the top" is fundamental to the success of innovative programs. To ensure that an organization realizes value from its investments in innovations, its leadership must foster a culture that facilitates change. This requires leaders to embrace behaviors that are very different from the traditional management paradigms.

As for the team, highly innovative employees are known for certain behaviors, including curiosity, courage, creativity, appropriate risk taking, lateral thinking, collaboration, and open-mindedness. The challenge for management is to ensure that performance evaluation and reward systems encourage these behaviors, and the corporate strategy and organizational values both explicitly and implicitly reinforce the importance of these behaviors (see **exhibit 8-1**).[1]

These are only some of the human factors that can facilitate or derail progress. Two additional areas that are pertinent to internal audit's ability to embrace innovation are employees' resistance to change and acceptance of risk.

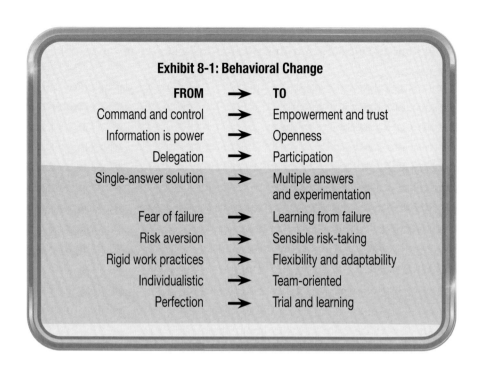

Exhibit 8-1: Behavioral Change

FROM		TO
Command and control	→	Empowerment and trust
Information is power	→	Openness
Delegation	→	Participation
Single-answer solution	→	Multiple answers and experimentation
Fear of failure	→	Learning from failure
Risk aversion	→	Sensible risk-taking
Rigid work practices	→	Flexibility and adaptability
Individualistic	→	Team-oriented
Perfection	→	Trial and learning

Resistance to Change

A study undertaken in the 1990s, *Enhancing Internal Auditing Through Innovative Practices,*[2] had two objectives: 1) to collect and describe a sample of innovations, and 2) identify characteristics and issues common to their implementation. While it has been a few years since the study was conducted, I think some of the observations have enduring value.

Even where there was agreement that change was needed, every internal audit activity in the study faced some degree of resistance from staff to the selected innovations. Staff expressed concern that workloads would increase, unrealistic expectations would be imposed, they were being asked to perform tasks usually not associated with internal auditing, or the innovations would dilute the core mission and purposes of internal auditing. In some cases, staff said it was unprepared to assume new roles, especially when those roles involved higher levels of responsibility and accountability.

General lessons learned about the successful implementation of innovation within internal audit departments included the following (and still ring true today):

1. Innovations always have costs.
2. Reception to innovation within the internal audit organization will be mixed.
3. Reactions outside the audit organization will be mixed as well.
4. Audit clients should be carefully chosen for the selected innovations.
5. Innovations need ongoing support.[3]

Acceptance of Risk

During my brief hiatus from internal audit in the 1980s, I served on a cost analysis team that prepared extensive studies about the cost of moving Army bases and closing Army installations. In one of my first projects, I created a cost model designed to show how much it was going to cost to move family housing quarters from point to point. This was quite early in my career, and personal computers were still relatively new. I was really proud of my model and the fact that my numbers were being put into major cost studies.

But one day I discovered I had made a mathematical error of approximately $100,000. I went to my boss and explained the situation. He responded, "It's not a decision-altering error; don't worry about it." He was right. We were looking at cost options totaling in the hundreds of millions of dollars. While my error seemed like a lot to me, it would have no effect on the overall decision.

His reply was a liberating moment for me. I realized that, as internal auditors, we can get so hung up on the details (including risk) that we forget to maintain perspective. As innovators, if our ultimate goal is to develop strategies that hit home runs for our stakeholders, we have to be prepared to strike out occasionally. Innovators understand and respect the potential impact of risk, but they do not fear it or allow it to impede their progress. Rather, they maximize these opportunities to communicate risk, as we will explore further in the next chapter.

CHAPTER 9
Communication Must Be Continuous

Throughout my career, from entry-level associate to where I sit today, effective communication has been critically important. I learned early in my tenure as a CAE that it is important to communicate not only well, but frequently, too. But in no job was this ability more important to my success than when I served as inspector general of TVA.

TVA is a wholly owned corporation of the U.S. government. As its IG, I had some of the most important and visible stakeholders any CAE will ever encounter. Not only did I work for TVA's Board of Directors, I also counted among my key stakeholders members of Congress and the president of the United States. Communicating with TVA's board was not a new experience for me because, as the USPS deputy IG, I had assisted the Postal Service's IG in carrying out this critical responsibility before I moved to the power authority. But having to communicate with the likes of Congress and the White House was uncharted territory for me. While required by law to deliver semi-annual reports to all members of Congress, I knew that the lawmakers most interested in TVA were those whose constituents relied on TVA-produced electricity—a group that consisted of 14 senators and 14 House members.

I made a commitment early in my tenure at TVA to establish relationships with as many of these congressional stakeholders and their staffs as possible. I routinely flew from Knoxville to Washington and walked the halls of Congress to foster and sustain these important relationships. The initial rounds of visits were to introduce myself. Subsequent meetings were designed to gain a better understanding of the needs and expectations of the senators and representatives. As we delivered on the lawmakers' expectations, and the number of meetings in Washington multiplied, I began developing strong relationships with certain contacts, particularly key congressional staff members.

Just a few months after TVA's board hired me as IG, Congress added the post to the list of IGs that from then on would be appointed by the president. I expected to remain in the job until the president nominated someone for confirmation by the U.S. Senate, so I added the Office of Management and Budget (OMB), an arm of the White House, to my list of Washington stakeholders, visiting there whenever possible. Several months after the bill was passed that made the TVA IG position presidentially appointed, I received the long-awaited call from the White House that the president was preparing to nominate a permanent IG for TVA. While such nominees were required by law to be qualified for their appointed posts, they typically were also connected politically in some fashion. So, when the caller from the Office of Presidential Personnel advised me that the president wanted to nominate me as TVA's first presidentially appointed inspector general, I was astounded. Only later did I learn that key members of Congress had weighed in with the White House to indicate their desire that I remain in the job.

Ultimately, I declined the nomination so I could retire from government and start a new career. Still, my efforts to build and sustain key relationships with members of Congress and their staffs through continuous communication had resulted, as an unintended consequence, in my becoming a nominee for appointment by the president of the United States. It's a lesson about relationship building and continuous communication—learned on one of the world's biggest stages—that I have never forgotten.

As the speed of risk has accelerated dramatically, the need for continuous communication has never been more critical for internal auditors. Yet, continuous communication is a struggle for many of us. Many in the profession are introverts; communicating with other people doesn't come naturally to us. As internal audit professionals, we are often recognized for the many outstanding skills and characteristics that we bring to bear in executing our important role within businesses, government agencies, and other organizations. But our inability to communicate effectively can impede our attempts to build and maintain rapport with stakeholders.

Year after year, survey results undertaken by The IIA indicate that a core competency that stakeholders value most in an internal auditor is an ability to communicate. CAEs are also consistent in signaling that communication is one of the top two or three most prized attributes when recruiting new staff for their internal audit department.

The communication starts long before an audit engagement; it begins with the relationships you cultivate with stakeholders and others within your organization. When it's time to conduct the audit, you will look for managers and others within the company to open up to you and share details about the kinds of things that keep them awake at night, what they see as their biggest challenges, and what they want you to do to help them. If you don't have the ability to converse with these people informally and build positive relationships with them *before* you start the audit, you will find yourself at a great disadvantage during the engagement.

As a CAE, you have to make a point of having regular luncheon meetings or other social interactions with those executives. You may be uncomfortable with that—you may prefer to spend that lunch hour eating at your desk—but if you truly want to understand the vulnerabilities of your business and the risks it faces, you have to be willing to have such conversations. Effective communication is also critical to building a successful relationship with the audit committee and, ultimately, delivering value to the company.

COMMUNICATION

The internal audit professional…

1. Secures the trust of others through positive use of communication.
2. Fosters open communication.
3. Demonstrates respect for others and customizes messages to reflect the needs of the target audience.
4. Organizes and expresses ideas clearly and with confidence in order to influence others.
5. Extracts key information from a variety of sources to support communication.

6. Selects appropriate communication forms (verbal, nonverbal, visual, written) and media (face to face, electronic, paper-based).

7. Employs the technical conventions of the language (spelling, punctuation, grammar, etc.) correctly.

8. Listens actively, asking questions as required to check his or her own understanding.

9. Solicits feedback from the audience to gauge the effectiveness of the communication.

10. Anticipates reactions to communications and plans responses in advance.

11. Discusses audit findings and their impacts professionally and confidently with appropriate levels of the organization.

12. Interprets and uses body language to reinforce communication.

13. Uses graphical methods to communicate processes and other complex information.

14. Delivers information in a structured fashion to foster learning and development among members of the audience.

15. Applies appropriate communication skills in interviews.[1]

You Need Strong, Effective Communication Skills

Strong, effective communication skills—especially effective interviewing skills—are as important to your annual and internal audit engagement cycles as the planning of your engagements' tactical elements. "Communicates effectively" is one of The IIA's Core Principles for the Professional Practice of Internal Auditing.

If we are going to be effective in this profession, we have to be familiar and comfortable with all the nuances of communication. The simple truth is: If you don't like to write or speak to other people, find another job.

Effective Communications: An Enduring Challenge

As with most professional characteristics, any gaps in effective communication often start at the top—in our case, with the CAE. In an earlier chapter, I identified being a dynamic communicator as one of the nine attributes critical to success as an internal auditor. In this section, I want to drive home that point by outlining the complaints I frequently hear about internal audit communication from stakeholders. Unfortunately, the following observations by audit committee members, managers, and others are far too common:

- Reports are too voluminous or not well written.
- Committees receive too many reports or too much content.
- Audit results are "not synthesized" in a way that allows users to "connect the dots."
- Internal auditors are "introverts by nature" and reluctant to communicate informally.
- The CAE and senior internal audit staff don't give effective presentations.
- The CAE is reluctant to offer or issue opinions.

I could go on, but I suspect you get the point. As an internal audit professional, you should candidly assess your communication skills and continuously hone and develop them. Be confident in what you are communicating, whether it's spoken or written. Speak and write with conviction, passion, and authority. Be clear in what you say or write. Don't try to sound like someone else—be yourself—but articulate your thoughts so they are understood. Believe in what you are saying; your clients will quickly spot any hypocrisy. And don't talk *at* people, talk *with* them. Ask provocative questions and listen carefully to what they have to say.

Closed Lips Are Missed Ships

During World War II, people were reminded of the dangers that enemy spies and submarines posed to wartime shipping with the phrase "loose lips sink ships." But when it comes to asking questions during an internal audit engagement, the danger is more often that "closed lips miss ships." Much of the information an internal auditor receives comes from interviews with managers and employees, and questions are the tool most commonly used to elicit that information. The reliability of that information depends in part upon how clearly the internal auditor is communicating with those being audited.

Be sure the questions you ask your clients are appropriate and designed to get you the information you need. Questions that elicit general or nonspecific responses are not productive and won't help you to identify any core problems.

Open-ended questions will encourage the client to disclose all relevant information. Pay attention to what is *not* said and follow up when appropriate. Don't make assumptions based on incomplete information.

Regardless of how specific and complete your interview questions are, they are useless if you do not listen to the answers you're given. Hearing the words isn't enough; that just means you're aware of the sounds the person is making. Listening means you're paying attention to what it is they're saying and making a sincere effort to understand the meaning and significance of their words. Once internal auditors begin asking questions, they must demonstrate an appreciation for the answers by remaining alert, undistracted, and attentive. Ways to accomplish this and convey your efforts to the person speaking include the following practices:

1. **Monitor your nonverbal behavior.** Maintain comfortable eye contact and assume a posture of involvement by facing the speaker and perhaps leaning in the person's direction.

2. **Listen for feelings as well as facts.** As people speak, they usually reveal emotions as well as information. The speaker's tone, choice of words, and apparent frame of mind can be just as important as the information provided.

3. **Learn to listen reflectively.** A good way to confirm whether you have been listening well is to summarize what the speaker just said and ask if you have understood correctly.

4. **Listen with an open mind.** Don't let preconceptions about the person or the topic you're asking about cloud your understanding of what's being said. If you have preconceived notions about people or their answers, you're likely to selectively focus your attention on only the information that supports your expectations. Other ideas may be filtered out.[2]

Keep in mind that sensitive issues—such as management's failure to manage strategic or operational risks, ethically questionable behaviors, even allegations of fraud—could arise at any time, in which case the CAE and relevant internal audit staff must possess highly developed oral and written communication skills to ensure the information is conveyed to all concerned stakeholders in a timely and appropriate fashion. The communication of sensitive issues is best handled through well-established channels of formal and informal communication with management and board members with whom the CAE and internal audit have strong relationships based on trust and credibility.[3]

Setting the Tone During an Entrance Conference

Another time when effective communication is vital is during an engagement's entrance conference. If you have been in internal auditing for a few years, you've probably seen this happen. You start your entrance conference and everything is going smoothly. You've prepared carefully for the meeting and have cordial relationships with your audit clients. Suddenly, your clients are frowning and the communication seems to have become a one-way street. It's almost as if someone flipped a switch. Management's arms are crossed in a defensive posture, and they seem to disagree with everything you say.

What went wrong? You may never know. All you do know is that an opportunity to discuss the scope, timing, and objectives of an upcoming audit with the relevant clients in a nonconfrontational atmosphere has slipped away. There are ways to help ensure it doesn't happen again, however. Every situation is different, but here are a few things you should avoid saying at entrance conferences because they seem to raise some people's hackles.

"We are here to help you." It's always good to establish and maintain a cordial tone throughout an entrance conference, but sincerity is the key. Clichés such as this are often referred to as "the oldest fib in internal auditing." The second-oldest is management's response, "We're glad to have you." Your clients might actually be happy to see you, or you might be as welcome as the last government auditor to review their personal income taxes. If that's the case, your cheerful opening comment might unexpectedly fall flat.

"We are here because your area ranked high on our risk assessment." Any suggestion at an entrance conference that internal audit has already decided that problems exist will usually spark tension with management. You are undertaking this audit to assess the effectiveness of management's controls

and risk management—if you think about the engagement from management's point of view, you can probably come up with a more compelling explanation for the audit.

"Our objective is to assess the overall effectiveness of your area." It is important to articulate possible audit objectives as clearly, specifically, and precisely as possible. Broad terms such as *efficiency* or *overall effectiveness* are difficult to assess in the absence of widely accepted criteria. And remarks about an operation's "overall effectiveness" can give already anxious managers the jitters—the implication is that you are on some sort of "fishing expedition" from which the client cannot possibly emerge unscathed.

"We will brief you on the results at the conclusion of the audit." Communication must be continuous. Holding the results until the end of an audit will invariably frustrate management and reinforce the stereotype of internal auditors as snoops with a "gotcha" mentality. It's okay to let clients know that you may not talk with them again until the conclusion of your visit—but only if you also make it clear that there will be no surprises at that meeting. An entrance conference should soothe unnecessary fears, not create anxiety about problems that may not exist.

"We don't have anything to tell you today. We just wanted to know if you had any questions." If you schedule a meeting at which you have nothing to say, you are not just missing an opportunity to build relationships, you are wasting management's time. An entrance conference should be about sharing information, and you should prepare in advance so you can introduce the team members and talk about how the audit came to be, its preliminary objectives, projected milestones, and what may be expected of management. If you don't have anything to tell your client, stay in your office.

An internal audit's entrance conference is more than just a chance to say hello. It's an opportunity to make a strong first impression, establish or reinforce healthy working relationships, and motivate clients to work with you toward a positive outcome. It can set the tone for the entire engagement. Unfortunately, an entrance conference can also damage working relationships; too often, mistrust is created or other barriers erected simply because of a thoughtless remark or errant phrase.

Avoiding Communication Breakdowns

As a young internal auditor, I was never more frustrated than when I presented what I knew to be a great recommendation or idea to an audit client, only to be met with waves of skepticism and negativity. I knew my message was important, but at times it was a real challenge to overcome the mistrust and fear seemingly engendered by the mere fact that the recommendation had come from an auditor.

I didn't understand why I sometimes had difficulty "selling" my recommendations until one particular exit meeting that was unusually frustrating. Almost every recommendation from internal audit elicited skepticism from the client—until a more experienced internal auditor joined the conversation. My colleague went back over several of the recommendations I had presented just a few moments earlier, and suddenly they seemed completely reasonable to our client.

Why was the other auditor so much more persuasive? I believe the difference was that the senior auditor had built a solid working relationship with the client and had firmly established his credibility.

Even when internal audit recommendations are sound, younger or less-experienced internal auditors may lack the credibility to make them stick. Sometimes the problem is simply a lack of internal audit experience, but many times the problem stems from the auditor's communication skills. The good news is that communicating your credibility—the trust you inspire in others through honest and fair dealings with them—is a skill you can actively work to improve.

Here are some tips that should help you avoid at least a few of the frustrating exit meetings I faced early in my career:

1. **Maintain your enthusiasm.** We all tend to view people who are enthusiastic and passionate about their work as more credible than those who are not. It's difficult for others to buy into our ideas if we are seen as ambivalent or negative. Maintaining a positive tone is particularly important when critiquing others. It's not enough that we are enthused by the

situation; we must also stoke our client's enthusiasm for the changes we recommend. It's easier to develop enthusiasm when we concentrate on solving problems, not on finding fault. The next time you are tempted to say, "You did it wrong," try saying, "Let's see if there's a better way to do this."

2. **Demonstrate your concern.** If you demonstrate genuine concern for your audit clients and their areas of responsibility, you will be well on your way to establishing some credibility (and building relationships). Yes, delivering promised results is critical for personal credibility, but nothing is more critical than constructive communication while delivering those results. When you show genuine concern for your clients, you are helping convince them that your audit recommendations are in their best interests.

3. **Be professional.** It may not always seem fair, but we are judged not only by the quality of our ideas but on how we present them as well. If you tend to dress sloppily, use slang or profanity, keep a disorganized work area, show up late for meetings, or chew gum throughout an exit meeting, don't be surprised when some clients assume you are also sloppy with your work. Being organized and professional in dress, speech, and behavior helps ensure that your ideas are taken seriously.

4. **Communicate continually, candidly, and (almost) completely.** Ongoing communication throughout an engagement can solidify your reputation as someone who is open to discussion, even when those involved may not agree. Visibility is also critical. If co-workers and clients can't remember your name or face, you cannot establish any credibility. I'm not suggesting that you monopolize meetings or bombard people with huge amounts of minute detail; I also don't mean to imply that discretion isn't important. Auditors often deal with sensitive information, and nothing can destroy someone's credibility faster than gossip or some other failure to preserve a client's confidentiality. Conversely, internal auditors must be particularly careful about agreeing to remain quiet about a potentially bad situation. You can't be credible as an internal auditor if you agree to hide anything immoral or illegal—it might even cost you your career.

5. **Follow through on commitments.** A reputation for dependability is essential in establishing credibility, and following through on your tasks and promises shows your clients and co-workers that you are trustworthy and reliable. Communication is essential if you realize you are going to miss a deadline or a commitment. But even if you apprise all relevant parties of the pending delay, too many excuses will damage your credibility further. Perhaps the dog really did eat your audit report, but that doesn't change the fact that the report was not delivered when promised. It's important that you don't make promises unless you are sure you can keep them.

6. **Be prepared.** If you arrive unprepared for meetings or don't know what you are talking about, you will lack credibility no matter what else you bring to the table. Preparation is especially important for auditors because each audit takes us into a new working situation. Asking questions is a key communication skill and can help build credibility, but it's important you do your homework first so you don't ask unnecessary questions. If you have not prepared for an audit ahead of time by learning about the industry and reading the files of previous audits, you are both destroying your credibility and wasting management's time.

7. **Get it right!** As Nathaniel Hawthorne said, "Accuracy is the twin brother of honesty; inaccuracy, of dishonesty." Whether an inaccuracy is a careless mistake, a deliberate exaggeration, or a downright lie, an internal auditor with a reputation for errors is always going to have credibility problems. If you're not sure of your facts, check them. If you're not sure about your audit procedures, get a second opinion.

Building credibility through effective communication takes time, but a solid reputation for honesty and fairness can follow you for the rest of your career—so, for internal auditors, it is well worth the effort. It is hard to be seen as honest and fair if you lack the ability to communicate tactfully and diplomatically.

Tact and the Art of Bringing About Positive Change

Isaac Newton once said, "Tact is the art of making a point without making an enemy." Being tactful is just that—having the ability to communicate our messages clearly while being sensitive to those around us. Being tactful does not mean that internal auditors should ignore the facts or hide what we believe. It does mean we should present our ideas in ways that make them more palatable. In the long run, it will usually lead to better decision making and client relationships.

There is a common misconception that internal auditing is simply about finding what's wrong and telling people how to fix it. If only it were that simple. At its essence, internal auditing is the art of bringing about positive change. But we all know that getting people to do what you want takes more than telling them what they should do. Paradoxically, the more forcefully we argue our points, the more likely our clients often reject them.

One of the first client meetings I ever attended was also one of the least successful. From the minute the internal auditor opened the meeting by going through a laundry list of things we found that were "wrong," it put our client immediately on the defensive. As a result, the client pushed back, the auditor stood his ground, and the conversation degenerated into little more than an argument.

"But this is wrong. You need to fix it," the internal auditor complained. "You just don't understand my department," the client shot back. "You are an auditor. What makes you think you know so much about our operations?"

It became difficult to come to any agreement, even on minor points.

As the newest auditor on the team, I felt trapped. I was at the meeting only to observe, but things obviously were not going well. An internal audit manager finally stepped in—far too late, in my opinion—and tried to defuse the situation. But the damage—both to any chance of a productive meeting and to the overall relationship—was done. Eventually, we decided to push pause, end the meeting early, and try again another day.

That day was one of the few times when I wondered whether I had chosen the right profession. Would all client meetings become this contentious? What would I have done?

When we returned to our offices that day, we reported the problem to the CAE, who calmly helped us determine what we might do differently the next time. Some of those tips stick with me today. To avoid any internal audit meeting from going wrong, always deploy tact and diplomacy, and remember to:

1. **Start off on a positive foot.** It's easier to come to agreement on difficult issues if you've already established a rapport. So, rather than tackling what may be the most important, and potentially most contentious, issue first, start with something you know that you and your client are likely to agree upon.

2. **Avoid becoming defensive.** It's natural for anxious internal audit clients to sometimes become defensive, and they might "strike back" inappropriately. But if you let yourself become defensive too, any discussion will quickly turn into battle. Stay calm and confident, even if your client does not.

3. **Ask for their opinion.** A firm demand to "fix it" can raise hackles, while the phrase "I wonder what would happen if" can lead your client to seriously consider alternatives. Tactfully worded questions are almost always a good way to get your client to consider their options. Consider asking, "What do you think would happen if we tried doing this?" or "What do you think about?" By asking for their opinion, rather than demanding action, you are showing respect and leaving them feeling in a position of decision maker.

4. **Demonstrate that you are on the same team.** Instead of saying, "You really should," try phrases such as, "We might consider" or "Do you think we should try?" By framing your recommendation in terms of "we" instead of "you," you can demonstrate that you are on the client's side.

5. **Accentuate the positive.** Even when a process is broken, you often can find something good to say about it. So, instead of "This doesn't work," try "This part of the process is working really well. Do you think it might be even more effective if we follow up by...?"

6. **Give an inch, gain a mile**. If you're willing to concede certain points to help make your case, you will often have a stronger position. Of course, proceed with caution. We can't decide to not report an important issue, but there's often more than one "right way" of doing things. You may be able to surrender on a minor, non-reportable issue or on an insignificant wording change. In doing so, you may find that your client is more likely to have an open mind to other, more substantive issues.

7. **Talk less, listen more.** The person who talks the most doesn't necessarily win an argument or convince anyone of anything. Listening courteously and taking the time to understand your client's point of view can help you to convince them of alternatives. If you learn to recognize the goals, beliefs, and motivations behind their remarks, you are halfway to bringing them to understanding your point of view.

8. **Do your homework.** It's important to know all the facts before making suggestions. You will gain credibility if you thoroughly understand both sides of the situation and can illustrate your point with solid examples and facts.

9. **Dangle the carrot, withhold the stick.** It's much easier to change points of view by demonstrating benefits than by making threats. If you are able to convince your client that they will directly benefit by accepting your suggestion, the odds of winning them over rise dramatically. The trick is to be enthusiastic without "overselling" your ideas. Most people tend to become wary of promises that sound too good to be true, but if you are honest about the expected payoff and positive about the benefits, you will likely gain your client's agreement.

10. **Establish mutual respect.** You will rarely convince anyone of anything if they believe you do not respect them. It should go without saying, for example, that you need to maintain eye contact and never interrupt when your client is talking. Negative body language or inattention to their point of view can result in lasting damage to important client relationships.

Continuous Communication—A Conduit for Information

During the many years I worked as an internal auditor and leading internal audit departments, I never envisioned becoming a CEO. But now that I am, I know my effectiveness as an executive leader is because of my experiences in internal auditing.

Having served as the CEO of The IIA, I oversee stakeholders that include about 200,000 members, leaders in more than 100 affiliated international institutes and 160 North American chapters, more than 200 staff at The IIA's global headquarters, and 17 members of The IIA's Global Board of Directors. You can imagine that communicating frequently with such a diverse and dispersed set of stakeholders is challenging and, yet, necessary.

As CEO, I routinely use lessons I learned as a practicing internal auditor when communicating with stakeholders:

- Learn their needs and expectations.
- Understand the key metrics by which they will judge the organization's success.
- Identify and mitigate key risks faced by the organization and profession.
- Share news about key opportunities and accomplishments, as well as my assessment of organizational and industry risks.
- Serve as a conduit for information from one key stakeholder group to another.

I encourage you to take the lessons you learn in your current role to sharpen your communication skills in order to share information with your stakeholders. Listen to them; seek to understand their viewpoint to help them identify key risks and opportunities; and become a channel for communication between management and the board. In so doing, you may find opportunities that will take you to the next level in your career.

CHAPTER 10
Failing to Plan Is Planning to Fail

When I first joined the USPS as deputy assistant inspector general for audit, I included among my responsibilities the task of reviewing all draft audit reports generated by the engagement teams. This was a frustrating process for everyone in the early going. The teams brought me their draft reports, proud of all the information they had collected and analyzed, but as I reviewed each of them ahead of their release to USPS management for comment, a common set of problems often emerged.

The audit's purpose and objectives were not clear in many of the draft reports, and both the scope of the audit and the methodology employed to conduct it were not well defined. Initially, I assumed the audit teams were simply struggling with how to tell their story, but I soon discovered that the root cause of the confusion went all the way back to the planning phase of the audit's engagement.

On more than one occasion, a disillusioned team had to retroactively craft a plan to serve as the basis for the audit. In some cases, the team then had to return to the field to gather additional evidence and make extensive revisions to the report—which inevitably was delayed, diminishing its value to management accordingly.

Poor engagement planning is the first, and perhaps the biggest, mistake that internal auditors make in conducting and reporting their audits.

Timeliness in the Digital Age

Two decades into the twenty-first century, we find ourselves in a digital age, with information moving instantaneously not only through mass media but through personal computers and various consumer devices, such as smartphones, virtual assistants, and tablets.

With the advent of digital text, images, and video, the speed and accessibility of information now defies imagination. I rarely find myself reaching for a TV remote anymore to find out on CNN or some other cable television outlet what is happening in the world. Instead, I pick up my smartphone to scan news sites, check my email, or engage others on a social network. This world of instant news and information is where internal audit's clients and stakeholders live on a daily basis. Many organizations have installed enterprise systems with computerized "dashboards" that place vast amounts of real-time information at company executives' fingertips.

Yet, timeliness continues to be a challenge for internal auditors. When I joined the profession, very little time was dedicated to planning an audit engagement. We often used some kind of "canned" template for our plan, charging off to conduct the audit much like a motorist with an old road map in the glove compartment. Some internal audit teams actually conducted internal audits without a plan at all, crafting one at the end of the process for filing with the rest of the engagement's workpapers.

Anyone who has tried to navigate a trip along a new route with an outdated map (or no map at all) knows it is easy to make wrong turns or become lost entirely. The same is true of an internal audit. If you don't plan an audit effectively, you are essentially planning to fail.

Forget auditing at the speed of risk. A poorly planned internal audit is likely to move at the speed of glaciers! Careful planning at the outset of an engagement can eliminate many of the timeliness issues that internal auditors encounter during the actual engagement and reporting stages of their work.

An Expectations Gap

The internal audit profession has not made speeding up stakeholders' access to information much of a priority. The typical audit process today is much as it was 40 years ago before the introduction of mass-market personal computers. We use automation more now than we did then, but it can still take an internal audit department two months or more to deliver an audit report to management.

Meanwhile, managers and the board of directors—our customers—live in the "Google era," with instant answers available to almost any question with a few keystrokes, and so they no longer consider two months, or even two weeks, very timely. This has created an *expectations gap* that is not often discussed in internal auditing.

Look at how the profession divides its energies and you'll see that an illustration of what internal auditors typically emphasize resembles an inverted pyramid. At the top is a large, wide band that represents accuracy; historically, we spend an incredible amount of time and resources to ensure the accuracy of our information, as well we should. Below that is a smaller band that represents usefulness; we spend a little less time focused on the degree to which our clients can use our information. And below that, the little triangle at the bottom represents the time we spend on our information's timeliness.

"Sometimes," George Bernard Shaw is reported to have quipped, "it's better never than late."

Management often needs to make urgent decisions. If they come upon a real or suspected problem, they might invite internal audit in to assess the situation or provide some assurance that the situation is under control, or they could be faced with a high-profile problem. I certainly encountered many of those during my years in government, particularly as an inspector general, when the morning newspaper might disclose a risk or problem that required me to deploy an audit team to quickly get to the bottom of it.

Deadlines imposed from outside the department can also be a problem. The CEO may ask the CAE to conduct an audit within a specific time frame, which is to say, "I need the answer within a week!" Health or safety concerns sometimes drive the need for quick turnaround of internal audit results.

And then there is the simple need to become more efficient. The faster we can wrap up an audit and distribute a report, the sooner we can move on to the next one, and the more audits we can produce in a year. That means more risks will be addressed each year, enhancing our ability to audit at the speed of risk. The challenge of balancing audit *quality* and *timeliness* has been around for a long time—I've faced it on and off for more than 40 years. While the digital age has radically accelerated the flow of information, I haven't seen a whole lot of change within our profession.

The Planning Phase

Improving the timeliness of internal audits should start with the gap that now exists between what the profession continues to do and what its stakeholders have quickly come to expect. Each phase of the engagement process, starting with the planning stage, can then be transformed to ensure that audit reports are not only accurate and reliable but timely as well.

The IIA's *Standards* mandate that internal auditors undertake a "preliminary assessment of risks" at the outset of every engagement and use the results of that risk assessment to build the audit program. Yet, only about half of the internal audit engagements I have reviewed during the past decade included evidence of such a risk assessment.

Important Considerations During the Planning Phase

The planning phase should be where internal audit teams typically spend most of their time and resources. However, many teams—impatient to arrive onsite, roll up their sleeves, and conduct the actual audit—make only a half-hearted effort to document a plan before diving in. Here's what I suggest to internal auditors who work with me on an engagement.

Establish the Objectives

The first step in an internal audit engagement is to "conduct a preliminary assessment of risks relevant to the activity under review."[1] The engagement objectives must then reflect the results of the assessment. Assuming that management has already assessed risks in the area to be audited, consideration of management's assessment of risks is often the best place to start. In that regard, the internal auditor should consider:

- The reliability of management's risk assessment
- Management's process for monitoring, reporting, and resolving risk and control issues
- Management's reporting of events that exceeded the limits of the organization's risk appetite
- Risks in related activity to the activity under review[2]

Once the risk assessment has been completed, the engagement's formal objectives must be framed. To foster a timely audit, engagement objectives should be as precise as possible. In *Performance Auditing: A Measurement Approach*, Steve Morgan, and my good friend, the late Ronell Raaum, offered some excellent advice on crafting precise objectives for performance audits. They recommend that to ensure objectives are precise as possible, they:

- Identify the audit subject
- Identify the performance aspects to be included
- Identify the finding and reporting elements the auditors expect to develop
- Be answerable[3]

Regardless of whether an internal audit is a performance audit or designed to pursue other objectives, I almost always advise internal auditors to pose them as questions that should be answered by the audit. For example: "Do departmental contracting procedures conform to corporate contracting policies?"

All other things being equal, there usually is a linear relationship between the number of questions we try to answer and how long it will take to conduct the audit. But audit timeliness can be affected by objectives that are framed too broadly, or as open-ended questions, which can become "black holes" swallowing time and resources. For example, an objective "to assess the overall effectiveness of departmental contracting procedures" is likely to take a long time to pursue should the criteria for "effectiveness" be too broad or ill-defined. Also, management might take strong exception if we were to conclude that the contracting procedures were "not effective" based on criteria that we developed. And such disagreements would further delay the final audit results.

Too many engagement objectives can actually be a bigger problem than having too few. That's because a large number of objectives may:

- Add time to the survey and planning phases of an audit.
- Increase the scope of the engagement—expanding how much we have to look at and how much of it has to be documented.
- Generate an overly complex audit plan, because each objective will need to be fleshed out in terms of specifying the procedures for identifying, analyzing, evaluating, and documenting information during the engagement.
- Increase the size and elevate the expertise of the team needed to complete the assignment.
- Increase the time required for doing fieldwork.
- Increase the quantity of workpapers eventually needed to document the audit's results.
- Increase the complexity and size of the report.

Based on my experience, limiting the number of objectives is one of the best ways to complete an audit in a timely manner. In deciding how to limit the number of objectives, the first step is to prioritize objectives based on the engagement risk assessment results discussed earlier. If I only have 200 staff hours or four calendar weeks to complete the engagement, then I want to ensure that the most significant risks are addressed with the resources or time constraints available.

Next, internal auditors should ask themselves a few questions about those who will use the information that the internal audit will likely generate:

- Is it going to be used by management?
- Is it going to be used by a board of directors?
- How quickly will the information be needed?
- Who is going to rely on it?
- What information are they seeking or do they need?

When framing objectives, I often advise internal auditors to think about what they already know. The traditional elements of an audit finding are *condition, criteria, cause and effect, and recommendations.* There are times when management will readily concede a condition and sometimes readily concede the cause and effect. When crafting an audit's objectives, there is no point in spending a lot of time documenting a point that management or those being audited concede at the outset. In such cases, it may be more prudent to frame that objective so it asks, "*Why* did the operating department exceed its budget by $1 million in the preceding year?"

Incremental Auditing

One way internal auditors can ensure that their results are delivered timely is through a technique I call *incremental auditing*, which involves taking an inventory of your audit's risk-based objectives and dividing them into a series of smaller engagements. If you have five objectives, you could decide to address the two objectives related to the biggest risk or the urgency that your stakeholders need the information in one audit, the two related to the next-biggest risk in a second audit, and the remaining one in a third audit. I have seen this approach work well in circumstances such as an audit designed to assess the response to a natural disaster.

Whether you use incremental auditing, there are times when it is critical that information from an audit report gets to management as soon as possible. That is when interim reports can be useful. The IIA's Implementation Guide 2410-1: Criteria for Communicating states that an interim report "[c]an be used to communicate information that requires immediate attention, to communicate a change in engagement scope for the activity under review, or to keep management informed of engagement progress when engagements extend over a long period."

Frame the Scope of the Audit

Once the objectives have been established, the scope of the engagement must be determined. Since an engagement will rarely cover everything that can be audited related to the objectives, scope statements must be specific about what is and is not included within the engagement. Such statements may include:

Boundaries of the process—Defines at what point in the process the engagement will begin and where it will end.

In-scope versus out-of-scope locations—For processes that cover multiple locations, perhaps only some of those locations can or will be included in the engagement.

Subprocesses—Larger processes may be composed of a series of subprocesses.

Components—Certain portions, or components, of a process may be omitted.

Time frame—States the specific period of time covered by the engagement.

In addition to limiting your objectives, it is important to limit the scope of the engagement, because the scope also affects timeliness. If the scope is too broad or unrelated to the objectives, it will take more time to complete the audit. I've seen engagements that included an objective to provide assurance on a certain aspect of operations in the current year, yet the engagement team decided the scope of the audit would look at three years' worth of operational data.

Ideally, your objectives should yield self-evident time periods. If a move is made to further limit a scope aligned with the audit's objectives, you may need to refine your objectives. Also, guard against "scope creep" during an audit engagement. If you find something interesting while testing records or results, don't expand your testing beyond the period for which you are trying to provide assurance without first seriously considering your reasons or the consequences. Obviously, if fraud is suspected or detected, expand the scope as needed.

Allocate Resources

Another way I have sped up the planning phase of an engagement is by engaging "functional experts" to assist the team in navigating the learning curve that invariably comes with planning the audit of a particular area for the first time. I have found that bringing in people with expertise in the area you are auditing, at least during the planning phase, will help you shorten the learning curve. Sometimes it is essential that you get such help, especially if you're studying a highly technical area in which you lack expertise.

Generating internal audit results in a timely manner is much easier if you or someone on the team is knowledgeable about the area you are studying. Implementation Guide 2230-1: Engagement Resource Allocation notes that consideration should be given to the availability of external resources where additional knowledge and competencies are required.

You could hire these functional experts as permanent members of your staff, though that is often not practical. For example, at the USPS, we hired some engineers because of the vast complexities of the agency's real estate. You can contract with such specialists, which is probably the more common approach. It may also be possible to borrow such people from within your organization, though that can raise objectivity issues, so I would urge caution.

Develop the Engagement Work Program

Standard 2240: Engagement Work Program talks about the need to develop work programs that will help achieve internal audit's objectives. These work programs can become very detailed and cumbersome, further undermining an audit's timeliness.

The form and the content of these work programs will vary depending on the area you are studying and the complexity of the audit plan for that area. The engagement program needs to include:

- The objectives of the engagement
- The technical requirements, processes, and transactions that are to be examined or tested
- The nature and extent of testing that will be required
- The procedures for collecting, analyzing, interpreting, and documenting information during the engagement

When the Wheels Come off During the Audit

Developing the internal audit plan is not the end of planning. Rather, we must continue to plan throughout the engagement, whether it be the logistics, communications, or even staffing. In general, most issues that arise when the wheels come off during internal audits stem from a single root cause—inadequate engagement planning. It can be tempting to cut engagement planning short, especially when we're still trying to wrap up the last audit. But when we resort to shortcuts, the results can be disastrous. In the words of Benjamin Franklin, "By failing to prepare, you are preparing to fail."

Here are a few examples of how things can go wrong when internal auditors fail to adequately plan:

- I once heard about an internal audit that got off to a disastrous start simply because the auditors didn't explain to the client during the planning phase why they were coming and what they hoped to accomplish. To be sure, they had intended to detail the audit objectives and process at the beginning of fieldwork, but before they could do so at the kickoff meeting, their nervous new client was already in a defensive meltdown mode.

- Another internal audit department was proud that it gave clients plenty of notice about upcoming engagements—six full months ahead of time, in fact, when the annual plan was approved. But when the team flew in for fieldwork in Europe, the client wasn't there. Once again, the problem turned out to be poor communications during the audit planning stage. The engagement supervisor failed to check back with the client in the weeks immediately before the audit, and the client simply forgot about the upcoming engagement. I heard about an internal auditor who reviewed the results of a previous internal audit during the planning phase but did not consider the work of other assurance providers. Testing was well under way when the exasperated client pointed out that the compliance department and regulators had both reviewed the exact same things a month earlier and neither had noted any problems. Naturally, there were some red faces in the internal audit department.

- If you've ever had to stay at a hotel two hours away from your client's location because you postponed making reservations until nearby hotels had no vacancies, you're not alone. If you've ever spent a weekend driving to a distant audit location because you waited a little too long to reserve a flight, you're not alone in that regard either. "Didn't anybody arrange for a rental car?" "Wasn't somebody supposed to reserve a conference room?" "When do you think we can get access to the system?" I often hear of logistics problems that could be avoided simply by starting the planning a little earlier and using a checklist to help ensure details are not overlooked.

- The most common "rookie" planning mistake is simply failing to ask for advice or help when it is needed. I have known several internal auditors who tried to go it alone when they did not have the knowledge or skills necessary to perform parts of an engagement. I have known others who tried to avoid the problem by eliminating audit procedures that should have been performed. Both approaches can lead to poor outcomes, yet a simple conversation with a supervisor might have solved the problem easily. For example, a new internal auditor might have been partnered with someone who knew more about the organization, an auditor might have been reassigned to make better use of his or her individual knowledge and skills, or training might have been available.

- Two internal auditors on one of my teams once found evidence of significant problems in a process under review. After weeks of testing, they shared their results with the client. The client told them that he was aware of the issue, which was why a decision had been made several months earlier to discontinue the process. New equipment was already on order. If, during the planning phase, the auditors had inquired about operations that might be changing in the future, they could have saved themselves weeks of work.

- Another team of internal auditors did not learn until the start of fieldwork that a new technology had already been implemented. Unfortunately, the assigned auditors were not qualified to review the new technology, so they canceled the engagement and rescheduled an audit for the following year. But the worst was yet to come. Due to a staffing change, nobody told the next year's engagement supervisor about the canceled audit. Once again, audit planning was minimal; once again, the wrong auditors were assigned to the review; and once again, the audit had to be canceled after it had begun. I'm told that the client's reaction was "memorable."

Each of these situations reflected poorly on internal audit, frustrated the internal auditors and the clients, and illustrated the type of inefficiency and ineffectiveness that internal auditors are supposed to prevent, not foster. But, in some cases, we may not be aware of the extent to which poor audit planning damages our reputation and our ability to add value.

Effective planning is the key to the successful completion of any type of project. This is true of the internal audit engagement. Communication takes place throughout the engagement process, as the team touches base with the audit's client about important matters on an interim basis—not just at the end of the process in the final engagement communication.[4]

An engagement's planning phase is the first, and perhaps most important, step in conducting a successful internal audit. Without adequate planning, the chances of missing relevant control weaknesses or encountering engagement-related problems increase considerably. Equally important, ineffective or inadequate planning can easily set you on the wrong path, undermining the timeliness of your work before you have even started.

CHAPTER 11
Fight the Temptation to Over-Audit

Shortly after assuming the role of CAE for the first time in my career, I noticed that individual internal audits in my department were taking an unusually long time to complete. A closer look revealed that my internal audit teams were spending an inordinate amount of time preparing the workpapers for each engagement, and I soon learned there was informal competition among the department's auditors to see who could generate the most voluminous workpapers. I joked that the only thing missing was a copy of the phone book, but then I found one among one audit's set of workpapers!

A small investigation on my part revealed what was fueling the competition. In the past, the internal auditors' names were displayed on the filing cabinet drawers that held their workpapers. This made it easy for them to monitor each other and measure who had the most workpapers. Team members equated the sheer size of their paperwork with their relative proficiency as internal auditors. While an extreme example, the competition was fostered by an internal audit culture that rewarded comprehensiveness and accuracy at the expense of almost everything else. As the old saying goes, what gets measured gets done.

From the outset of my career, it has been my experience that most internal auditors tend to over-audit. Blame it on the highly risk-averse nature of our profession. Being accurate and reliable is so ingrained in us early on that we end up auditing and documenting more than we really need to. The IIA's *Standards* are not overly prescriptive in terms of the methodology that must be deployed during internal audit engagements and do not mandate that workpapers contain specific things. However, the policies of many internal audit departments, as well as other audit standards, are often very prescriptive.

For example, the 2018 edition of Generally Accepted Government Auditing Standards (also known as the Yellow Book) includes almost 40 pages of standards prescribing how performance audits should be planned, conducted, and documented. Thirteen pages alone are dedicated solely to prescribing how sufficient and appropriate evidence is to be obtained and how audit evidence is to be documented.[1]

Laboring under the pressure to ensure accuracy above all else, it is no wonder that internal auditors spend so much time on the *fieldwork* phase of their engagements. Whether you call the actual conducting of the audit *fieldwork* or simply talk about *performing the engagement*, as the *Standards* does, you are actually gathering, collecting, and analyzing evidence based on the audit's objectives so that you can draw basic conclusions that ultimately will be documented in your audit report.

While there is no magic formula for reducing the amount of time spent on an engagement, I'd like to share with you several strategies I've identified during my career that may help your internal audit department reduce its overall engagement cycle time.

Audit Techniques

To talk about performing the engagement is to talk about the techniques the internal audit team uses during its fieldwork. IIA Standard 2300: Performing the Engagement states, "Internal auditors must identify, analyze, evaluate, and document sufficient information to achieve the engagement's objectives." The techniques employed should yield sufficient and competent evidence and ensure that the engagement is swift, yet done with due professional care.

Selecting the appropriate techniques can directly affect how long it takes to produce results. From my experience, certain techniques can improve the timeliness of internal audits.

Sampling

Historically, sampling has been a very effective time-saving tool. Before technology made it easier to gather and evaluate larger pools of data, sampling allowed us to limit the number of actions an auditor had to perform, or the number of documents that had to be collected, or the number of locations that had to be visited, without materially affecting the results. Sampling allowed us to draw conclusions about transactions or balances without spending the time and money to examine every transaction. Sampling is still used when it isn't efficient to review 100 percent of the available records, which is often the case if only hard-copy versions of the records are maintained. Sampling is also useful if inventories of physical assets are necessary. It also may be used if records are in remote locations, or other circumstances make it difficult to review all of them electronically.

Flowcharting and Process Mapping

Flowcharting processes and activities allow you to quickly evaluate all the steps that occur during an activity or function in a department for which you are conducting an audit. Flowcharts, by the way, can add stakeholder value to an audit. I've had clients who were more excited about the flowcharts that we developed and included in our workpapers than they were about the final audit report. Some even posted copies on the walls above their desks, or maintained them on their desktops for easy reference.

Flowcharts are a great tool to visualize complex systems inside an organization, and often they are easier to understand and less time-consuming for others than a narrative would be. Flowcharts enable the auditor and the client to quickly grasp the big picture. And in the current age of digital technology, it is relatively easy to create a flowchart. It is also easier to update the information in a flowchart than it would be to rewrite a narrative description of the process being audited.

Regression Analysis

Regression analysis helps you identify anomalies using advanced analytical techniques and then, based on an analysis of those anomalies, tells you where you need to focus your efforts. That can save you time and money.

It can also be very useful during the planning phase of an engagement, when you are trying to determine the objectives and scope of the audit. *Sawyer's*

Guide for Internal Auditors defines regression analysis as a "Statistical technique used to establish the relationship of a dependent variable to one or more independent variables. For example, an internal auditor might estimate payroll expense based on the number of employees, average rate of pay, and the number of hours worked, and then compare the result to the recorded payroll expense."[2]

Thanks to the availability of modern, off-the-shelf software such as Microsoft Excel, tools like regression analysis are easy for internal auditors to use.

Collecting and Documenting Audit Data and Evidence

An important element of the audit engagement is the collection of evidence to be used in evaluating, preparing, and communicating the audit results to your client. There are several types of audit evidence that can serve as a basis for conclusions.

Testimonial Evidence

Testimonial evidence is what people say to the auditor. It is considered the weakest form of evidence, though certain testimonial evidence is stronger than others. For example, the person who performs a task could provide stronger evidence of how that task is actually performed than could a supervisor who may know only how it *should* be performed. As a general rule, people who are independent of, but knowledgeable about, the activities being reviewed will provide more reliable testimonial evidence than will the people who are actually involved in the activities.

When documenting testimonial evidence, try to avoid long, detailed transcripts of your interviews, unless they reveal significant anomalies such as material waste, mismanagement, or fraud. Instead, I have coached my auditors to summarize the interviews, particularly if they are corroborated by other types of evidence.

Documentary Evidence

Documentary evidence is contained in some sort of a permanent record form, such as a hard-copy version of an audit report or a supplemental IT system digital archive. This is the second strongest type of evidence, though it may not be as strong as it appears. It is important to consider the source of the document. A written memo is not much stronger than testimonial evidence, for example, because it proves the person said what is in the memo but does not prove that what is said is true.

Documents from sources external to the organization are much stronger evidence than internal documents. External documents from external sources sent to the organization are usually stronger than internal documents, though they are not as strong as those sent directly to the internal auditors.

In working with internal audit teams, I have always advised them that it is not necessary to include paper or electronic copies of every document examined in the audit's workpapers. In my experience, much of that documentary evidence amounts to what I call "happy workpapers."

Happy workpapers are simply evidence that everything is fine—that observed conditions conform to criteria. Such documentation does not need to be included in its entirety, though the workpapers should note what was observed and include notations that would enable an experienced internal auditor to retrieve the same documentation and draw the same conclusions. Documentary evidence indicating conditions that do not conform to criteria should be included in the workpapers, particularly if fraud is involved. This type of documentation has a tendency to "grow legs and walk away" after the audit is completed, if management elects to dispute the audit results or if someone is accused of wrongdoing.

Physical Evidence

Physical evidence is evidence the auditors see with their own eyes. This is considered the strongest form of evidence, though it is important for the auditor to consider what the evidence proves and what it does not prove.

With the advent of the digital age, it is very easy for internal auditors to capture images of physical evidence. During my tenure at the USPS in the late 1990s, the inspector general's office documented safety and environmental conditions at an older postal facility using video technology. With the advent of smartphones and other digital technology, documenting physical evidence in the field is even easier and faster.

Analytical Evidence

Analytical evidence is obtained by comparing, computing, or otherwise analyzing data. Analytical evidence—assuming the data analyzed is accurate—proves that certain relationships exist among the data. This usually has to be investigated further to determine why the relationships exist.

IIA Standard 2310: Identifying Information states that "Internal auditors must identify sufficient, reliable, relevant, and useful information to achieve the engagement's objectives." It interprets each of these criteria as follows:

> *Sufficient* information is factual, adequate, and convincing so that a prudent informed person would reach the same conclusions as the auditor.

> *Reliable* information is the best attainable information through the use of appropriate engagement techniques.

> *Relevant* information supports engagement observations and recommendations and is consistent with the objectives for the engagement.

> *Useful* information helps the organization meet its goals.

One way to improve the timeliness of an audit is to shorten the process in the way you gather your evidence. Avoid over-auditing by taking care to document your findings with the strongest type of evidence, which then makes it unnecessary to gather weaker evidence for the same findings. If gathering the stronger evidence would be too time-consuming, you may be able to accomplish the same thing by quickly gathering several weaker types of evidence that corroborate each other. And remember, it is not necessary to include all of these types of evidence in every set of your internal audit's workpapers.

Workpaper Contents and Preparation

I am probably more liberal than many of my peers when it comes to documentation and workpaper preparation. I always remind myself that workpapers are a means and not an end. By that I mean that workpapers are an important element of the audit's system of quality controls, so they must be comprehensive enough to form the basis of any conclusions we reach and communicate to our clients, but those clients rarely see them.

Although I am sometimes critical of the prescriptive nature of the Yellow Book, I believe that its discussion in Paragraphs 8.132-8.134, "Requirements: Audit Documentation," conveys the right message about the contents of workpapers:

> "8.132 Auditors must prepare audit documentation related to planning, conducting, and reporting for each audit. Auditors should prepare audit documentation in sufficient detail to enable an experienced auditor, having no previous connection to the audit, to understand from the audit documentation the nature, timing, extent, and results of audit procedures performed; the evidence obtained; and its source and the conclusions reached, including evidence that supports the auditors' significant judgments and conclusions.
>
> 8.133 Auditors should prepare audit documentation that contains evidence that supports the findings, conclusions, and recommendations before they issue their report.
>
> 8.134 Auditors should design the form and content of audit documentation to meet the circumstances of the particular audit. The audit documentation constitutes the principal record of the work that the auditors have performed in accordance with standards and the conclusions that the auditors have reached. The quantity, type, and content of audit documentation are a matter of the auditors' professional judgment."[3]

Automated Audit Management Systems (AMS)

Audit technology has evolved from basic electronic working papers to comprehensive, fully integrated audit management systems that now cover the entire audit process, including risk assessment, scheduling, electronic workpapers, end-of-audit reporting, system-wide issue tracking, and audit committee reporting.

When properly implemented, the benefits of using robust audit management technology drive increased productivity and efficiency, enhance audit's transparency, facilitate compliance with the *Standards*, and reduce the demands on stakeholders.

Risk Assessment

Today's risk assessment functionality allows audit departments to quickly develop true risk-based audit plans. Self-assessment capabilities in today's systems allow audit departments to gain valuable risk and control input from all relevant process owners through automated distribution and follow-up of risk and control surveys. These systems aggregate all of the risk and control data and present an audit universe that is risk ranked along with all of the supporting details and reports. Advanced systems also facilitate more frequent and even continuous risk assessments that are demanded in today's dynamic risk environments.

Scheduling

Audit scheduling tools can quickly and automatically provide draft schedules based on auditor skillsets and availability and automatically create draft schedule and also for allow convenient drag-and-drop scheduling functionality. Most systems today are automatically linked to time and expense capture systems, which also include mobile functionality for easy input, tracking, and reporting.

Electronic Workpapers

Today's e-workpapers remain the backbone of most AMS. E-workpapers are web based and allow auditors to document and review audit work anywhere at any time, whether on a laptop, tablet, or smartphone. Advanced features include smart planning whereby controls and related audit steps can be automatically imported into the audit file based on the risks identified.

Reporting

Fully automated draft audit reports, comprehensive issue tracking functionality, and rich visual audit committee dashboards that are updated in real time are just a few examples of features that are increasing productivity and allowing both auditors and stakeholders to spend less time chasing details and more time understanding and mitigating potential threats to the business. Mike Gowell, a former PwC colleague who went on to be the general manager and vice president of TeamMate in Tampa, Florida, was involved in creating the first audit management system and anticipates that audit technology will continue to evolve as the audit profession evolves.

As the profession demands more coordination across the lines of defense (Standard 2050, for example), technology is already evolving to facilitate this enhanced coordination with features that drive the consideration and consolidation of enterprisewide risks, the detailed plans of various individual assurance providers (e.g., compliance, IT, legal, health, and safety) in the second line of defense, and a consolidated reporting database that contains all issues facing an organization—eliminating or reducing siloed reporting.

AMS will evolve into complete audit management platforms with APIs that allow real-time communication with most major reporting systems, thereby facilitating real-time continuous control monitoring. Audit management platforms will also include components such as real-time reporting for audit committees, continuing education modules for auditors, continuing professional education (CPE) tracking, knowledge databases and benchmarking data, and integrated data analytics.

Data Analytics, Data Mining, Data Requisition

Areas where electronic auditing tools have evolved considerably include data analytics, data mining, and data requisition. Such systems allow auditors to access 100 percent of the information for testing in areas of concern, such as duplicate payments to vendors. In the past, information could only be sampled. Thanks to data analytics, an auditor can ask IT to generate a list of every check cut the previous year grouped by vendor.

Data analytics uses IT files and IT interrogations to do audit testing. It allows for continuous controls monitoring. Reports can be run automatically every night, if necessary.

These systems have quickly become fundamental tools of internal auditing. They can greatly improve a department's efficiency and effectiveness, and the quality of its work. An internal auditor or audit department that is not using these systems is simply not going to produce audits as effectively or timely as they could be.

Closing the Effectiveness Gap

Internal audit departments are constantly being offered new technology designed to improve their work. But these new electronic systems are of no value unless CAEs have at least a rudimentary understanding of how to use them and require their staffs to incorporate the technology into every audit they complete.

CAEs realize the importance of leveraging technology. According to The IIA's Audit Executive Center, five key strategies can help make that happen:[4]

1. **Set the tone at the top.** If the CAE doesn't make an effort to embrace the technology and doesn't make it a strategic priority, the internal auditors aren't likely to either. The CAE has to articulate the benefits of such technology to the staff and require that it become a priority for every audit. The CAE must also budget resources for training.

2. **Make electronic tools mandatory for every audit.** Unless you start by making it compulsory, the gap will linger.

3. **Invest in training.** When CAEs have been surveyed on how they trained their teams in the use of new technology, and how proficient their teams were in using it, did they bring in an outside instructor? Organize formal instruction and classes led by someone in the department? Or settle for on-the-job training? The correlation between type of training and staff proficiency couldn't be more obvious. Those departments that chose on-the-job training had the lowest rates of proficiency among their staffs. On-the-job training doesn't seem to always cut it where use of technology is concerned.

4. **Hire someone with technology skills.** Not every internal auditor will become an expert user of the latest technological tools. Some CAEs are

finding it hard to transform just any auditor into a data analytics expert. Instead, they are hiring an IT expert and making that person the internal audit department's technology champion. An added benefit of this arrangement—having such an expert within the department ensures that internal audit will not miss out or be slow to learn about emerging technologies. Teams that budget money for training and hire a technology champion seem to have shorter learning curves.

5. **Measure what matters.** Have metrics in place to measure the return on investment from your new technology and to show others you are not licensing technology and then failing to use it effectively. If you can show the audit committee or CEO a return on the organization's investment, they will be more inclined to support your technology initiative.

The Interview Process

No discussion on streamlining fieldwork would be complete without addressing the processes by which interviews are conducted. During an engagement, internal auditors derive a significant amount of their information about the operations under study, as well as related control activities and deficiencies, from interviews with other people. As I discussed in an earlier chapter, active listening is as important to an internal auditor as the ability to solicit, verify, compare, and evaluate information. Important techniques for effective listening include making eye contact with speakers during individual and group encounters, expressing your interest through questions, restating what someone has said to ensure clarity, avoiding unnecessary interruptions, looking for subtle meanings and feelings that may not be overtly expressed, and responding appropriately to what you have heard.[5]

I once spoke with an auditor who had just spent the previous week combing through contract provisions, painstakingly gathering supporting documents for what he thought would be an important finding, only to discover that the contract provisions were no longer in force. If he had asked a few more questions at the beginning of the week, he would have discovered that, because of a series of change orders, many of the provisions in the original contract were no longer valid. The audit was still a success because at the end of the week—and well before the closing meeting—he asked his client to explain what appeared to be numerous discrepancies. But who knows what else might have been accomplished during that week of lost productivity.

Develop Effective Interviewing Skills

When I taught accounting during evening courses at a local university, I would often tell my students, "The only stupid question is the one that is never asked—unless the question is, 'Would you postpone the next exam?'"

My years as a college instructor coincided with the early years of my career in internal auditing, my day job at the time. And so I came to appreciate that in internal auditing, as elsewhere in life, there really are very few stupid questions.

The most successful internal auditors are not necessarily the smartest or the most experienced; often, they are simply the most inquisitive. Of course, it also helps to be intelligent and well prepared for what's to come, but when internal auditors miss a finding, too often it's simply because they weren't curious enough to ask all the questions they should have.

Consider this: If you cite an issue or problem in your draft report that does not exist, management will usually object vehemently and provide ample evidence that your conclusions are erroneous (which is why I often cite management review of a draft report as one of the best forms of quality control during an audit). But if you fail to cite an issue or problem that really does exist, is management likely to speak up and say, "Excuse me, but you've missed a major deficiency in my area"? Let's just say that, in more than 40 years on the job, I have never seen it happen.

We also need to be able to assess risks, plan engagements, conduct fieldwork, analyze situations, and advise our clients appropriately. But the overall process (and each step within it) starts with asking well-informed questions.

How Smart Internal Auditors Ask Smart Questions

The best internal auditors know that there are times when we need to "break the rules" when conducting client interviews. Few skills are more essential for internal auditors than knowing how to ask the right questions. With effective questioning skills, we can build rapport, strengthen understanding, and encourage openness. Without these skills, we can damage working relationships or overlook essential information.

Even the world's best analytical skills are useless if we fail to uncover the information we need because of faulty questioning techniques. That's why most internal auditors receive formal training on how to conduct internal audit interviews. Training is essential because it can provide important rules regarding how to interview people.

Open-Ended or Not? Take, for example, the standard rule that open-ended questions work better than yes/no questions. That's usually correct, particularly when you have a candid, trusting relationship with your client and you plan to talk about nonthreatening subjects. But recent research indicates that it's important for questioners (regardless of profession) to assess whether a discussion is more cooperative or competitive in nature before asking questions. In "competitive" interviews or when a client seems evasive, open-ended questions may simply lead to lies by omission.

When Negative Is a Positive. Internal auditors generally are advised to maintain a positive, upbeat tone during audit interviews. Certainly, tone matters. And it's rarely helpful to sound accusatory or to telegraph anger when we meet with clients. But, at times, we need to temper the positive attitude with realism. Internal auditors need to ask difficult questions, and when the answer to a question is likely to be adversarial (when a deadline is going to be missed or a production estimate is overly optimistic, for example), some experts suggest framing the question pessimistically. If you ask, "That's not going to be on time, is it?", you are giving your client "permission" to be truthful by showing you understand the situation. The trick is to frame your question negatively but ask it in an empathetic, nonaccusatory manner.

Sequence Matters: Ask in the Right Order. It seems natural to start an audit interview with light, nonthreatening questions. Generally, this approach is recommended because it helps to put our clients at ease. But there are times when asking the easiest questions first can be a mistake.

New research indicates that people are likely to respond more fully to questions if you lead off with your more sensitive and intrusive queries.

According to a report published in the *Journal of Consumer Research*,[6] people were more willing to reveal sensitive information when questions were asked in a decreasing order of intrusiveness because subsequent questions felt relatively less intrusive. The researchers pointed out that, if you start with asking "Have you ever had a fantasy of doing something terrible to someone?", then subsequently ask "Have you ever called in sick to work when you were perfectly healthy?" becomes less intimidating. (I would not recommend starting an audit interview with either of these questions, but they make a good point.)

The danger is that starting a discussion with the toughest questions first can be hard on a client relationship. It's probably not a tactic you should use during the kickoff meeting for your next audit, but every time you plan to meet with a client, it's important to consider the best sequence for your questions.

Prepare More, Ask More. When we ask questions that we should already know the answers to, we waste everyone's time and risk aggravating our clients. However, while asking the wrong questions is a relationship killer, most internal auditors could actually improve client relationships by asking more questions. According to research published by the *Journal of Personality and Social Psychology*,[7] people who ask more questions are seen as more likable. Intelligent questioning can create a bond of trust and empathy that leads to better audit results.

The point is that, even when we think we know the essentials of effective interviewing skills, there may be important exceptions to those rules. Effective interviewing is more involved than simply asking for information. It is a mixture of art and science that can determine the success or failure of an audit career. That's one of the many reasons the best internal auditors believe in lifelong learning, practicing their skills, and preparing thoroughly before every client meeting.

Avoid Drive-By Auditing

Nothing undermines the value of an internal audit more than delivering the results once it's too late to correct a problem or prevent further fraud, waste, or mismanagement. But at the other extreme are what I call "drive-by" internal audits that rely on canned programs or checklists. These quickie audits are sometimes conducted at the branch or store level in the financial services and retail industries.

Don't get me wrong—drive-by audits can provide important assurance on the effectiveness of internal controls and compliance matters. They can also help deter fraud. But their use does not always comply with our professional standards, and they rarely provide management with real value. I often think of these down-and-dirty engagements as "inspections" rather than true internal audits.

To avoid becoming a drive-by auditor, I recommend you assess your approach by asking yourself these five questions:

1. **Is the engagement the result of an annual or ongoing risk-assessment process?** Drive-by audits are often cyclical: "We are going to audit you this year whether you need it or not."

2. **Is the audit program or engagement plan based on an assessment of risk?** As noted earlier, the *Standards* mandate that, in planning an engagement, internal auditors must consider significant risks to the activity, its objectives, resources, and operations. Drive-by audits often use canned audit materials, with little consideration given to the risks facing the specific business unit or activity that is the focus of the engagement.

3. **Is the same audit program being used at each drive-by location?** As indicated above, an audit program should be tailored to the risks of the specific unit. But there is an even bigger problem with repeated use of the same program at multiple locations: Management will quickly ascertain the areas subject to audit and prepare themselves for the auditor's arrival

at subsequent locations. Even if a new audit program is used each year, I have seen instances where management from the first business unit audited as part of the annual cycle alerts their colleagues further down the schedule to "what the auditors are looking at this year." Naturally, that can undermine the effectiveness of the entire audit process.

4. **Does the final audit report offer recommendations or simply provide findings or observations?** Although it's rare, some drive-by internal auditors don't even attempt to develop customized recommendations for taking corrective action in response to the findings or noncompliance issues cited in their audit report. The final report is nothing more than a list of transgressions compiled by the auditor before heading off to the next location. Rather than a drive-by internal audit, this should be classified as a "hit-and-run" internal audit.

5. **Does the audit process and final report provide management with any added value?** Sadly, in the case of drive-by audits, the answer is often "no." The reports are often very clinical, with no indication of management's accomplishments, insight on operations, or opportunities for improvement beyond the boilerplate "these things are not in compliance—correct them."

Every phase of the internal audit process must be reengineered with an eye toward producing more timely results. But while new digital tools for the planning and fieldwork stages, such as automated workpapers, have certainly streamlined internal auditors' work, the most daunting part of the process in terms of timeliness is the reporting phase. In the next chapter, I will share with you the challenges I have faced in the reporting phase, and how I learned to deliver timely, effective reports.

CHAPTER 12
Better Never Than Late

It would be nice if a typical internal audit, well planned in advance and employing the latest technology to speed up the fieldwork, was then destined for swift delivery to the audit's client. Unfortunately, crafting the actual internal audit report and obtaining management's concurrence with applicable findings and recommendations can be the most time-consuming—and frustrating—phase of all.

In his iconic book *Sawyer's Guide for Internal Auditors*, Larry Sawyer nails it when he describes the process of writing an audit report this way: "Few sources of friction within the auditing department exceed that caused by the process of report writing. The most brilliant of analyses and the most productive of audit findings seem to be forgotten during the trauma of report writing."[1]

Given the speed at which risks emerge and can wreak havoc, internal audit departments should have zero tolerance for slow reporting processes. Failure to deliver a final report after it's too late for the results to avoid further impact is not an option. That isn't even protecting organizational value, much less enhancing it.

Typical Challenges in the Reporting Process

As a young internal auditor, I was certainly frustrated now and then by the writing of internal audit reports. But I imagine it is much more frustrating for new auditors today.

The challenge to produce internal audit reports in a timely manner, for clients now accustomed to instantaneous transmission of information in the digital age, competes with the other criteria for communicating audit results to clients—especially accuracy. The same hurdle exists in the planning and fieldwork phases of the internal audit process.

We are trained from the outset of our careers that we cannot afford to generate inaccurate internal audit reports. We also strive to craft reports that pass muster with management and result in improvements or corrective action within the organization. Combine these demands with a multilevel review process within the internal audit department, and writing an audit report can become an exercise in delay and frustration.

The first time new internal auditors send in a draft audit report for review, they may naively think the audit is finished as they shift gears mentally to begin focusing on the challenges and uncertainties of the next engagement. Little do they know that the reporting phase of that audit has just started.

It helps to know what to expect when a draft is sent up the departmental chain for review; that is, someone will look it over and indicate desired changes to your carefully chosen words—and trust me, if it is your first audit report, there *will* be changes. The draft will be sent back to you for revision, and when you're done with it, again, the new version will be sent back to the first reviewer, who may or may not forward it to the next level of review, depending on how pleased they are with your revisions.

If your internal audit department is large enough, a second reviewer might then take a more strategic view of how the report should be written, and they often append extensive comments. Back will come the report to your audit team, and once the questions are answered and additional revisions made, it will then be forwarded back up the chain through the first two levels of review.

At this point many audit groups require a process called *referencing*. Referencing is an accuracy check that involves cross-referencing every word in the report with a source document or other supporting evidence from the audit's workpapers. This can take a surprising amount of time (particularly if you didn't heed the advice on workpapers in chapter 10), after which the draft report will make its way back down through the same review channels for questions or comments about the cross-referencing results.

Next, if you are part of a really large internal audit department, a professional editor may review the draft report before it's issued. Many internal audit departments also send their drafts to the general counsel or legal department for review, particularly in government settings where audit reports tend to generate newspaper headlines. At each point in the process, fresh comments, questions, and revisions may demand your attention.

Discouraged yet? Don't be; there's more to come. Until a few years ago, some internal audit reports were pulled from the files independently reviewed as a quality-assurance measure long after the conclusion of the engagement. But the quality-improvement programs at a growing number of organizations now require peer reviews of all audit workpapers *before* a draft report is issued. So all workpapers must be well crafted, too, because your report may resurface again with additional comments and questions.

Given the number of safeguards built into the report-review process, it's not surprising that it sometimes takes weeks or months to get a draft out the door—at which point that frustrated new auditor may learn, as I did early in my career, that an explosive reaction to the draft report from the audit client can trigger parts of the review process to start over again. You may find yourself immersed in a weeks-long process of negotiation involving numerous explanations and clarifications before the client accepts the findings.

The good news is that there are ways to sidestep many of the pitfalls in the audit-reporting process. And, if all else fails, there are some fundamental strategies that may help save some time.

Time-Saving Strategies

Often, information in an internal audit report is urgent. But even when the findings or recommendations don't need immediate attention, speedier delivery of audit reports is becoming more essential as clients' expectations rise amid the ongoing explosion of information in the digital age. We all like to know where we stand when we're being examined. Imagine for a moment that you're still in college and your professor has just told the class he won't have your grades until four months after the final exam. Oh, sure, a few students might be pleased with the delay, but most of you will likely be grumbling in the hallways and perhaps even complaining to the dean!

Obviously your internal audit clients are not college students, but if an audit report is not out the door four months after the fieldwork is complete, you're likely to hear some grumbling around the water cooler. When people stop what they are doing at work to talk about the results of an internal audit, chances are good you are making a difference in your organization; but if they drop what they're doing to grouse about an audit report that they expected to see months ago, the difference you're making in the organization is not necessarily something to be proud of.

During my career, I have worked with quite a few audit departments that have taken on the challenge of audit reports' timeliness. Many of them have achieved enviable results in reducing their reports' "cycle time." Based on my observations, there are at least six strategies that, if deployed effectively, can substantially reduce the amount of time it takes to issue internal audit reports.

1. Share internal audit results with clients "as you go."

Client "pushback" against an audit report can be intensified by the shock effect of seeing all of the results at once. Providing the client with results incrementally can help. Once the internal audit team gets to the point in the engagement where they are satisfied there is a reportable condition, you should share the information with your client, either informally or through an interim audit memorandum. Regular communication with clients during the audit—including sharing draft findings and recommendations in writing—goes a long way toward fostering a positive reaction when the full report is presented for comment.

2. Eliminate or reduce levels of review.

Multiple levels of review within the internal audit department are often a major source of delays in audit reporting. Streamlining the review process and reducing the number of reviewers can shorten and speed up the process.

Large organizations in particular seem to get quite a few people involved in crafting their engagement reports yet, in my experience, the reports produced for these organizations are not necessarily better than reports written elsewhere that undergo only one or two reviews. Many of the organizations I've worked with over the years have found that, if you eliminate some of the additional reviews, the reports move along much more quickly. Others have delegated the reviews to lower-level staff. Such tactics entail some risk; every additional review provides a fresh viewpoint and a different level or type of expertise, while having more-senior staff do reviews ensures more experienced eyes will examine the drafts. Sacrificing those could affect reports' accuracy, clarity, and constructiveness; for example, considerations that should be weighed when attempting to speed up the process. Reducing levels of review is a way to move the audit along faster, but it pays to consider the risks.

3. Use an editor earlier in the process.

Larger audit organizations such as national offices or U.S. federal IGs tend to have professional editors; and in my mind, the editor should have first crack at revising the draft report. As soon as a draft is available from the engagement team, the professional editor should take over. There is no point in having auditors higher up the ladder worry about correcting grammar and syntax; the time of these amateur editors is best spent focused on actual audit issues. Using the professional editor earlier in the process can move things along quickly.

4. Use team writing to condense the process.

Bringing the audit team together with all of those who will edit or review the draft report for a single editing session can reduce reports' cycle time dramatically. This approach allows the internal audit team and the department's upper-level supervisors to discuss the draft report and propose changes without the endless back and forth of the usual editing process. This is a strategy I used when working for the USPS OIG in the late 1990s.

Team writing brings together the engagement team, the first-level and second-level reviewers, the editor, the referencer, and the lawyers (if any are involved). Everyone sits around a table in a conference room, with the audit report projected onto a screen at the front of the room, and each person commits to not leaving that room until the review process is complete.

This is one of the fastest ways to reach consensus on a draft report, but it can actually be more costly in terms of total staff hours than conventional review processes. At the USPS, it generally took us about an hour per page to edit the draft, and each person there was committed to spending the entire time on the review. If we began with an eight-page draft report, it often took upwards of a day of each person's time to complete a team-writing review.

But when team editing is done correctly, once you're done, you are done. You don't have to worry about anyone circulating new versions of the report, and the draft report gets out the door much sooner.

Team editing is a powerful tool for shortening the report process and improving the timeliness of an organization's internal audits. The group dynamic also allows newer auditors to gain valuable insights about report writing from the team's more experienced members. I recall one instance at the USPS when we were able to deliver a fully coordinated draft audit report to management for comment only 48 hours after the fieldwork was complete!

5. Report conferencing.

Report conferencing is a somewhat more daring version of team writing. Similar to team writing, because it brings all reviewers together in the room, report conferencing also brings your audit clients to the table—so the people you have audited can offer their two cents' worth before the draft report is issued.

It makes many internal auditors nervous to have their clients in the room while the audit report is being drafted or edited, and you do need to build in safeguards when using this approach. Obviously, the internal auditors have to retain control of the final product, but overcoming clients' objections is always part of the reporting process, and those I've talked with who have tried conferencing are generally positive about the approach. It certainly eliminates management's frustration with reports that don't show up for weeks or months, and when done successfully, it can cut the time between a draft and the final report to almost nothing.

6. Streamline the audit report.

Internal audit departments that have successfully reduced their reports' cycle time generally produce leaner audit reports, which makes them not only easy to edit but easy to read. The shorter a report is, the less time it typically takes to write and edit. Complexity can also slow the review process, so generally speaking, simpler is better, too. And reaching consensus with clients can become onerous with longer reports, so streamlining formats pay dividends throughout the process.

I have on occasion seen internal audit reports that exceeded 100 pages. I am convinced reports that long are not read in their entirety by all of those who were likely to benefit from the information. It's always tempting to include more detail in an internal audit report than the minimum needed to make your point, but my advice to new auditors is to tell your story clearly and succinctly. There's nothing worse than working hard and coming up with a good report that people then ignore. Think of it this way—the longer your report, the less likely it will be read by those in a position to take action on your recommendations.

Some internal audit departments model their reports on those issued by large accounting and consulting firms. At first glance, this seems logical. Those firms have tried-and-true report formats that work extremely well for them. But our reports are usually not intended for public audiences, so it may not be necessary to include lengthy company descriptions, legal disclaimers, or minutely detailed descriptions of our methodologies in every report. I once saw an internal audit report about payroll processes, for example, that included the year the company was founded, its location, its motto, its vision statement, and descriptions of each of its major product lines—all before it said anything about payroll processing. When I asked why that information was included, I was told it was standard procedure to include it in every report issued by the department. Presumably, the company's audit committee had long ago learned to skip ahead when opening a report. One can only hope they didn't skip all the way to the back cover, though that is a danger whenever an audit report doesn't make every word count.

If your department is considering streamlined report formats, remember that electronic report formats allow you to embed hyperlinks in the copy that direct readers to additional information if they think they need it. A hyperlink might open a source document, for example, thus eliminating the need to spend much time describing that source information in your report. This can result in a concise report designed to meet the needs of different audiences by providing details only for those readers who seek them.

The Three-Inch Audit Report

Perhaps the most extreme example in my experience of streamlining a report and speeding up the reporting process occurred during my first assignment as a CAE for the Army. As fighting ended in the 1990–1991 Gulf War, I helped deploy a military internal audit team to the Mideast as part of Operation Desert Storm. Resources over there were limited, and everyone throughout the Army was operating under very constrained conditions, including those of us in internal review.

The commander at one military facility was a three-star general who was director of logistics in the war. Every morning, the general met with all of his direct reports, including internal audit. He told his deputies, all of the generals and colonels reporting to him, "If you have a problem, you come to me with it. But I am only going to take problems or challenges written on 3-by-5-inch index cards. I'll assign them out for solutions or corrective actions."

"But we have to give you our reports!" the internal auditors said. The general was unimpressed—managing such a complex military operation depended on responding rapidly to concise reports from every group in the room—internal audit's included. The auditors were limited to the same 3-by-5-inch index cards as everyone else.

With some effort and creativity, the internal auditors were able to condense their audit issues and recommendations so they each fit on a standard index card while meeting applicable audit standards. The general took the 3-by-5-

inch cards and handed them out during his morning staff meetings to the appropriate individuals for corrective action.

Every organization is unique, and I assume you will never have a 3-by-5-inch limit imposed on your internal audit reports. But you do need to find innovative ways to produce those and improve their timeliness. And the strategies outlined above have worked in numerous organizations around the world. Who knows—maybe someday internal audit reports will be distributed as lengthy text messages by some innovative audit department.

Dealing with Pushback

The first time management takes strong exception to one of your draft audit reports is likely to be a significant and emotional event—for you as well as the client. You might be tempted to lash out or become intransigent, though neither of these options would serve you well.

Difficult, emotional client meetings are often best handled with the calm assistance of more seasoned members of the internal audit team. In all likelihood, your supervisor or the CAE have plenty of experience with contentious audit results and have likely built relationships with management that can mean the difference between success and failure, while helping to resolve the standoff as painlessly as possible. If you have not yet experienced such a situation, I strongly advise that, when it does happen to you (and sooner or later it *will* happen if you stay in internal audit long enough), you should immediately seek help from a more experienced auditor.

No matter how emotional a client might get, in my experience that client's objections to your report are often not as severe as they might first appear. You may discover that you concentrated so hard on "selling" your findings and recommendations that you forgot to deliver a *balanced message*. The problem may not be what you have written as much as what you didn't write. I frequently find that most of a client's frustrations can be relieved merely by adding a few sentences of context to a report that highlight accomplishments observed or look at the findings in terms of the organization's overall operations.

It is easy to fall into the trap of reporting only negative results. After all, finding problems is what they pay us for, right? But we shouldn't limit our assurance to what isn't working well, and when a draft report fails to indicate satisfactory performance as much as warranted, clients may conclude that we are not presenting an objective image of their operations.

During my career, I developed a growing appreciation of the need to choose my words carefully. I came to understand that a well-written internal audit report, while a call to action, can result in inappropriate actions—or no action at all—because of a single poorly chosen word or phrase. I witnessed cases where poor report writing actually harmed an internal auditor's reputation or made it impossible to build or continue effective working relationships with others.

By the time I became a supervisor, I no longer considered my supervisors' editing of reports as unreasonable as it had once seemed. As a CAE, I found myself editing my team's audit reports as rigorously as my former supervisors had edited mine. I did try, however, to resist perpetuating the age-old tradition of changing "happy" to "glad."

Tone of the Report Is Important

Regardless of how well we communicate during engagements, our clients often remain sensitive or fearful about internal audit reports. You may be confident that your report is timely, accurate, and *perfectly crafted*, yet it still might be received with a resounding thud. Sometimes it can't be avoided, but with practice we can often keep that from happening. You've probably heard the old saying, "It's not what you say, it's how you say it that counts." Well, in internal auditing, it's a combination of both. The content of our audit reports must always add value to the organization, but the way we communicate in our reports will determine how those findings and recommendations are received.

What we perceive as objective reporting can sometimes trigger fear or anger from those being audited. They may feel as though their integrity or judgment is being attacked; they may also be reading the report while thinking, "How will my bosses react when they read this?" Even if they do not view a report as needlessly critical, they may think their triumphs and successes have been neglected by a process designed to highlight flaws and vulnerabilities. Sometimes a little well-deserved recognition can offset a whole lot of valid criticism in an audit report.

For internal auditors, it is absolutely necessary not only to be able to articulate a problem—what the potential impact is and how it can be fixed—but also to inspire corrective action. If we fail to inspire change, the entire audit process is a waste of time. And when it comes to inspiring change, there are times when a little recognition can be more motivating than a mountain of criticism. Emotion and perception are not things we talk about very often, but they can have a significant effect on how an audit report is received.

Ultimately, I think, internal audit is judged by its ability to improve the organization, and to accomplish that, we can't afford to be tone deaf when dealing with others in that organization. People want and need to feel appreciated and like to be recognized for their accomplishments, not just in our reports but throughout the engagement.

10 Things You Shouldn't Write in an Internal Audit Report

The time-saving strategies discussed earlier are some of the most effective ways to ensure engagement reports are issued quickly. But one of the easiest ways to speed up a review is simply to avoid writing things that will inevitably be edited out of your reports. This is my "Top 10" list of things you should *not* include in an internal audit report. Avoiding (or, in a few cases, at least limiting your use of) these things isn't going to save you huge amounts of time later, but doing so will reduce the degree of client pushback and the number of unnecessary rewrites. You might even develop a reputation for clear and effective writing.

1. **"Management should consider..."** Internal audit reports should offer solid recommendations for taking specific actions. When our recommendation is merely to "consider" something, it puts even the most urgent call to action at a disadvantage. No internal auditor wants management to respond to a recommendation with a simple, "OK, we'll consider it."

2. **Weasel words.** It's tempting to hedge our statements with phrases such as "it seems that" or "our impression is" or "there appears to be." But if you hedge too often, there's a danger that those reading your report will conclude that you are not presenting well-supported facts. They need to know they can rely on your findings and recommendations, but weasel words can make them sound more like hunches. If your report contains weasel words, don't be surprised when those reviewing it kick it back and ask you for more information.

3. **Intensifiers.** Because they add emphasis, words such as "clearly," "special," or "very" might seem to be the opposite of weasel words. But these intensifiers are so non-specific they can amount to another type of weaseling. Intensifiers raise questions such as, "Significant, compared to what?" and "Clearly, according to whose criteria?" If you use intensifiers too freely in a report, different readers of the same report may be left with very different impressions of what you're saying. Numbers such as 23 percent or $3 billion help tell a story, but just what does "very large" mean?

4. **Absolutes.** It's good to avoid vagueness, but there's a danger in words such as "everything," "nothing," "never," and "always." "You always" and "you never" can be fighting words to clients, prompting them to start looking for exceptions to the rule rather than examining the real issue. It's safe to say you tested 10 transactions and none were approved, but it's overstating your results to state that transactions are never approved.

5. **Blame.** Internal audit reports are supposed to bring about positive change, not assign blame. We're more likely to achieve consensus when our reports come across as neutral rather than confrontational. The goal is to get to the root cause of the problem rather than call out the name of the guilty party. It's fine for a report to identify the party responsible for acting on an audit recommendation—not so fine to say, "It was Fred's fault."

6. **Failure.** Statements such as "Management failed to implement adequate controls" will invariably annoy those to whom we are looking for solutions. Simply stating the problem, without assigning blame through words like "fail" or "failure," is much more likely to result in the needed

corrective actions—while helping preserve our relationship with management for the next time we conduct an audit of their area.

7. **"Auditee."** A few years back, people undergoing an audit were most often referred to as "auditees." But that's old school. Many experts now consider the term to have negative connotations and imply that the client is having something done *to* them by the auditor. Internal audit has become a collaborative process, and terms such as "audit client" and "audit customer" indicate that we are working *with* management, not working *on* them.

8. **Jargon.** Every profession needs a certain amount of specialized language, but the more we can keep technical jargon out of our internal audit reports, the clearer our message will be. If you use terms such as "transactional controls," "stratified sampling methodology," or "asynchronous transfer mode" more than once a page in your audit report, don't be surprised when you discover that some of those reading it check out before getting to the end.

9. **Subtle bragging.** While it is tempting in internal audit reports to use phrases such as "internal audit found" or "we uncovered," management will often bristle when you take credit for identifying something that wasn't all that well hidden to start with. From their point of view, it's as if, after throwing them under the bus, you have it back up and run over them again.

10. **Verbiage.** You want those reading your audit to remember your recommendations and take action to carry them out, so don't bury them under mounds of pompous words or bloated phrases. For example, don't say "by means of" when "by" will do, or "at the present time" when you mean "now," or "so as to" when "so" is the way to go.

I like to use the seventh-grader test when reviewing an audit report—if an intelligent middle-school student couldn't understand it, then it may be needlessly complicated. Take, for example, this 65-word sentence from an actual internal audit report that basically tells you, "Little things can add up":

"During the aforementioned examination of the accounts under-taken by the internal auditors, the team evaluated the cumulative impact of individually immaterial items and in doing so relied on the assumption that it was appropriate to consider whether such impacts tended to offset one another or, conversely, to result in a combined cumulative effect in the same direction and hence to accu-mulate into a material amount."

Enough said; and then some.

Coping with the Review Process

Let's assume for a moment that you just wrote the world's first absolutely perfect draft of an internal audit report. It is clear, concise, accurate, fair, helpful, and everything else you could wish it to be. The tone is faultless, the issues are straightforward, and the recommendations are convincing. Not a comma is out of place.

Congratulations. You have just accomplished the impossible. But regardless of your report's perfection, it will now be edited.

Because internal auditors don't enjoy being criticized any more than our cli-ents do, your first reaction to the editing of your report might not always be the best one. The key is to know how to cope with the editing process.

Extensive editing of your report can be frustrating, even disheartening, but it's important not to overreact. You need to understand why the edits were made and learn from people who have more experience than you. If there is time in the schedule, you may want to put the report aside for a day or two so you can go back over the list of requested changes with a fresh eye.

If you still think the edits are inappropriate, the best approach is to make your case rationally and without emotion. Differences of opinion will always exist between internal auditors; there is merit in having more than one point of view brought to bear on an assignment. But if you can't come to complete agreement with the rest of the team about every word in the report, you may have to accept that the final decisions will be made by those ultimately accountable for the quality of the overall engagement.

Small Stones Can Cause Big Waves

Every internal audit professional looks forward to career milestones—those "big impact audits" that we can look back on later with the satisfaction of knowing our work made a real difference. Whether it's in internal auditing or life in general, we all aspire to make this world a better place, even if only in small ways. What makes internal auditing especially rewarding is that it can bring about significant change in an organization, the kind that prompts senior management and board members to sit up and take notice.

But often it's the little things, not the big ones, that attract the most attention. We assume that those who read our reports will assess the significance of our findings and recommendations using the same criteria as we do, but that's not always the case.

Early in my internal audit career, I learned how easy it is for something relatively insignificant to have far-reaching ripple effects. Findings in an audit report can often be taken out of context or assigned much greater significance than warranted. No matter how well you conducted your audit, it is important to manage such situations. I call this phenomenon the "small-stone effect," when something with the financial significance of a rounding error starts out as a ripple, like those made by a pebble tossed in the water, but grows into a tsunami of overreaction or negative publicity as it spreads outward.

Alien Presence at TVA

During my tenure as inspector general at TVA, we received a complaint that some employees were using their computers for a study-at-home initiative called the Search for Extraterrestrial Intelligence, or SETI. Software had been downloaded onto the employees' computers, allowing them to help sort through radio-signal data collected by the giant Arecibo radio telescope in Puerto Rico.

When TVA's employees signed up for the program, they received a free computer screensaver and software that allowed the study-at-home coordinators, when the employees' computers were inactive, to access TVA computers via the internet to help search the radio signals from outer space that could indicate the presence of extraterrestrial intelligence. No proof of intelligent life elsewhere had been found to that point, and we recommended that the software be removed.

It was a fairly modest report. We identified 19 employees who had been using their work computers for the SETI project. We shared the report with management and, as required by law, I included a reference to it in my semiannual report to Congress. The local newspaper picked up on it and, lo and behold, it went viral. I remember it making the news in Australia.

At the time, the SETI computer program, which came from the University of California at Berkeley, had been downloaded by more than three million computer users worldwide. The TVA security breach was a violation of the agency's written policy but was not considered a serious one. We recommended that administrative action be taken against the employees—something IGs, though not internal auditors, occasionally do. TVA employees were warned that any future computer security violations could result in dismissal.

The "Lavish" Satellite Office

Although my tenure at TVA was shorter than my other stops along the audit trail, it was packed with action in terms of small stones triggering tsunamis in the form of media coverage. While reaction to the SETI software had been global, the most intense media coverage from a TVA audit conducted during my time there involved "lavish" spending to refurbish a satellite office for the agency's board of directors.

TVA's headquarters is in Knoxville, Tennessee, but many of its operations are based about 100 miles west of there in Chattanooga. The board decided to relocate and upgrade a small office in Nashville, about 180 miles from Knoxville. The new space would include an office for the agency's chairman and a boardroom. At the request of a member of Congress, we initiated an audit of the project and identified several examples of furnishings that generated intense publicity and strong congressional reaction—including a $53,000 conference table, a $42,000 glass backdrop, and $326,000 spent to transform hickory trees from President Andrew Jackson's historic home in Nashville into paneling for a new library adjacent to the chairman's office.

Once again, for an agency the size of TVA, with an annual budget totaling $8 billion, these were not material examples of waste, and no fraud was detected. But that audit report created waves of publicity.[2]

The Nashville office was front-page news in Knoxville and Chattanooga, and the region's largest newspaper, the *Atlanta Journal-Constitution*, did an in-depth report. Members of Congress weighed in too, calling the project a "boondoggle." The public was incensed that a government-run utility that helped set their electric-power rates was spending money on such extravagances. There was little I could do about this as the IG; I had an obligation to report the findings. We avoided characterizing the expenses, though others had no problem attaching terms such as "excessive" and "dubious."

It's a Matter of Perspective

I wish public officials and the media had paid as much attention to some of the truly consequential examples of waste and inefficiency in the internal audit reports I worked on or supervised during my years in government auditing. But if you analyze enough audit reports about $640 toilet seats and $53,000 conference tables, you can begin to see why certain findings resonate with stakeholders and the public in ways that much more important findings do not.

People's reaction to findings of waste or inefficiency in an internal audit report have less to do with the amount of money involved or the consequences of the error than they do with how much they identify with the problems, usually in a negative way. In the age of social media, it can take only one tweet about a finding in an internal audit to set off a tsunami of negative reaction.

So, what's an internal auditor to do? I learned early on the importance of putting my report observations in perspective. If the amount of money involved is not material and the problem or error cited is not systemic and poses no threat, then the observation may not even warrant inclusion in the report;

you can still review such issues with management so they can be addressed without the turbulence of the "small-stone effect."

The Fine Art of "Fence Repair"

When coaching internal auditors, I remind them that audit reports are often the basis for evaluating management's performance, and unfavorable results have been known to cost executives bonuses, promotions, or even their jobs—especially if the report includes some sort of rating system. It may not seem fair, but as a result, adverse internal audits can damage relationships between internal auditors and management, a situation I call a "broken fence."

It is practically impossible to avoid breaking a fence now and then in our line of work. Internal audit reports must be accurate, and if an issue is significant enough to be in the report, it should not be negotiated out of the report or downplayed into virtual nonexistence. No matter how congenial you might be as an internal auditor, if you are doing your job correctly, there will be times when you have to "call it like it is," and that can create hard feelings or damage relationships. But no internal auditor can function effectively if surrounded by broken fences. A successful auditor learns, over time, the fine art of fence repair.

How do you mend broken fences? First, work tirelessly to avoid breaking them in the first place by anticipating the potential consequences of your internal audits and mitigating the damage before it occurs. For example, I have always discouraged the use of ratings in internal audit reports if used as a punitive measure, and I avoid inflammatory words and phrases. We should always strive to ensure that the tone of our reports doesn't lead to lingering animosity on management's part.

If a fence is broken, you need to consider a fence-mending mission. Here are a few of the strategies I have used to mend damaged relationships:

- Engage in frank and open discussion with the offended party or parties. Ask them to share with you their candid feelings about the accuracy or fairness of the report and what they think internal audit could have done better. (*Warning*: *These sessions can become contentious, so check your ego at the door.*)

- Solicit feedback from all of your internal audit clients using a customer satisfaction survey or similar mechanism. The ability to vent without a face-to-face confrontation can be therapeutic for some of those who take offense at your reports—and you might just learn about a few fences that you hadn't known were broken.

- Demonstrate genuine empathy when engaging someone who feels wronged by your report. If an internal audit costs someone their bonus, I put myself in that person's shoes when talking about our relationship going forward.

- Own up to your mistakes, whether made by you or the team as a whole. View mistakes as opportunities to improve.

Why should we care about broken fences? Well, as internal auditors we have to "live where we eat," and once a fence is broken, managers in that part of the organization will not want you auditing them again. And every internal audit conducted in that area from then on will occur under a cloud of mistrust and contention. Effective fence mending takes time. While a well-established relationship can be destroyed in a second, rebuilding trust between internal audit and a client is a slow process. If management thinks that trust has been compromised, it will take time for them to recognize again that our work is balanced and fair. So be patient; almost any fence can be mended.

CHAPTER 13
Culture Is Often the Culprit

In the opening chapter of this book, I noted that sometimes we learn valuable lessons late in our careers, and the down side to that is we have little time to apply them. The most significant lesson that fits that category for me is that internal audit must assess the role that corporate culture plays in governance.

When I launched my internal audit career, the idea of auditing the "softer" side of an organization's culture was anathema to the profession. Back in the day, it was believed internal audit should focus on hard controls, such as codes of conduct or human resources policies. Evaluating concepts as intangible as trust, ethics, competence, and leadership styles was something for psychologists and pop-culture gurus to worry about. In retrospect, a lot of heartache and failure across a multitude of organizations might have been prevented had internal audit taken on the full spectrum of culture 40 years ago. As it is, the concept is only now gaining broader acceptance among internal auditors and their stakeholders. All I can say to that is, it's about time!

Some longtime practitioners might say that auditing corporate culture is nothing new. After all, we have been talking about tone at the top for decades. But that doesn't quite capture the significant value a thorough and ongoing assessment of culture can when it comes to preserving an organization's ethical well-being. Just as important, understanding and monitoring culture can protect an organization from misguided or even toxic influences that might serve short-term goals but threaten the organization's long-term success and even survival.

Others question whether internal auditors can develop the skillsets to successfully audit corporate culture, which I believe is possible. The profession has undergone significant changes on multiple occasions through the years, and each time practitioners have pivoted successfully to meet stakeholder needs. When it comes to assessing corporate culture, I believe internal auditors will answer the call to action again.

Even if we set aside the question of whether internal auditors have the skills and mandate to fully audit culture, there are practical concerns that will inexorably push the profession in that direction. The speed at which risk related to culture has been exposed is an enormous threat to organizational well-being. There have been too many big companies and organizations getting into trouble in recent years over actions that clearly had cultural components, from FIFA and Volkswagen to Wells Fargo and Uber. Even the most reluctant among us should acknowledge that culture is a big risk, and risk must always be an area of focus for us.

What Is Culture?

To audit culture one must first begin with a clear understanding of what culture is—and isn't. One definition describes culture as the "moral fabric" of the organization. Another describes it as "the self-sustaining pattern of behavior that determines how things are done." I tend to prefer a much simpler definition: Culture is "how we do things around here."

This short phrase packs a big punch as much for what it says as what it doesn't say. It's important to understand that culture is defined by the actual day-to-day operations, interactions, and influences within an organization, not what a mission statement, CEO speech, or employee policy manual says it is. Culture is not what is said; it's what is done.

A perfect example of this can be found in one troubled company's well-publicized code of ethics that said, "…We are responsible for conducting the business affairs of the companies in accordance with all applicable laws and in a moral and honest manner." Had the company's executives simply followed this lofty guidance, maybe the name Enron would not be synonymous in the minds of so many with corruption.

When organizations blindly latch onto a slogan or focus more on branding rather than executing what they portray, trouble isn't far behind. Too many governance failures and resulting corporate scandals were born from senior management and boards believing the hype and being out of touch with reality.

Now that we have a basic understanding of what culture is, we can get down to *why* it's important. I should acknowledge that many things influence an organization's ability to succeed, including how its leaders address strategic, business, operational, compliance, and financial risks, its ability to adapt, the strength and reliability of its workforce, competition, strategy, and more. But the power of corporate culture and the speed with which the strongest companies can be brought down when culture goes bad cannot be overstated.

Maybe the best way to express this is to share two relevant quotes from noted business experts. Patrick Dixon, one of Europe's leading futurists who has been ranked as one of the 20 most influential business thinkers alive, has a deep understanding of business risks and opportunities. He identifies a sound strategy as critical to success. "Business strategy is a battle plan for a better future," he says.

Dixon is undoubtedly right. However, I believe Peter Drucker, a management consultant, educator, and author who has written extensively on the modern business corporation, puts business strategy and culture in proper perspective when he says, "Culture eats strategy for breakfast." Yes, business strategy is important for an organization's success, but it's the culture that strongly influences whether that strategy will succeed or fail.

Healthy vs. Toxic Cultures

Organizational cultures are complicated, and trying to grasp how they develop and change is no easy task. Yet, we can get a basic understanding of conditions that exist in or contribute to poor cultures by understanding those conditions in healthy cultures. We can begin by going back to our definition of culture—"How things are done around here"—and asking the questions, "How should things be done around here?" and "How do we say things are done around here?"

This should be well within the comfort zone of any internal auditor. It is not difficult to find practices and protocols that are universally accepted as contributing to healthy cultures (e.g., codes of ethics; conflict of interest declarations; corporate governance codes; conformance to laws, regulations, and organizational policies; equal and judicious application of rules; etc.). By establishing a foundation of conditions that support healthy culture, we can more easily identify the signs of weakened or eroded ones.

However, monitoring those baseline positive influences is more than just making sure everyone signs a code of ethics or updates their conflict of interest statement each year. It's easy to proclaim a positive intent or goal, but it's much harder to achieve it.

When I make presentations about culture, I encourage auditors to understand the difference between talking the talk and walking the walk. In other words, "practice what you preach" or "actions speak louder than words." This suggests that the concept is not unique to corporate culture.

What auditors should be mindful of when auditing culture is how far the talk deviates from the walk. **Exhibit 13-1** depicts what can be termed a "Culture Gap." As the space between "how things should be done around here" and

---

Exhibit 13-1: Culture Gap

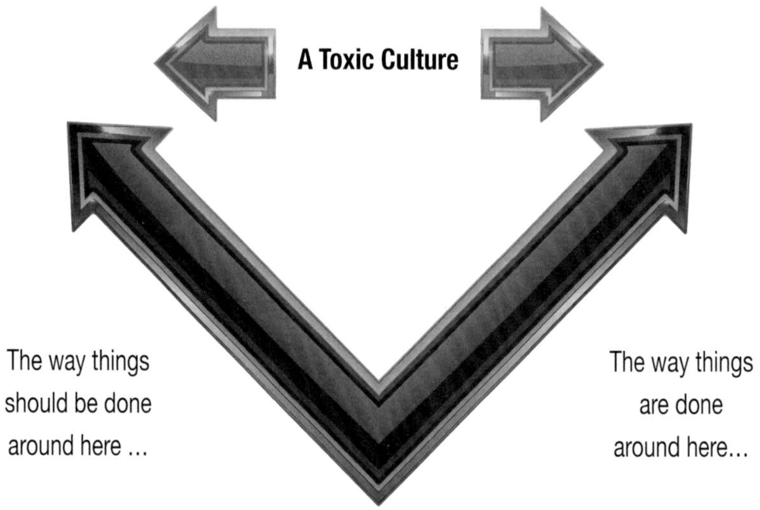

A Toxic Culture

The way things should be done around here ...

The way things are done around here...

"how things are done around here" grows, so does the likelihood of developing a toxic culture.

There are telltale indicators of an eroding or toxic culture. For example:

- Loss of confidence in leadership
- Groupthink and judgement errors
- Unethical or illegal behavior
- Erosion of the brand and reputational damage
- Erosion of shareholder value

Each of these symptoms can be explained away as isolated incidents or temporary setbacks. Indeed, not every hit to the share price, embarrassing social media event, or instance of fraud means the organization's culture will lead to disaster. But internal auditors must be attuned to the frequency and severity of such symptoms and become comfortable considering culture as a possible root cause of control weaknesses uncovered in engagements. The concept of incorporating a culture component into every engagement is a fundamental shift for many internal audit functions, but it is one that must become the norm.

Another measure of the health of corporate culture is senior management's relationship with internal audit. Ideally, internal audit should operate in an atmosphere that allows it to function independently and have the resources necessary to perform its job well. It must have separate administrative and functional reporting lines to the CEO and board (or audit committee), respectively. It should have a clear and positive relationship with senior management that fosters open, transparent communication without the fear of retaliation, and experience a similar relationship with its audit committee and/or board.

When an organization's senior management treats its internal audit function positively, it's an indication that internal audit has senior management's assurance to routinely undergo scrutiny from an informed and independent outside perspective. It also reflects management that understands its role and that of the board and audit committee, and one that is eager to identify risks and control weaknesses and improve on those areas. It takes such commitment to transparency from confident leadership that does not fear that its actions fall outside the lines of established risk appetites, business strategies, or ethics. Most importantly, it sets a tone at the top that signals unequivocally that doing things right is a hallmark of its culture.

Conversely, a relationship where senior management attempts to undermine or hamper internal audit's ability to do its job signals something potentially dire. Leadership that shuns scrutiny and takes steps to obstruct or avoid feedback sets a negative tone at the top that can ripple throughout the organization.

Telltale signs that can indicate an unhealthy culture when it comes to the organization's treatment of internal audit include:

- **Attitude toward internal audit.** Management's response to internal audit's inquiries is to circle the wagons and limit access to information.
- **Carousel of chief audit executives.** Management cycles through a number of CAEs seeking one it can most easily control or manipulate.
- **Pressure to change or hide findings.** Management makes clear it doesn't want to hear the truth.
- **Redirecting or misdirecting internal audit.** Management manipulates the choice of audits based on an agenda other than one based on the organization's risk.
- **Suppressing internal audit's budget.** Management limits resources in staff, access to expertise (co-sourcing), or travel to limit internal audit's ability to do its job.
- **Limiting internal audit's access to the board or audit committee.** Management wants to control the message from internal audit to the board.

Each of these is an example of senior management avoiding accountability and transparency. It does not mean an organization is operating unethically or illegally, but it does suggest a fundamental disregard or misunderstanding of good. It also hints at an organization that has work to do on its culture.

Why Audit Culture?

Now that we know what culture is and isn't, and some of the signs of good and bad culture, it's time to look at why we should audit culture. Some of the first suggestions that internal audit should look at culture came from financial services regulators who noted the role culture played in financial services firms leading up to the global financial crisis of 2008. Since the topic first arose, the idea of internal audit assessing organizational culture has become more widely accepted. There is a growing recognition that culture is such a significant risk in the twenty-first century that it cannot be ignored, and internal audit is being viewed in some organizations as a natural choice to take on the task.

It is not internal audit's job to ensure a healthy culture. However, it seems an unavoidable conclusion that, because of internal audit's promise to "protect and enhance organizational value," it simply cannot ignore a risk that can have such profound and negative effects on the organization. Fortunately, there is evidence that suggests culture is increasingly viewed as a risk to be reckoned with by both internal audit and its stakeholders.

In 2017, the National Association of Corporate Directors (NACD) Blue Ribbon Commission on Culture as a Corporate Asset called on boards of directors to take a proactive approach to culture oversight as one way to sustain success and long-term value creation. That's the good news.

The bad news is that an NACD survey found less than half of directors reported that their boards assess the alignment between the company's purpose and values and its strategy. Only 50 percent say they understand the "buzz at the bottom"—the collective behaviors, norms, and values at the front lines of their organizations, among their rank-and-file employees.[1]

Responses to the 2018 IIA North American Pulse of Internal Audit survey paint a similar picture of a dangerous disconnect between the recognized need to monitor culture at the highest levels and follow through by boards and senior management to do so. The survey finds a correlation between CAEs who rank governance/culture risks high or very high and organizations where the audit committee is less involved in assessing culture. Indeed, the data is startling considering the growing evidence of culture's role in a number of high-profile scandals.

Among those CAEs who rated the risk as high or very high, 43 percent disagreed that their audit committee assessed culture. In contrast, among those CAEs who rated the risk as low or very low, only 18 percent disagreed that the audit committee assessed culture. The correlation is supported when the data is broken down by the type of organization. Public sector audit committees scored lowest for assessing culture (22 percent), which is consistent with the finding that the public sector had the highest reported risk level for governance and culture (31 percent). Conversely, publicly traded organizations reported the highest percentage of audit committees assessing culture (39 percent) and the lowest risk level (13 percent). It should come as no surprise that CAEs would be more likely to rate governance and culture risks higher when their audit committees have little or no involvement.

Despite this, auditing culture today remains more of a "nice to have" in most organizations. Fewer than 6 in 10 CAEs who responded to the Pulse survey reported that their audit plan includes an allocation for governance and culture. Among those who do audit governance and culture, the average audit allocation was a scant 7 percent of the audit plan. The average allocation for all respondents (includes those who reported not allocating any time to governance and culture) drops to 4 percent. These troubling statistics should serve as fodder for CAEs to speak up and convince audit committees of the risks of ignoring culture as a component of governance.

Recognition that the right corporate culture helps contribute to long-term success is not new. Indeed, 48 percent of CFOs surveyed in 2016 rated corporate culture among the top three things that contribute to their organization's long-term value.[2] The strategic plan, operating plan, and CEO each rated lower.

It also appears there is growing recognition that culture's influence on day-to-day operations requires monitoring and nurturing and should be part of a comprehensive approach to governance. How that monitoring and nurturing is accomplished varies depending on the organization, but there are substantial reasons and a history of success that points to internal audit being the natural choice to lead that effort.

Monitoring culture, recognizing the signs of an eroding culture, and speaking out when culture goes awry require skills that are natural to internal audit:

- Speaking up
- Connecting the dots
- Displaying courage
- Understanding pressure points
- Being willing to "throw in the flag"

Auditing culture is not easy, and it is certainly not in most internal auditors' comfort zones. But if this chapter accomplishes anything, it should be to convince you that culture is too important to ignore. A couple of straightforward approaches to adding culture to internal audit's growing scope of work follow, but the first step is overcoming the resistance to take it on. CAEs should see culture not as an obstacle but as an opportunity. CAEs should eagerly embrace the important role that internal audit can play in engaging the organization's culture and bringing transparency and attention to its strengths and weaknesses.

Considerations when Auditing Culture

The first step in auditing culture may have nothing to do with the skills required to do the audit, yet everything to do with the audit committee and senior management trusting internal audit to undertake such a role. Despite acknowledging the importance of culture on an organization's ability to achieve its goals, boards and senior management can sometimes resist efforts to examine it. For example, a survey of participants in a recent IIA webinar on auditing culture found that nearly half said no one—not the board, management, nor regulators—was encouraging culture audits.

But that should not stop a CAE from raising the issue with the audit committee or board. In the past, internal audit has overcome resistance to expanding its scope into strategic and operational risks, but those areas are now commonly found in the annual plans of many internal audit departments.

I often encourage CAEs who seek my advice to ease into auditing culture. The first step should be to assess the effects of culture in every audit engagement. We are already compelled to identify the cause in any findings our audit produces. It's easy to lay blame on superficial causes (e.g., lack of training or resources) when controls are inadequately designed or implemented. However, if we dig deep enough, we might find that aha moment when we realize that the organization's culture is to blame. For example, we might discover that compensation is based upon the number of contracts awarded rather than compliance with corporate policies, resulting in sole-sourced acquisitions. The end to justify the means is at the root cause of a number of high-profile corporate scandals and, ultimately, the demise of its culture.

If culture is found to be a root cause for any risk management or control failures, it should be included in individual conclusion findings in the final engagement report. This approach introduces and nurtures a keen awareness of culture for all members of the engagement team. While culture will likely not be identified as the root cause in every engagement, it may be identified as something that masks or exacerbates deficiencies observed. As multiple audits are conducted that identify culture as a root cause, it may be time for a capstone or theming report the trends noted regarding culture.

As internal audit becomes more adept in assessing culture or identifying its impact on the organization's operations, the CAE may choose to expand internal audit's focus on culture to include entire lines of service, business units, or geographic operations. As with the results of individual audits that disclose culture as a root cause, reports on audits of culture within lines of service, business units, or geographic operations can be assimilated into a broader capstone report on culture. The advantage to this approach is that it permits internal auditors to gain expertise and build credibility in auditing culture without taking on the entire enterprise all at once.

Internal audit departments with the resources and expertise may be ready to take the next step and tackle enterprisewide audits of culture. I always caution those who don't have the expertise or resources for such an audit to avoid "biting off more than they can chew." We must recognize that management and even boards may be skeptical of our role in auditing culture.

That skepticism can be mitigated in part by establishing our credibility more slowly through commentary on culture in our individual audits and assessing the culture of components of the organization.

The mandate to audit culture on an enterprise level has raised many questions in the profession. The most basic question is, "How do we do it?" KPMG and other service providers have shared ideas on auditing culture. In *Five Steps to Tackling Culture,* KPMG breaks down the process of fostering and assessing culture into five familiar themes[3]:

- **Align** the organizational strategy with risk and compliance strategy to determine where the organization wants to be in terms of culture.
- **Understand** current culture and how it compares with the desired culture.
- **Define** what needs to be done to get to the desired culture and how to get there.
- **Implement** the road map and define measures of success.
- **Measure** progress against the road map and the evolution of the culture.

This approach incorporates all three lines of defense, but the key takeaway is aligning organizational strategies with risk and compliance strategies to help define an ideal culture. This identifies a clear target to aim for as an organization. From an internal audit perspective, the second and third points—understanding the current culture and defining what needs to be done to get to a desired state—are most relevant.

A final suggested approach is to look at culture audits the same way as any other engagement. The IIA offers a Framework for Auditing Culture (see **exhibit 13-2**) that identifies three basic levels of work: 1) collecting evidence, 2) analyzing and evaluating the evidence, and 3) reporting conclusions.

Collecting Evidence

The challenge for most internal auditors is collecting evidence that addresses and assesses soft controls such as competence, trust and openness, leadership expectations, shared values, and ethical standards. When evaluating evidence for any audit, IIA Standard 2310: Identifying Information directs CAEs to "…identify sufficient, reliable, relevant, and useful information to achieve the engagements objectives."

CAEs must consider whether organizational values are defined, promote clarity, make expectations clear, and drive the desired behavior. Because examining soft controls is particularly challenging, internal audit must use its expertise and judgment based on a holistic view of the organization. If it can aggregate the effectiveness of hard and soft controls and connect the dots to identify patterns, a clearer picture of culture can emerge.

Exhibit 13-2: A Framework for Auditing Culture

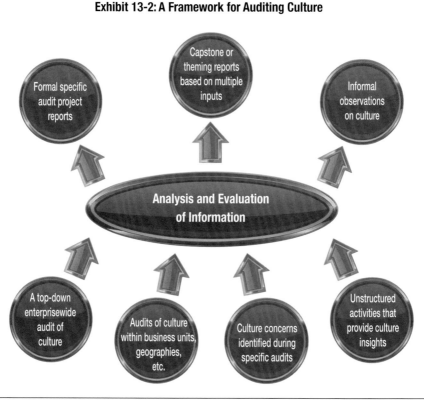

The framework identifies multiple sources of culture-related evidence that can be combined with more traditional evidence-gathering techniques, such as evaluation of training, customer complaints, employee turnover, or employee surveys. One caveat: As with any engagement, it is important to understand the limitations of surveys. For example, even in anonymous surveys, employees may be reluctant to be 100 percent truthful for fear of retaliation. A determination on culture can be helped by surveys, but they should not be the primary basis for any assurance on culture.

Analysis and Evaluation

Analyzing and evaluating evidence can be particularly challenging when it comes to auditing culture, and the tendency may be to assign less value to evidence that might be unstructured and hard to define. Internal auditors should resist this temptation and, instead, develop techniques to make the evidence less abstract.

One technique I encourage auditors to use is to drill down to the core issue by simply asking *why* until there are no more *why* questions to be asked. For example, an organization's employee survey finds strong support for senior management, but the sentiment conflicts with an extremely high employee turnover rate. Why? Employees may not be truthful in their survey answers about senior management. Why? They are fearful about speaking the truth. Why? Managers are quick to quiet any criticism of management. Why? Management bonuses are tied to positive survey responses.

Reporting Conclusions

IIA Standard 2410: Criteria for Communicating directs CAEs to make clear each engagement's objectives, scope, and results. Standard 2410.A1 further directs, "Final communication of engagement results must include applicable conclusions, as well as applicable recommendations and/or action plans."

Applying reporting standards to culture engagement can be tricky because of the potentially highly sensitive findings and conclusions. CAEs should weigh carefully how to report culture conclusions. The framework offers three options:

- Formal specific audit reports
- Capstone or theming reports based on multiple inputs
- Informal observations on culture

Treating culture audits the same as routine or traditional audits might have the effect of souring management's view of them. Earlier in the book I noted that adverse internal audits can damage relationships that later will require mending fences. A CAE can avoid breaking fences on culture if they are judicious in how they report their findings. While a direct written report will be clear and leave less room for interpretation, it provides little opportunity for engaging management. Raising concerns about culture might be better communicated through a preliminary notice prior to the final report. Preliminary or informal discussions can go a long way in smoothing the delivery of difficult findings, gaining management acknowledgment and acceptance of culture problems, and improving the chances of making positive changes to organizational culture.

Where Auditing Culture Fits In

Culture clearly presents risk in organizations. Driven by either a genuine concern about culture's impact on the organization or increased pressure from regulators and the investor community, more boards and senior managers are grasping the need to understand and monitor "how we do things around here." Internal audit can either be a leader in that movement or allow stakeholders to direct how we do the work. I believe we cannot allow the latter scenario to take hold. We must lead the movement by embracing the challenge and developing the skills to audit the "soft" as well as the "hard" side of culture.

CHAPTER 14
No One Is Immune to Ethical Lapses

During my first assignment as a CAE in the Army, one of my responsibilities was to provide direction and oversight to our CAEs in subordinate/subsidiary organizations. One day, a CAE of one of the subordinate organizations called seeking my advice. Her department had identified several problems during an internal audit of the organization's IT function. The IT director had concurred with the report and asked if the lead internal auditor for the engagement could help the IT office implement the audit recommendations. The CAE asked if I thought temporarily assigning the internal auditor to the IT department to help with the corrective actions would pose a problem.

"I don't think you want to do that," I responded. "It will impair your department from going back to audit in this area later on. But you and your organization need to make that call."

I soon forgot about the conversation. A few months later, I received a subpoena from a federal judge to appear before a labor relations hearing. An employees' union had filed a grievance against management for allowing an internal auditor to undertake work that the organization's IT staff could have performed. I was called to testify regarding any breach of Government Auditing Standards (Yellow Book) resulting from the action.

I was puzzled because I had assumed the CAE had decided against allowing the temporary transfer. When I asked her why she had ignored my advice and agreed to let the internal auditor work in IT, she dropped an even bigger bombshell. She said IT made her a promise. They said, "We'll give you all new computers if you send this auditor over to help us out."

"I couldn't pass that up, right?" she added.

I was almost speechless at the news. "You do realize that now your decision impairs you even more?" I responded. "How are you possibly going to go back and audit the IT department when you are on the hook because they gave you all those computers?" The CAE hadn't done anything illegal, but her twin decisions—to allow an internal auditor to help implement recommendations in a department her office would have to audit again, and to accept equipment from that very department in exchange for the favor—were serious ethical lapses that had tainted her office's reputation.

When Ethical Lapses Turn Serious

"Ethics is so boring, until you go to jail," was how a post on Twitter summed up the problem that some people have with ethical standards. I am not suggesting that internal auditors are likely to end up in jail, though it is not unprecedented, unfortunately. What we do need to worry about is how often our behavior and our decisions fail to promote an ethical culture within our profession and the organizations we serve.

The first decade of the twenty-first century had no shortage of high-profile ethical lapses in the corporate world. Remember Enron Corporation? It is still the poster child for corporate fraud and ethical lapses in this country, and its collapse was partly responsible for the passage of Sarbanes-Oxley. The debacle at WorldCom was another massive accounting fraud that happened at about the same time. IIA members who worked there played a key role in exposing the fraud in 2002. Similar ethical meltdowns were reported at Parmalat, Adelphia, Tyco, and elsewhere.

The reality is that corporate executives often get caught in ethics scandals. To our shame, the internal auditors responsible for monitoring these executives and the operations they manage have ethical lapses too. In recent years, CAEs in several instances have been caught up in foreign bribery scandals or fraud cover-ups.

My heart stands still each time such a case appears among the headlines on the internet, because I fear the damage it can do to our profession. "How is a company supposed to avoid corrupt payments when the individual tasked with finding out about corrupt payments [the internal auditor] and reporting them to the Board of Directors is himself complicit in the bribery scheme?" Howard Sklar asked in a blog post on Forbes.com.[1]

People often ask me what keeps me awake at night as the head of The IIA. It isn't our operations or our finances, and it isn't concern about our professional standards or certifications coming under attack. What keeps me awake at night is the possibility of more headlines about internal auditors violating our Code of Ethics.

Ethical misconduct is not a matter of isolated instances. During a roundtable of about 70 CAEs at one of our annual IIA General Audit Management Conferences, I asked those present, "Have you ever discovered or witnessed ethical lapses within your own internal audit function?" Nearly one-third of the CAEs acknowledged they had.

What Causes Ethical Lapses?

Various motivations have been mentioned for the ethical violations that internal auditors have been accused of committing in recent years, including:

- Loyalties to other senior executives
- Desire to protect the organization
- Protection of career opportunities
- Conflicts of interest
- Lack of courage and integrity
- Disregard of The IIA's Code of Ethics

Internal audit professionals sometimes do things that raise questions about their ethical behavior without them even recognizing the situation as an ethical lapse. If we are professionals and expect others to think of us as such, then we must hold ourselves to an ethical code. And it has to be about more than just *how we do our work;* it has to be about *how we behave.*

If you are a certified internal auditor (CIA), then you are already aware of The IIA's Code of Ethics. A vast majority of internal audit departments have compliance with the code somewhere in their internal audit charters, which require them to comply with the code and other mandatory guidance in The

IIA's IPPF. But I wonder how often we as individuals really think about the code or what it means to our work.

The stated purpose of The IIA's Code of Ethics is "to promote an ethical culture in the profession of internal auditing." It has two components: the Principles and the Rules of Conduct. The Principles express the four ideals to which internal audit professionals should aspire as they go about their work, while the Rules of Conduct describe 12 behavioral norms.

Let's take a quick look at the four principles:

1. **Integrity:** The integrity of internal auditors establishes trust and thus provides the basis for reliance on their judgment.

2. **Objectivity:** Internal auditors exhibit the highest level of professional objectivity in gathering, evaluating, and communicating information about the activity or process being examined. Internal auditors make a balanced assessment of all the relevant circumstances and are not unduly influenced by their own interests or by others in forming judgments.

3. **Confidentiality:** Internal auditors respect the value and ownership of information they receive and do not disclose information without appropriate authority unless there is a legal or professional obligation to do so.

4. **Competency:** Internal auditors apply the knowledge, skills, and experience needed in the performance of internal audit services.[2]

Blind Spots

At first glance, complying with the four principles may seem like a straightforward proposition. But many ethical lapses are committed as the result of "blind spots." I became familiar with this concept years ago when I picked up *Blind Spots*, a book by Max Bazerman and Ann Tenbrunsel.[3]

Most of us would think that people who commit fraud or some other ethical breach intend to do so. But Bazerman and Tenbrunsel suggest that, when people have a vested interest in seeing a problem in a certain way, they are no longer capable of objectivity. And that, I think, presents a serious challenge as we try to keep our personal ethics compass pointing in the right direction.

My good friend, Cynthia Cooper, writes extensively in her own book about the challenges she experienced while working at WorldCom.[4] At one point near the end of the book, she warns her readers:

> Guard against being lulled into thinking you're not capable of making bad decisions. Each of us is imperfect and must protect against giving in to temptation. Keep in mind that what is legal and what is ethical are sometimes different.[5]

Real-World Blind Spots

I have faced ethical dilemmas during my career, and I have seen blind spots at work within the internal audit profession. As you read through the following real-life scenarios, ask yourself, "Have I ever seen or done that?" That's the trouble with blind spots.

1. **"They really aren't good policies anyway."**

An auditor was assigned to review his organization's travel policies. He soon discovered that his client was not conforming to policies requiring purchasing the lowest airfare and documenting receipts, but he also knew the internal audit department was not complying with the policies either. He had to decide whether to include the violations in his report or ignore the problem.

As he struggled to make a decision, he rationalized, "They really aren't good travel policies anyway." That rationalization led him to reason that internal audit wasn't following the policies because they weren't sound business practices. So he didn't include the issue in the final report.

I stumbled on this omission as we were conducting a quality assurance assessment of that very same department, so I called the auditor in to talk about the situation. "You know, I couldn't write them up because we don't follow the policies either," he said.

That auditor's attempt at an explanation is the kind of rationalizing that can start early in your career if you decide, "There is some room for interpretation as we go through an internal audit if the results might somehow reflect badly on us."

2. **"Conducting the audit during the holidays will disrupt the business."**

I was once involved with a company whose business cycle was particularly heavy around the annual winter holidays, from mid-December into the early part of January. It was in an industry that had to deal each year with an inherently high degree of risk involving its logistics and customer service during the busy holiday period.

The team working on an internal audit of the company in this particular instance was aware of operational problems. There had been problems in prior years regarding deadlines and merchandise shipments during the busy year-end season. Internal audit had rated the risk as high in the company's annual risk assessment, and so the audit plan specified that the engagement team would complete the current audit during the holiday season, because that's when the problems usually occurred.

But when it was almost time for the audit to start, several internal auditors asked the department director, "Are you really going to make us work on Christmas Eve and Christmas Day, and those days right around the holidays? On those days, we want to be with our families."

At the same time, the director was hearing from the company's operating managers, "For goodness' sake, don't audit us that week, because that is the most difficult week of the year from an operations standpoint. Your auditors will disrupt things if they come then."

The audit director was finally persuaded to delay the audit because his staff also had plans for the holidays, and he had originally planned to vacation during the holiday season too. He issued a memo to the operating officials, stating, "We will defer this audit due to potential disruption of your business operations."

Whether the decision to delay was the right one or not, the audit director hadn't come clean. He was at least as influenced by his team's desire for time off as he was by the effect that a holiday audit might have had on the business.

If the internal auditor in this case felt strongly that the audit should be delayed, he should have stated that he was deferring it for both reasons—at the request of the operating managers being audited *and to allow his staff to spend the holidays with family*. Sure, he came across as the good guy to management and his auditors, but I believe his approach raised serious ethical questions because it wasn't completely honest.

3. **"I don't recall if this was going on when I was here."**

A woman who joined the internal audit department after working in one of the company's business units was scheduled to audit the area where she had previously worked. Internal audit policy was that you cannot be involved in an audit of your former work area for at least a year, but the proper amount of time had passed.

During the audit, she found several control deficiencies that she suspected had existed when she was responsible for that area. She also knew that if she reported the deficiencies, the current audit client would likely say, "But this was going on when you were here."

She feared damage to her reputation if she put herself in the position of defending her earlier work. At the same time, she didn't want to ignore the problem completely in her report because it was clearly documented in the workpapers.

So she reasoned to herself, "I don't know whether or not this was going on when I worked there, but that's irrelevant. I don't think it's important enough to include it in the report as a finding. We will just put it in the back of the report in a section that we call *other areas for management consideration.*" She did not bury the deficiencies, but she didn't treat them as she would have had she not had a prior connection to the problem before joining internal audit.

In the preceding scenarios, the internal auditors did not view their actions as unethical. They rationalized their decisions and convinced themselves and others that they were in the best interest of the department or the organization.

4. **"It's not worth damaging a personal relationship."**

An internal auditor assigned to lead the audit of a business unit managed by a close friend—the best man at his wedding—unearthed problems during the audit. Significant risks weren't managed well and controls weren't effectively implemented. The auditor knew that if he reported the problems, they could damage the friend's reputation or destroy a long friendship—or both.

So he told himself, "I can't exactly bury the issue or ignore it. But if our objective in doing the audit is to improve the organization, why do we have to write a big finding about it, embarrass the guy, and make him look bad in front of everybody else in the organization? I'll just talk to him about these areas. I'll walk him through these deficiencies and he will fix them. He will understand that this is something that should be taken care of and, because we found it during the audit, it *will* be taken care of."

In the internal auditor's mind, he had addressed the issue properly. The problems were fixed, after all. But another auditor might have seen the situation in an entirely different light. All internal auditors have friends and established relationships throughout their organization, but it's important to remember that personal relationships can easily create conflicts of interest and lead to ethical lapses.

5. **"First impressions are lasting impressions."**

A new CAE who was not yet fully aware of the skills and capabilities of the internal auditors in his department decided that, based on an updated risk assessment, a team needed to audit the deployment of a new system in the IT department.

So he turned to one of the department's young internal auditors who had already been in to meet him (only some of the staff had yet briefed him on what each of them was doing) and said, "I need you to lead this audit, and here is what we need to do."

The young auditor knew full well he wasn't the best choice to lead an IT audit; there were others in the department who had done such audits before and were much more qualified to lead the engagement. But he wanted to make a good impression, so he said, "Yes, sir."

I saw the audit report later during an external quality assessment and didn't find anything that I thought was particularly deficient in it. But I also knew that, because I had reviewed information about the internal audit department's staff and their qualifications, this internal auditor wasn't even in the top five on staff who should have been assigned the audit.

The IIA's Code of Ethics precludes internal auditors from taking on work for which they are not qualified. Had this auditor behaved unethically for not having said, "I'm not the best person to do this"? In his case, he wanted to prove that he *could* do it, and he wanted to lead the team. But was his decision ethical?

6. **"Better no external quality assessment than a bad one."**

IIA Standard 1312: External Assessments states:

External assessments must be conducted at least once every five years by a qualified, independent assessor or assessment team from outside the organization. The chief audit executive must discuss with the board:

- The form and frequency of external assessment.
- The qualifications and independence of the external assessor or assessment team, including any potential conflict of interest.

That standard has been in place now for more than 12 years, yet many internal audit departments have never undergone such a review—*even in cases where the requirement is clearly spelled out in their charter and approved by the audit committee.*

In a case I observed a few years ago, a CAE who had been in place for some years had every intention of getting the external quality assurance (EQA) assessment done. She knew it needed to be done and was preparing for it, but just a few months before the EQA was to be scheduled, a new CFO and a new audit committee chairman joined the company.

The CAE faced a dilemma. "I don't know how the EQA will come out," she thought to herself. "We haven't had one before and I don't want to risk having the results make internal audit look bad in front of a new audit chair and CFO. That would undermine the credibility we hope to build with those key stakeholders." So she decided to delay the EQA for a year. In her mind, it was better to have no EQA than to have an unfavorable one.

7. "Of course we can absorb those reductions."

The economy was slumping and the CAE was informed that internal audit's budget was to be cut by 25 percent, which would require eliminating 25 percent of the department's staff positions. The CAE knew that would mean delaying or cancelling several internal audits of high-risk areas scheduled for the coming year, but the CEO and the CFO were clear about the situation, saying, "This is it; don't argue. Take your share of cuts just like everybody else in the organization."

When the audit committee was made aware of the internal audit staff cuts at its next meeting, the chairman turned to the CAE in executive session and said, "Now, let's go back to these reductions that we talked about earlier. Will the reductions impair your ability to address the key risks that we have told you are important to us?"

The CAE knew the answer was more than a simple *yes* or *no*. There were risks that fell into that category that he would not be able to cover adequately, but he would have real problems with the CFO and the CEO if he told the audit committee his team may not be able to address all of its important concerns. So his response to the chairman's question? "No, no. As I said earlier, we can take these cuts and still get the job done," he said. "We'll be fine."

This is a situation many CAEs will face eventually. During a CAE forum, I asked those present how comfortable they would be in sharing information with the audit committee that they had not discussed first with the CFO or their direct supervisor.

I was surprised at the responses. Quite a few willingly said, "Yeah, I would not be comfortable doing that at all."

But that's what they pay us to do. That's why CAEs get the "big bucks," right? To make tough calls and to acknowledge, "I know this isn't going to go down well with the CFO or the CEO. But I'm going to be asked a direct question by the audit committee chair, and I cannot hide this or lie."

8. **"I won't fit in later if I do that now."**

A lot of audit departments have positioned themselves as a pipeline of talent to their companies in recent years by employing developmental or rotational programs at the end of which internal auditors rotate into a business unit. I think there is real value in sharing internal audit's talent with other departments and becoming a source of such talent within the organization. But some departments have set up very rigid rotational cycles, so that the individual knows that he or she will come into the internal audit department, spend approximately three years there, and then be expected to move into another business unit.

Some companies that have a rotational audit staffing cycle want the internal audit staff to have the chance to audit the areas within which they next want to be assigned. I see an inherent conflict of interest if auditors are assigned to an engagement in a business unit into which they hope to be rotated; it challenges their objectivity. I was talking to some of the staff attending an internal audit conference a few years ago, many of whom were earmarked for transfers soon to new positions within their companies. I asked them, "Have you audited the area you want to go into?"

"Yes," one of them replied.

"What did you do?" I asked. "Did you find any problems in that area?"

"Yes. I identified some internal control design and implementation issues," he said.

So I asked, "Did you report them like you normally would?"

His response: "I was concerned, because if I put them in the report, I was worried that maybe the folks in the department would decide I might not be a good fit. But we worked that out. I talked them through it and they fixed the problems, so I didn't need to put them in the report."

A disturbing theme runs through this and several of the other scenarios. When a conflict of interest exists, whether we recognize it or not, we aren't likely to handle audit issues the same way we would if we were truly objective about the situation. The first step to avoiding such ethical lapses is to recognize a conflict of interest when we see it.

9. **"Don't Worry, Be Happy."**

The Foreign Corrupt Practices Act (FCPA) prohibits the bribery of foreign officials and employees who work for foreign governments. But while bribery is illegal, the federal law allows for *facilitation payments,* which are payments "designed to facilitate the execution of clerical or ministerial government tasks" such as making provisions for telephone, water, and power service; police protection; mail delivery; business permits; and inspections tied to contract performance or the shipment of goods.[6] Thus, the line between bribery and facilitation payments can sometimes be very thin.

In a case I didn't experience personally but that made national headlines, a company's internal audit staff had documented numerous FCPA violations. The CAE conferred with the company's general counsel, who read the draft report and probably responded with something like, "You can't say that."

The CAE's likely response? "Well, this is what we found."

So they met again about a week later. "Our legal staff has looked at everything you gave us," the general counsel said, "and I want to assure you that you don't have any FCPA violations. What you found were merely facilitation payments, which are perfectly acceptable. If you put these matters into the audit report, you are going to look bad. You will force us to go in front of the audit committee and tell them that you don't know what you are talking about. You need to take our advice here and back off."

So the CAE did just that, though he came to regret it. The general council spun it in a way that made the CAE back away, essentially reassuring him that legal and management were OK with the payment while simultaneously threatening to confront him before the audit committee in a battle of wills management expected to win. But that didn't change the facts as the CAE's staff knew them to be. When the bribes were eventually exposed and a scandal ensued, the company ended up in much more trouble than if everyone had addressed the issue openly—back when it was first identified by internal audit.

This particular type of blind spot is certainly not limited to FCPA compliance. Have you ever been in a conversation with general counsel, or another corporate executive with specific expertise in audit results, during which you were pressured to take a different view of something or word a report differently? I'm not blaming general counsels; they get paid to do one thing, we get paid to do another. But we shouldn't defer to them if we are sure of our findings and recommendations.

After those run-ins with the general counsel, I would hope that I pressed forward and presented both points of view to senior management and the audit committee. Looking back later, I would not want to be the one who had said, "They are the lawyers; I'm just the auditor."

10. "This could wipe out the whole company."

Occasionally, an internal auditor comes upon significant financial reporting fraud; for example, earnings that have been manipulated or overstated. In some cases, the external auditors didn't catch the issue, so internal audit needs to blow the whistle on the problem.

If you are new to this profession, I recommend reading *Extraordinary Circumstances: The Journey of a Corporate Whistleblower* by Cynthia Cooper, former vice president of internal audit at WorldCom. In 2002, Cooper and her team of auditors uncovered a $3.8 billion fraud at World-Com, the then-giant telecom company. At the time, it was the largest accounting fraud in U.S. history. WorldCom's CFO and others in the company clearly pressured Cooper to not report the enormous ethical violations she had discovered.[7] They gave her all kinds of excuses, such as it's just a temporary thing; they insisted it's going to reconcile. She was so determined not to get caught in the ethical quicksand that she had her staff work at night to keep them out of top management's sight. Cooper knew what the discovery would do to the company, her colleagues, and the community, but she also understood her ethical obligations.

Modeling Ethical Behavior

I like to think internal auditors really are guardians of trust for the organizations they serve. Yes, individual auditors have ethical lapses, but as a profession, we strive to behave ethically every day. It's what I call the vision of internal audit leadership in ethical organizations.

Seven Traits of Ethical Internal Auditors

Having been fortunate to meet many internal auditors who exemplify ethical leadership, I have identified seven traits that ethical internal auditors share.

First and foremost, ethical internal auditors are *honest*. They don't lie, they don't conceal; they are open and transparent. They would correctly be described as honest individuals.

Second, they are *courageous*. They are willing to make really tough calls. As an internal auditor, if you never have bad news to deliver, something is seriously wrong, because no matter how well-run your organization, mistakes always occur and there's always room for improvement. You must have the courage to say what needs to be said.

Third, they are *accountable*. If they do something wrong or bad, or have a department that isn't meeting standards, they admit it and take responsibility for the problem.

Fourth, they are *empathetic*. They realize they are auditing other human beings as well as business units and departmental processes. Those people face challenges and are wrestling with issues of their own, and ethical auditors work to understand and share their experiences and feelings without sacrificing their objectivity for the job at hand.

Fifth, they are *trustworthy*. They are dependable, good, effective, and honest.

Sixth, they are *respected*. They are seen by colleagues throughout the organization as someone to be admired for all of the other ethical attributes they bring to their role.

Finally, they are *proactive*. They do not wait until after an ethical transgression has occurred to speak up if they see it happening.

Throw a Flag Before the Play

In American football, which I enjoy watching, the referee sometimes throws a penalty flag even before the ball is snapped and the play begins. For instance, the referee will throw a flag for a "false start" if certain players on offense move before they're supposed to.

Throwing the flag before a play starts because something isn't right is, I think, exactly what internal auditors should do in their role as corporate watchdog and fiduciary and a key part of their organization's conscience.

More than once in my career, I have had to interrupt the process to warn of an impending mistake or a crisis in the making in the hope it would spur management to action and prevent the problem. I think I added far more value to the organization by doing so than if I had simply shown up afterward and written a report critical of the situation and recommended what could be done differently next time. For me, it was the ethical thing to do.

I have discussed with others the various roles internal auditors can play across what I called the "ethics continuum." On rare occasions, when internal auditors get directly involved in a fraud or unethical conduct, they become *accomplices*; sometimes they are partly at fault simply because they sat on the sidelines and failed to expose the inefficiency, waste, fraud, or mismanagement. I consider such internal auditors to be *spectators*.

Most of the time, however, internal auditors are *referees*. They monitor the series of plays that constitutes the normal course of a business's operations and blow a whistle or throw a flag only when they identify a mistake or transgression that has already occurred. They objectively determine whether a penalty, foul, or other infraction has occurred.

Just as a football referee will interrupt the game if there are too many offensive players in the huddle, and a baseball umpire won't allow a pitcher to throw until a hitter is settled in the batter's box, internal auditors must be willing to call for a halt to the action if they see a problem looming. I call this being part of the *conscience* of the organization.

A good example of when internal auditors should have blown the whistle or even thrown a penalty flag was the rolling out of the federal Affordable Care Act's health-insurance website—healthCare.gov—in the latter part of 2013. The site's debut was a fiasco, with consumers unable to research or purchase medical coverage for days, weeks, or even months. The software and related systems obviously had not been ready for prime time, which suggests that opportunities may have been missed for someone to sound a warning. Either auditors in the U.S. Department of Health and Human Services' Inspector General's Office weren't proactive enough in warning agency officials of potential risks or failures, or they were less than effective in preventing the disaster once they had warned the agency.

The time for internal auditors to get involved with complex IT systems for business or government is when they are being designed; if the auditors observe lax planning, internal controls, or system design, the time for them to speak up is before the new equipment is deployed. Waiting until deployment risks the reputation of the very organization they are entrusted to serve. It is internal audit's obligation to raise any concerns early on and often, and to proactively warn management of the potential for failure.

In the case of HealthCare.gov, the result was a big, long-running, public relations nightmare for a presidential administration that had placed much emphasis on health-care reform.

Ethical Internal Auditors Must Be Courageous

Earlier, I listed seven traits of ethical internal auditors with courage as number two, but it really could be tied for number one with honesty. Over the decades, countless practitioners have put their livelihoods on the line to bring wrongdoing to light. Like many others, I have long believed that Cynthia Cooper is the model of courage in our profession. In *Extraordinary Circumstances*, she counsels internal auditors to "find your courage."

But courage doesn't suddenly blossom within an internal auditor simply because there is an expectation or strong case for it. I go back to Cooper's admonition to "find your courage," which requires practitioners to examine what courage is and under what circumstances their own internal fortitude may be tested.

In *Trusted Advisors*, one of the nine key attributes I examine is ethical resilience, and in speeches about the book, I frequently talk about internal auditors needing to be ethical *and* courageous. I have known many ethical internal auditors who kept their heads down rather than confront highly contentious risks, issues, or results. But being courageous often requires being the lone voice.

The Audit Executive Center survey conducted as research for *Trusted Advisors* identified courage as "being brave enough, even in the face of professional or personal danger, to do the right thing." A number of survey respondents ruminated on the importance of courage:

- "Courage: the ability to express one's opinion and give advice even when the ideas are not popular or wanted.

- Courage to stand alone, if needed, when tough issues need to be raised to management and the board."

In addition to understanding what it takes to be courageous, internal auditors should also be attuned to whether their own organizations' corporate cultures support or discourage speaking out. If organizations foster an environment in which retaliation is unacceptable for those who raise concerns, they tend to be better off in the long run.

I've written many times that those aspiring to become CAEs should know what they're getting into and be prepared emotionally, professionally, and financially to do their talking with their feet if it comes to that. I've also written that great internal auditors do not fear difficult or uncomfortable topics. They courageously sail toward the storms to alert management and the board when risks are not being managed and controls are not adequately designed and implemented.

To be clear, I do not take lightly that acting in the face of adversity may pose great professional and personal vulnerabilities. But internal audit's ability to provide assurance, help organizations overcome risks, and become trusted advisors to our stakeholders depends greatly on our willingness to speak out.

By definition, courage is not easily achieved. It can involve danger and personal sacrifice. But courage is not courage when there's nothing on the line.

CHAPTER 15
Always Remember—We Are Auditing People, Too

Today's internal audit professionals must understand the possibilities and flaws of human nature so they can develop strategies to maximize the possibilities and minimize the pitfalls in their day-to-day work.

As a young internal auditor, I concentrated on learning the technical skills needed to succeed in the profession. I learned early in my career about the importance of developing a comprehensive plan at the beginning of every engagement, documenting the work, and writing a clear, concise report. I also learned about the business area I was auditing and how it operated. These skills served me well throughout my career, but I can honestly say that learning the technical skills was easy compared with cultivating the people skills that I also needed to succeed.

Over the course of my career, I have led or served on scores of audit teams involving an array of industries and military or government operations. In doing so, I noticed that, regardless of the type of function or operation I was auditing, they had a lot in common in the way the people behaved. Overall, the many people whose operations I have audited have been good, decent, and hard-working professionals. Many had thankless jobs at which they toiled tirelessly without complaining. But I also learned that human nature is a complex thing. You can't always take what people say or do at face value.

Smart People Can Do Dumb Things

It's easy for internal auditors to become intimidated when auditing an area led or filled with intelligent, seasoned professionals. They can dazzle you with their deep understanding of the area's operations, and their knowledge can appear unassailable. Yet, I have frequently observed some of these bright folks doing some pretty dumb things. For example, I have uncovered instances when violations of internal controls in their area turned out to be deliberate circumventions that they had instigated in the belief that their experience or expertise didn't warrant such controls. Don't assume smart people always do smart things.

How do internal auditors accomplish their work in the face of such uncertainty about their clients? New auditors tend to see the world in black-and-white terms. "Should we do an audit?" "Should we issue a finding?" "Am I maintaining a healthy degree of professional skepticism?" For many new internal auditors, such questions point unerringly to a single, yes-or-no answer. But with experience, an internal auditor comes to realize that the answers to these kinds of questions are more nuanced than that. The issue is not merely whether we should perform an audit, but whether risks in the program, function, or activity warrant an audit compared with other areas where the risk may be greater; whether sufficient resources are available; and how soon the audit would be needed. The issue is not just whether to report a finding, but how significant the finding is relative to others in the audit, and how strongly to word the description if we write one.

The same thing applies when we attempt to draw the line that separates a healthy amount of professional skepticism from harboring unwarranted suspicions about the people we audit and the areas they operate. Professional skepticism means we take nothing for granted. We continuously assess audit evidence and other information, and we question what we see and hear. We take pride in never missing a clue or warning sign and remaining alert for hidden messages that other auditors might miss. It is a quality that is essential to our work as auditors.

The flip side of skepticism is that too much of it can actually hamper an internal audit's effectiveness. I once had a hyper-suspicious auditor who worked for me. He always assumed his clients were guilty of something and his primary job was to "blow the whistle" on them. Not surprisingly, his working relationships with management and with me deteriorated over time; managers were less than forthcoming during risk assessments and audit engagements when he was involved. His overly suspicious nature eventually led to a breakdown in communication and weaker audits. There is a fine line between skepticism and suspicion. As internal auditors, we must know where that line is drawn.

The written performance goals for many internal auditors might include initiatives to building working relationships with key stakeholders and fostering business partnerships with management. Unfortunately, the need for professional skepticism means we can never completely trust the very people in our organization who want us to be their partners. And that means management is less likely to think of internal auditors as trusted advisors, especially when compared with their "partners" in other departments.

Finding an appropriate level of professional skepticism and knowing how to express it are critical to an internal auditor's long-term success. One size does not fit all; some internal auditors rely more on building relationships, while others are more inclined to "dig out the truth" in the form of hard facts. The trick is to exhibit *just the right degree* of professional skepticism in any given situation.

If only we had a standardized rating system for determining our level of skepticism! Unfortunately, accurate and flexible ratings are not likely to appear anytime soon. Imagine a checklist with statements such as, "The client seemed nervous and was sweating profusely. Add three skepticism points." Or, "The sample size was statistically significant. Deduct one skepticism point."

For me, the secret is simply to approach each situation with an open mind and communicate in a way that demonstrates my underlying trust and confidence in management. I will still need to ask tough questions, but I will also use tact in asking those questions and in deciding when and how to ask them.

"Trust but verify" was a signature phrase of former U.S. President Ronald Reagan, who used it often in the 1980s when discussing superpower relations with the former Soviet Union. For internal auditors, "trust but verify" should be words to live by. We need to demonstrate trust in our co-workers and continually verify that our trust is well placed.

Good People Can Do Bad Things

When we think of fraud, we tend to associate it with nefarious characters who deliberately set out to do something they know is wrong. But many of the fraudulent or illegal acts uncovered by internal auditors are committed by otherwise decent people whose blind spots caused them to lose their way. Often, these people were under extraordinary financial or personal pressures outside the workplace; they often rationalized their initial actions and didn't intend for them to morph into a full-blown fraud. As internal auditors, we should not assume that everyone is doing bad things, but our professional skepticism should remind us that even good people can do bad things.

The first time I stumbled onto a fraud was during my very first internal audit job at a large regional bank in Atlanta. Working in the bank's internal audit department proved to be a great experience for me. I learned about internal audit processes and the financial services industry. I had a chance to participate in branch office audits, which were fascinating. These were surprise audits; the internal auditors assembled about two blocks away from the designated branch office, and right at closing time the team showed up to look for any concealments, fraud, or violations of company policy. The audit also included counting all of the cash in the vault and on the premises.

Internal auditors were assigned to audit the tellers. Each teller had a "bank," so to speak, in their cash drawer. At that time, they had maybe $2,000 each in their banks to use throughout the day.

On one occasion, I began my audit with a female teller who did not even try to conceal what she had done with some of the money in her bank. "I have an IOU in here for some money that I've been using," she said. It was my first eye-opening encounter with fraud. I eventually learned that she was a sweet, good-hearted person who did not comprehend that she had committed fraud because, in her mind, she was going to pay the money back. She didn't think she was violating the law, but her actions could have resulted in a charge of embezzlement.

Why Does Fraud Happen?

Interviews with people who commit fraud reveal that most of them don't set out to commit such a crime. Often, they take advantage of an unexpected opportunity; many times, the first fraudulent act was triggered by an accident. Perhaps they mistakenly processed the same invoice twice, didn't correct the problem, and discovered that no one noticed. After that, their fraudulent acts were deliberate and became more frequent. Fraud investigators talk about the 10-80-10 law, which states that 10 percent of all people will never commit fraud, 80 percent will commit fraud under the right circumstances, and the remaining 10 percent actively seek opportunities for fraud. So internal auditors need to stop the 10 percent who are out to get us—and strive to protect the 80 percent from making mistakes that could ruin their lives.[1]

The Association of Certified Fraud Examiners' (ACFE's) 2018 Report to the Nations on Occupational Fraud and Abuse estimated the cost of internal fraud worldwide totals nearly $4 trillion in U.S. dollars, or 5 percent of all enterprise revenue.[2] And, as we all know, internal fraud is only part of the picture.

Everything is moving faster these days, including fraud. A rogue employee with a smartphone and a sufficiently weak control environment at work could transfer significant sums of money offshore in the blink of an eye. According to the ACFE, the average fraudster takes $130,000 out of a company in an average period of about 16 months.[3] Little of that money is ever recovered.

To be good at detecting fraud, internal auditors must understand exactly what it is. The IIA's *Standards* defines fraud as, "Any illegal act characterized by deceit, concealment, or violation of trust. These acts are not dependent upon the threat of violence of physical force. Frauds are perpetrated by parties and organizations to obtain money, property, or services; to avoid payment or loss of services; or to secure personal or business advantage."[4]

Detection technology is advancing as rapidly as fraud, with real-time transaction monitors exposing anomalous patterns that might otherwise have gone undetected. Systems for collecting tips (for example, fraud hotlines) and a robust internal audit function have also proven effective at detecting fraud. But detection should never be the first line of defense.

In fraud, as in medicine, an ounce of prevention is worth a pound of cure. Donald R. Cressey, the late criminologist, is credited with identifying the three ingredients necessary for fraud—motive, opportunity, and rationalization—that are known collectively as the fraud triangle.[5] With appropriate risk assessment and controls, an organization can effectively shrink the "opportunity" side of the triangle. But if you don't know what you're looking for, how will you know when you've found it?[6]

IIA Standard 1210.A2 specifies internal audit's responsibility in the fight against fraud:

> "Internal auditors must have sufficient knowledge to evaluate the risk of fraud and the manner in which it is managed by the organization, but are not expected to have the expertise of a person whose primary responsibility is detecting and investigating fraud."

As a federal inspector general, I had a key responsibility to prevent and detect fraud in my agency. I was fortunate to lead a well-resourced cadre of auditors and criminal investigators, and, looking back, I give us high marks for our ability to detect and investigate fraud where it had already occurred. But I continue to think that the real opportunities lie in fraud prevention. Leveraging our knowledge of the risks and getting in early—before the fraud can occur—would add so much more value for our stakeholders.

People Appreciate Recognition for Accomplishments

As internal auditors, we are told from the outset that our job is to provide assurance on the effectiveness of risk management, internal controls, and governance. But too often we forget to balance our assurance by reporting the good as well as the bad. Instead, our final reports head straight for the findings on inadequate risk management, internal controls, and so on. Many internal audit reports are submitted with no genuine recognition of management's accomplishments during the audit period, which serves to reinforce our reputation of being "professional fault finders." Based on my experience as an internal auditor, I have concluded that people are looking for an objective assessment of their operating areas. They understand we have a job to do, but they believe such an assessment includes some recognition of the things they accomplished or did well. Including a "management accomplishments" section at the beginning of an audit report can pave the way for general acceptance of our findings and the recommendations for corrective actions that follow.

The Importance of Recognition

Recognizing people's accomplishments both within the internal audit function and in management and executive positions within your organization goes a long way toward fostering an atmosphere of cooperation and support. Mutual recognition is an essential condition of effective relationships; to recognize someone is to acknowledge implicitly or explicitly that you are aware of and value their contribution to the enterprise. Taking time at the onset of an internal audit engagement to show appreciation for your client can set a positive tone for the entire engagement.

As the leader of an internal audit team, you should recognize the achievements of your team as a matter of course. Sincere and honest praise lets employees know you value their efforts. Such simple acts take little time but provide many benefits. With a few encouraging words and a pat on the back, you recognize and reinforce desired performance behaviors. And an employee who feels appreciated is likely to continue those desired behaviors.

As a CAE, you should make sure your staff knows they are valuable members of the organization. Praise creates and reinforces a positive self-image in employees, making each one feel like a winner. This is particularly helpful in confusing or unclear situations when an employee is trying to do the right thing but is uncertain where their performance falls on the departmental scale.

I have also learned that employees under stress also need a few words of praise to let them know they have done the right thing in a difficult situation. And when employees are assigned necessary but unchallenging tasks, they too should be praised for their contributions.

Don't Let Assets Become Liabilities

Are you one of the best and brightest internal auditors in the profession? Do you model all of the attributes of outstanding internal auditors? Are you a great communicator, a critical thinker, and a relationship builder? Great! But be warned: Your professional assets can become liabilities.

These kinds of qualities will usually serve you well in the internal audit profession. But all humans are fallible and, as we discussed earlier, our "blind spots" are often closely linked to our strengths. I have identified several traits usually possessed by successful internal auditors that, under certain circumstances, can become liabilities:

Are you the most dedicated auditor in your department?

Maybe you work long hours to verify just a few more facts or interview just a few more people. Normally, that's a plus for a career. But if your passion for completeness gets out of hand, you soon may find that "scope creep" gets the better of you and undermines the timeliness of your engagements (as discussed earlier). There are only so many hours in a day, so try to keep in mind that spending too much time on one internal audit might not leave enough time for the next one.

Are you widely admired for your industry experience and technical knowledge?

If so, you bring important strengths to the department and your career. But nobody's knowledge is complete, and the more experienced you are, the more likely you may begin to rely on outdated information should the situation change. Auditors viewed as "experts" are also tempted to live up to their reputations by offering opinions even when they don't have all the facts. And even the world's most experienced experts need help on occasion—though it may not occur to them to ask. A second opinion doesn't make you any less of an expert, and the people you ask for help will probably be flattered that you sought their opinion.

Is your work highly accurate?

It's great to have a reputation for professional infallibility. But everyone makes mistakes sometimes, and the danger is that, if you are almost always right, it may be difficult for you to spot or admit your mistakes when you are wrong. After all, you haven't had much practice!

Are you extremely detail-oriented?

Attention to detail is important in internal auditing, but if you are particularly detail-oriented, you may become so tightly focused that you lose track of the bigger picture. Too much detail in an audit report can actually hamper the delivery of its most important messages. We usually only need to tell the reader what time it is—not how the clock works!

Are you passionately committed to bringing about positive change?

Enthusiasm is important, but if you are particularly determined to bring your audit clients around to your point of view, remember that they may also have valid points to make. Internal auditors should consider new evidence fairly, even when that evidence doesn't appear until the closing meeting —or later.

Finger Pointing

Recent media coverage of corporations charged with violating U.S. anti-bribery laws has focused on the case of a globally recognized American company and the prosecutors who are scrutinizing a draft internal audit report to determine whether the company's executives ignored or tried to conceal the report's findings from the company's audit committee. If so, prosecutors think it could help show intent, which is a key element in obtaining criminal charges. Cases such as this raise an important internal audit issue that I think the profession needs to talk about: If an internal audit report is ignored or suppressed, whose fault is it?

One of a CAE's most fundamental roles is to ensure that members of management and the company's audit committee get the information they need to make sound decisions. When someone prevents important internal audit findings from reaching the audit committee, it undermines key tenets of our profession.

I recognize that many forces are at work when audit information is suppressed. The decision to censor or suppress important information rarely starts with the CAE. Still, ultimately it is the responsibility and obligation of an organization's internal auditors to make sure essential information gets to the audit committee in timely fashion and in enough detail for management and the committee to take appropriate action. Sure, there are obstacles, and at times the challenges can be formidable, but rarely is the task impossible.

IIA Standard 2420: Quality of Communications is clear: Communications must be accurate, objective, clear, concise, constructive, complete, and timely. The accompanying interpretation is also clear:

> *Accurate communications are free from errors and distortions and are faithful to the underlying facts. Objective communications are fair, impartial, and unbiased and are the result of a fair-minded and balanced assessment of all relevant facts and circumstances. Clear communications are easily understood and logical, avoiding unnecessary technical language and providing all significant and relevant information. Concise communications are to the point and avoid unnecessary elaboration, superfluous detail, redundancy, and wordiness. Constructive communications are helpful to the engagement client and the organization and lead to improvements where needed. Complete communications lack nothing that is essential to the target audience and include all significant and relevant information and observations to support recommendations and conclusions. Timely communications are opportune and expedient, depending on the significance of the issue, allowing management to take appropriate corrective action.*

The *Standards* are clear. But to me, this issue is more than a matter of complying with professional standards. The CAE has a professional and moral obligation to ensure that the audit committee is advised if there is evidence that the organization may be a party to criminal wrongdoing.

Management and the audit committee bear some of the responsibility for ensuring free and open communication between the organization's auditors and the audit committee. Audit committees that rarely meet privately with the CAE ought to consider rethinking the meeting agenda. If reporting lines don't ensure internal audit's independence, objectivity, and organizational stature, it may be time to reassess internal audit's reporting relationships.

Failures Can Be Keys to Success

I have concluded over the course of my career that how people respond to critical internal audit reports often speaks volumes about their character and probably indicates how they deal with criticism or disappointment in other parts of their lives. I think you can tell a lot about a person's character by the way they respond to any setback. I can't tell you how many people I've known over the years who have suffered setbacks and never recovered; they just couldn't resume their forward progress and get on with their professional or even personal lives.

I can recall at least three times when I dearly wanted a promotion or an assignment and didn't get it. Each time, failure presented me with a choice. I could press on and thrive, keeping an eye out for further opportunities, or I could quit—literally or figuratively—and let failure define me.

For me, there was really no choice. I can tell you that every time I failed to get something I wanted, I chose to persevere and wound up achieving much greater success down the road thanks to opportunities I might have missed had I been granted that earlier wish.

But don't take my word for it. History is full of similar examples.

Growing up, Milton Hershey thought he wanted to be a printer. I can't help but wonder what s'mores would be made with today if he hadn't been fired and then signed on as an apprentice candy maker.

Walt Disney's dream of becoming an ace reporter was shot down in flames when an editor at the *Kansas City Star* fired him for "lack of creativity."

Thomas Edison's teachers told his parents he was stupid.

And the greatest successes for Steve Jobs at Apple came only after he had been forced out of the company he had founded and then brought back into the fold to run the technology giant.

I was devastated when I did not even make the list of finalists for the deputy controller's job at a large Army command when I was working at the Pentagon. I look back today in awe at how limiting such a "prestigious" career assignment would have been for me and my subsequent career. I was disappointed again in 2004 when I was not selected to be The IIA's next president. Yet, I could not imagine the decade that followed without the exhilarating experience of being a part of the internal audit practice at PwC!

As you consider your career in the internal audit profession, never be sure what is right for you and never give up, even when you think you have failed to achieve an important goal. I'm not suggesting that failure guarantees future success. You should always examine the reason why you didn't succeed at something and try to learn from it. After all, learning is one of the greatest gifts of failure. I'm just urging you to not let failure define you. I would say the same of success. Both are merely mile markers on your personal audit trail. Neither is a destination.

As Rudyard Kipling, author of *The Jungle Book* and *Gunga Din*, put it in his poem "If":

> If you can dream—and not make dreams your master;
> If you can think—and not make thoughts your aim;
> If you can meet with Triumph and Disaster
> And treat those two impostors just the same ...
> Yours is the Earth and everything that's in it,
> And—which is more—you'll be a Man, my son![7]

Life and the careers we shape within it are really journeys. Speaking with the hindsight of more than 40 years in the workforce, I have probably at some point questioned every career move I've made, but I don't regret any of them today. Take adversity as it comes and never quit. You will always learn more in life's valleys than on its lofty peaks.

CHAPTER 16
Internal Audit Needs a Seat at the Table

Whenever I travel, I meet CAEs who long for an opportunity to secure the trust of key players within their organizations. The exact words vary, but the question they put to me amounts to this: "How can internal auditors get a seat at the table?" CAEs frequently seek my advice on the best way to secure and retain this seemingly elusive seat. Although there is no magic formula, I often share my thoughts on this professional quest.

When I arrived at TVA as the newly appointed inspector general, I was mindful of the rocky relationship my predecessor had with the board of directors in the years leading up to his retirement. As I contemplated a strategic approach for improving the Office of the Inspector General's relationship with TVA's board and executive management, I was struck by the current relationship, which was very much an *us versus them* arrangement—at least from management's point of view. For example, I knew that the board and management met regularly to review the giant electric utility's business strategy and its execution. I also knew that, as the inspector general, I was not invited to these meetings. I genuinely believed that getting a "seat at the table" was essential to better understanding the business and how its strategies and decisions were formulated.

Not long after I arrived, I approached TVA's CEO and said I wished to attend the meetings as a non-decision-making participant. Not unexpectedly, he was very apprehensive. No previous inspector general had attended management's meetings (though no previous IG had a background in auditing). He said he was concerned my presence would have a *chilling effect* on the candid discussion of business issues and exchange of ideas. He also worried that management would view my presence as an attempt to gather audit leads that the OIG would then use to *cherry pick* areas of weakness in TVA's operations for targeting in our annual audit plan. I assured him I would not take advantage of such opportunities.

In the end, we agreed that I would attend these meetings on a regular basis, but I would not attend every meeting. I recall the tension in the room the first time I showed up for a meeting. Several executives made no secret of their mistrust of the OIG, even if they didn't know me. I took the opportunity early on to address the "elephant in the room" when I delivered a brief presentation on the OIG's newly formulated strategic plan and informed the executives that our vision was to be successful in "illuminating today's challenges and tomorrow's solutions" for TVA. I also noted that one of our strategic objectives was to "enhance communications with stakeholders and deliver services that meet their needs."

TVA executives remained skeptical, but I followed up on my pledge to work more collaboratively by "walking the talk"—particularly during these important meetings. Over time, I came to earn the trust of several key officials. When I retired from TVA, more than one of the board members and executives who had initially been skeptical of my intentions indicated they had been proven wrong. They thought my seat at the table had helped improve relationships between the OIG and TVA's management. My experience there taught me an important lesson: *The process of earning a seat at the table begins long before you can pull up your chair. It starts with you building a trusting relationship with the organization's board and management.*

Why a Seat at the Table?

For internal audit departments to deliver optimum value, the CAE and the department's staff need a keen understanding of the organization. Such an understanding must include how the business strategy is formulated and how risks are assessed and managed. A "seat at the table" is simply a label for the CAE's attendance at and participation in meetings and discussions with senior management and the board.

In seeking a seat at the table, it's most important that you first examine why you want to be there. Too often, internal auditors treat a seat at the table merely as a sign of success, which is a mistake. You must be at the table for the right reasons, not because you hope that being with senior executives will make others view you as a senior executive. Securing a seat at the table is a means to an end, not an end in itself. Not preparing for it in advance may damage rather than enhance your chances of delivering added value to the organization.

It's also a mistake to view a seat at the table as a source of audit leads. If you leave your first management meeting with plans for an immediate audit of the operating unit discussed that day, you may not be invited to the next one. You need to add value, not prevent others from talking freely. And I mean add value. Management will benefit from our being at the table only if we are prepared to share, not just listen.

Think of guests at a dinner party; we want our hosts to invite us back. In the case of board and management meetings, it helps if we bring something fresh, interesting, and important to the discussion. Focus on making operations better in the future, not on past mistakes, and provide insight instead of hindsight. I understood that I would be more welcome at executive meetings of TVA if I was willing to share insights as the authority's IG on matters related to risk and control.

The table is not a training ground. We must be able to discuss critical strategies and business risks facing our organizations, and we must understand the organizations' core business and be aware of both internal risks and external factors affecting our industry. If we don't bring our own perspectives, we won't add value, but we must be able to defend our views by ensuring we fully understand the discussion.

Most internal auditors are prepared to offer such valuable insights long before they are invited to the table, because the invitation is usually the result of the relationships they have built throughout the organization. It's not what we write in an audit report that gets us to the table, it's what we say and do with management every day. Senior executives will want us there if they respect us and see us as knowledgeable, trusted advisors. By the time most internal auditors reach the table, they no longer see management meetings primarily as sources of audit leads because they are already fully informed on the subjects likely to be discussed.

Adding value at the table requires a different perspective from the one we use as internal control advisors. Most internal auditors can discuss internal controls for a new strategic initiative, but when management discusses the feasibility of such an initiative, controls may be just one facet. To act as senior management, we must add value to other parts of the discussion as well.

An important part of IIA Global's strategic plan in recent years has been to support internal auditors worldwide in their quest to obtain a place at the table. While The IIA can advocate granting auditors a seat at the table, ultimately decisions about the scope of the auditors' role will be made by boards and executives in the organizations where internal audit resides. Each CAE, therefore, must demonstrate the insight and ability to participate in the senior management team. Knowing what we want to accomplish and preparing diligently to accomplish it greatly increase our chances of getting to the table.

Are You a "Trusted Advisor"?

Many CAEs and internal auditors also long to be "trusted advisors" within their organizations. They want management and the board to seek them out for advice on matters involving risk, control, and governance based on their understanding of the business and an assured level of trust that they have fostered over time.

But aside from possibly making us feel good about ourselves, what does it really mean to be a trusted advisor? This topic is the focal point of my book, *Trusted Advisors*, as observed in the opening:

> "Trust is one of the most underused words in the internal audit vocabulary. Sure, internal auditors occasionally speak of trust when considering whether they can rely on documents and assertions by management and those they audit. Those in the profession ponder whether they can trust management's intentions, and whether management can be trusted to be forthcoming and transparent during an audit engagement... [W]hile we use the word *trust* on occasion, it is usually in reference to whether we can trust our stakeholders and those we audit. Rarely do we speak of whether *they* should

trust *us*, and rarely do we view trust in the same lofty and vaunted ways as do philosophers and playwrights. Why should that be the case? Shouldn't our stakeholders have 'a firm belief in the reliability, truth, ability, or strength' of internal audit? Shouldn't those we audit trust that we understand the business and will not simply be wasting their time over the course of the audit?"

When I speak of internal auditors as *trusted advisors*, I am using the term to encompass the full spectrum of an internal auditor's work, from providing consultation and advice at the request of management to generating recommendations for corrective actions as the result of an assurance engagement. In the end, I believe we are advisors in our professional roles every day.

If becoming a trusted advisor were easy, we could simply prepare a sign or add a line to our business cards. Surely management would then seek us out at the first signs of trouble, right? Not really. As I chronicle in *Trusted Advisors*, those who win and sustain trust in our profession typically model several critical attributes. With the help of more than 250 CAEs in research conducted for the book, there are nine characteristics that internal audit's trusted advisors model. As discussed in chapter 2, and as **exhibit 16-1** illustrates, these attributes array into three broad categories: personal, relational, and professional.

The attributes, as displayed, make sense if viewed starting at the bottom and working up. Successful internal auditors must possess the attributes

---

Exhibit 16-1: Nine Characteristics of Trusted Advisors

Professional	Critical Thinkers	Technical Expertise
Relational	Dynamic Communicators · Insightful Relationships · Inspirational Leaders	
Personal	Ethical Resilience · Results Focused · Intellectually Curious · Open-Mindedness	

in the personal category and apply them in every transaction—and every interaction—with others. The personal attributes of being ethically resilient, results-focused, intellectually curious, and open-minded are absolutely essential for internal auditors in achieving success.

At the mid-point of the diagram, attributes in the relational category demonstrate that how a person interacts with others conveys how he or she relates with them. Trusted internal auditors are great communicators who typically listen before they speak, build and sustain strong relationships throughout their organizations based on mutual trust, and are leaders who inspire others to achieve greatness.

Then at the top of the diagram—the professional category—are the capstone qualities that help pave the way to a seat at the table (multiple tables, really, from the boardroom table to the breakroom—each important in its own way). Thus, they have earned the respect that is essential to apply their professional intellectual abilities and well-honed technical skills to address business issues.

From Backroom to Boardroom

I would characterize internal audit's journey during the past two decades as having taken it from "the backroom to the boardroom." Following those spectacular corporate failures in 2001–2002—and the subsequent regulatory and legislative response—internal audit found itself front and center with the audit committee and other members of the board at companies around the world. The profession's rapid rise in stature is reflected in statistical studies. In 2002, for instance, The IIA found that only 55 percent of CAEs in the United States reported functionally to their audit committees. By 2007, PwC found that the number had jumped to more than 80 percent. In recent years, internal audit's emphasis on assessing the effectiveness of financial controls has abated significantly. Given the shift in emphasis, I think there is a real threat that some audit committees may lose their newfound interest in internal auditing.

I suspect my view is one not shared by many. After all, it will be argued, corporate audit committees have much broader missions than mere oversight of financial performance and controls. But is that really true? From my experience conducting quality assurance assessments of Fortune 500 companies, I was struck by how narrowly written audit committees' charters often were. As I noted earlier in this book, in many instances, they were heavily tilted toward oversight of the independent auditors as well as financial statement and disclosure matters. I have often found the emphasis in the audit committee charter was a reflection of the focus of its members, many of whom were primarily interested in receiving assurance from internal audit on the effectiveness of their company's financial controls.

Given the foregoing, I believe many CAEs face a significant challenge as they continue to rebalance their internal audit coverage to audit at the speed of risk and include greater emphasis on operational, compliance, and strategic and business risks. Their challenge will be to ensure the audit committee drives or embraces this direction and perceives the strong value that a comprehensive risk-based approach to internal audit coverage will bring. Otherwise, I fear some audit committees will grow bored with internal audit's coverage of nonfinancial risks.

As a profession, we have worked too long and hard to gain the stature we have enjoyed. Let's stay in the boardroom and retain the seat at the table with management, because it is there where we can share insight and foresight, which is valuable to those who lead the enterprise.

CONCLUSION
Becoming a Trailblazer

When I look back on my journey along the audit trail, I realize how many of the lessons I learned on the way corresponded with change in our profession. The flexibility and resilience of internal auditors have been tested many times in recent decades. Some of the change has been evolutionary, but some has been revolutionary. Regardless, we are not what we used to be. Throughout the book, the subject of auditing at the speed of risk reinforces the point that we can no longer afford the luxury of stargazing. Those who thrive in this environment are those who are uniquely equipped to pivot quickly.

Leading at the Speed of Risk

From military and world leaders to business entrepreneurs, a common theme is that taking no risks leads to earning no rewards. As Facebook's co-founder Mark Zuckerberg has observed, "The biggest risk is not taking any risk. … In a world that is changing really quickly, the only strategy that is guaranteed to fail is not taking risks."

The risk/reward dynamic takes on the added component of the harrowing speed at which risks can emerge, change, and impact. I have written often of the need for internal auditors to audit at the speed of risk, which is no easy task. Leadership at the speed of risk can be even more daunting.

Today's business leaders must decipher a vexing risk/reward puzzle that can include disruptions in global supply chains, geopolitical instability, cybersecurity threats, and technological breakthroughs that can morph yesterday's state of the art into tomorrow's quaint curiosity.

Those leaders who have excelled at finding the right balance among risk, reward, and speed are highly valued. From Zuckerberg to Jobs, the great entrepreneurs are those who comfortably anticipate and manage risk. Today's greatest business leaders are, in a word, risk-centric. They recognize that failure to identify and manage rapidly emerging risks can prove lethal.

I believe that contemporary leaders who excel in "leading at the speed of risk" share four risk traits that set them apart—risk awareness, risk intuition, risk acceptance, and risk courage.

1. **Awareness. Leaders who are risk aware** are those who can identify threats and manage situations so that those around them are attuned to the risks. These leaders understand that risks cannot be ignored until they impact the organization. They anticipate risks and successfully execute plans to mitigate them before it's too late.

2. **Intuition. Leaders who possess risk intuition** seem to have an innate ability to sense risk in situations and instinctively know how to navigate through it. But that intuition is supported by a commitment to improving their ability to identify and address risks. They understand there are better ways to manage complex risks than relying on what worked for them 20 years ago.

3. **Acceptance. Leaders who accept risk** understand that taking intelligent risks is the path to accomplishing organizational objectives. Successful strong leaders don't treat risk as one-dimensional threats to be avoided, but they understand the upside of taking smart, well-calculated risks.

4. **Courage. Leaders who possess risk courage** are not afraid of risk, they are adept at managing it. But they maintain a healthy respect for its potential to damage the organization. As former U.S. President Teddy Roosevelt observed, "Risk is like fire. If controlled, it will help you; if uncontrolled, it will rise up and destroy you."

In internal auditing, we encourage organizations to address risk holistically and to identify risk strategies and risk appetites. Audit plans are based on providing assurance on organizational efforts to mitigate the biggest perceived risks. But these tools and techniques can provide a false sense of security without strong risk leadership.

Management executives and board members in today's business environment can't be blamed for becoming more risk averse, particularly when one considers the growing list of challenges and responsibilities placed on them. But risk avoidance can in itself become a risk. Great leaders understand and respect risk. They also have the courage and knowledge to use it in their favor.

The Era of Hindsight

Not so many years ago, the "perfect" internal auditor was considered the one with 20/20 hindsight—that is, the person who could go back in time through skillful use of records and interviews to uncover every mistake and report each misstep in exacting detail. We perceived we added value by helping our organizations recognize past mistakes and avoid repeating them in the future. We were the hindsight experts.

Hindsight will always be important for internal auditors. We're often brought in to assess what happened, and when used well, hindsight helps others learn from experience and build expertise. But there are things hindsight cannot tell us. Hindsight alone could not have predicted the rapidly evolving legislation, the explosive technological growth, the mounting risks of cybersecurity breaches, the economic crises, the advent of artificial intelligence, or the many other changes we have experienced over the past few decades.

As the velocity of change continues to accelerate, I can say with some certainty, based on the decades that I've been a part of this profession, that internal auditing has seen more changes in the past decade alone than at any other time in its history. And while clear hindsight continues to be important, one of the most fundamental ways in which we have changed recently is that we are no longer focused mainly on the past. In today's relentlessly evolving business environments, yesterday's ways of doing things are often not good enough. Our vision of the "perfect" internal auditor has been transformed: We have advanced from providing 20/20 hindsight to offering real insight into our organizations' risks, controls, and operations.

...To Insight

By moving from hindsight to insight, internal auditors exponentially added to the potential value of their services. Insight has become a key element of internal audit's "value proposition." Hindsight analyzes the past to keep us from repeating our mistakes, but insight allows us to apply past lessons to new challenges. With insight, internal auditors are no longer content with after-the-fact reviews. Instead, we are at the front end of our organizations' strategic undertakings, helping with acquisitions, systems redesign, multinational business expansions, and other initiatives that can mean the difference between success and failure for our clients.

The addition of insight was an important advance for our profession. Yet, I believe internal audit's greatest opportunity to add value for its clients lies ahead. That's because we are only now beginning to explore the potential of moving beyond both hindsight and insight—and positioning ourselves to provide foresight.

...To Foresight

For internal auditors, foresight is the ability to peer into the future so we can judge the relative importance of what's ahead for our organization. With it, we can help our clients prepare for challenges or opportunities before they even materialize. And foresight can mean the difference between an engagement resulting in another routine audit—or a major success story.

Each of us has an innate ability to imagine the future; we do it every day. But foresight is more than just exercising the imagination, interpreting gut feelings, or guessing about future events. No one can perfectly predict the future, but we can work hard to develop the knowledge and skills necessary to understand better what the future may hold.

During my years in client service, I worked with several leading internal audit departments that already delivered real value to their companies by including foresight in their work—whether or not they called it that. For example, the internal audit department of a leading U.S. health-care provider routinely offers advice to its management about risks that could materialize depending on how different scenarios affect health-care legislation and regulations. The auditors weren't recommending which strategies to pursue; they were simply shining an informed, objective light on the future to gauge the hazards that may lie ahead. In my opinion, that is what foresight is all about.

Internal auditors have a strong head start in developing the knowledge and skills needed to demonstrate useful foresight. Pattern recognition, trend assessment, and analysis are second nature to many of us in the profession. Internal auditors also have exceptional opportunities to learn about all aspects of a business, adding depth and focus to our "future view." We tend to look at things with fresh eyes and are trained to challenge existing assumptions and paradigms. In studying past mistakes and current problems, we have become experts at assessing risk and spotting opportunity, which makes us ideal candidates to provide our clients with forward-looking advice as well.

Given that a clear-eyed view of the future requires so many of the skills we use in conducting audits, it seems almost paradoxical that internal auditors are not renowned for their foresight. But just because we possess the tools doesn't mean we know how best to use them when looking forward, rather than into the past. Developing foresight will require hard work. Internal auditors must consciously strive to think in future tense, applying forward-looking analyses to our organizations' strategic plans and operations. Developing these abilities won't guarantee the accuracy of our predictions, but they will mean our foresight will be grounded in the same principles and preparation that have made our hindsight and insight so valuable for so long.

We are more likely to be disintermediated by future technologies, such as artificial intelligence, when providing hindsight and insight than in providing foresight. If we are to thrive in the future and blaze tomorrow's trails, we must adapt, which will likely require a different skillset.

Tomorrow's Trailblazers

The changes in technological innovations and geopolitical and macroeconomics pressures will redefine how professions deliver value tomorrow. In others, change will diminish or eliminate professions altogether. For the internal audit profession, I believe the decades to come will offer a great opportunity for transformation that will bring us closer to becoming indispensable to effective risk, control, and governance. Those who adapt to the changing landscape will serve as trailblazers.

Internal Auditor magazine annually recognizes a distinguished group of men and women as "Emerging Leaders" in our profession. These are individuals who demonstrate many of the characteristics and attributes that are essential to leading the profession in the years ahead. As I anticipate the newly designated emerging leaders each year, it's hard to resist contemplating what internal audit's future leaders will look like. I believe those who will become trailblazers directing internal audit functions in the years to come possess six core characteristics.

1. **Genetically risk-centric.** As I noted above, truly risk-centric leaders must be able to "decipher a vexing risk/reward puzzle that can include disruptions in global supply chains, geopolitical instability, cybersecurity threats, and technological breakthroughs that can morph yesterday's state of the art into tomorrow's quaint curiosity." Although still a rare breed, tomorrow's internal audit leaders will need to possess risk-centricity in their DNA.

2. **Tech savvy and tech fearless.** Technology has always been a two-edged sword. Advances that make work easier, increase productivity and efficiency, and add convenience also can eliminate jobs, make supporting services unnecessary, and disrupt competition. The next generation of internal audit leaders will have to understand innately how technology can impact and change organizations and still have the courage to embrace and adapt to technological change.

3. **Incessantly curious and professionally skeptical.** Asking "why" is fundamental to the work of internal auditors, and a desire to dig deeper will be as important as ever in the future. Intellectual curiosity is one of the characteristics I single out in *Trusted Advisors.* In the future, this will be more than just a trait of the best; it will be table stakes to get into the game. However, tomorrow's internal audit leaders will need to walk a fine

line when it comes to skepticism. The axiom "trust but verify" will become critical for successful internal audit leaders.

4. **Ethically far-sighted.** Ethical resiliency is another of the character traits I identify in *Trusted Advisors*. The pace and unforeseen consequences of change will make having an unshakeable ethical foundation imperative for internal auditors of the future. Beyond this, however, they will need to understand and anticipate how technology and other factors that change our world impact and influence ethics within the organization and within themselves.

5. **Intellectually honest.** Seeking the truth, regardless of whether it agrees with one's personal beliefs, should be a principle by which every internal auditor lives. Yet, rapid change and pressure to be agile and innovative will test our ability to remain so. True leaders will not give in to pressure to compromise intellectual honesty for expediency.

6. **Not your grandfather's CPA.** According to the 2018 North American Pulse of Internal Audit survey, accounting and finance remains the most recruited academic degree for internal audit. However, IT-related degrees, such as data science or information systems, are now a close second. Demand for accounting and finance backgrounds will continue to decline as the scope of internal audit work changes, and I suspect IT could overtake the traditional finance backgrounds by the end of the decade.

In the future, internal auditors will increasingly come from nontraditional backgrounds, from engineering to chemistry, as demand for specialized skills grows in parallel to changing demands on the profession. This is especially germane as sustainability and enterprise risk management play greater roles in governance.

Macroeconomic and geopolitical pressures are here to stay. Despite efforts at isolationism, demands of the marketplace, global warming, population growth, limited resources, and other factors make it impossible for any nation or industry to be an island. As such, internal auditors of the future will have to be cosmopolitan—familiar with and at ease in many different countries and cultures.

Those are just some of the ways that tomorrow's internal audit leaders will distinguish themselves. Many are already achieving them, along with new job skills and outlooks. Since *Internal Auditor* magazine began identifying some of our profession's rising stars in 2013, alumni have been contributing to shaping internal audit's future. These visionary leaders who adapt to innovation and transformation will blaze their own trail in our profession.

Notes

Chapter 1
There Are No Speed Limits on the Audit Trail

1. Merriam-Webster, http://www.merriam-webster.com/dictionary/audit%20trail.

Chapter 3
Stakeholder Expectations Can Change Swiftly

1. The money that becomes available in a national government's budget when the country is at peace and can afford to reduce its defense spending. The term "peace dividend" is also used to refer to an increase in investor confidence that sparks an increase in stock prices after a war ends or a major threat to national security is eliminated. The money saved from defense spending is usually used toward housing, education, and other projects.
2. Angela Witzany and Larry Harrington, *Voice of the Customer: Stakeholders' Messages for Internal Audit* (Altamonte Springs, FL: The Institute of Internal Auditors Research Foundation, 2016).
3. Ibid, 2.
4. KPMG, 2017 Global Audit Committee Pulse Survey. Accessed at: https://home.kpmg/pl/en/home/insights/2017/01/2017-global-audit-committee-pulse-survey.html.

Chapter 4
Stakeholders Have the Last Word on Value

1. For more information about the Value Proposition, see "Value Proposition: Internal Auditing's Value to Stakeholders" (Lake Mary, FL: The Institute of Internal Auditors). Accessed at: https://na.theiia.org/about-us/about-ia/pages/value-proposition.aspx.
2. Ibid.
3. Rick Telberg, "The Scary New Outlook for Internal Audit," American Institute of Certified Public Accountants, *Career Insider*, April 22, 2010. Accessed at: http://www.cpa2biz.com/Content/media/PRODUCER_CONTENT/Newsletters/Articles_2010/Career/ScaryOutlook.jsp.
4. Ibid.
5. Ibid.
6. Ibid.
7. This section provides the Executive Summary from The IIA's International Professional Practices Framework (IPPF) Practice Guide, Developing the Internal Audit Strategic Plan.

It will be necessary for the internal team to review this entire practice guide and use the information to prepare its own comprehensive strategic plan for meeting the expectations of its stakeholders. The practice guide can be accessed at: http://www.theiia.org/bookstore/downloads/9764013237511/1121_Developing%20IA%20Strategic%20Plan.pdf.

Chapter 5
Relationship Acumen Is Essential to Success

1. *Sawyer's Guide for Internal Auditors, Volume 1, Internal Audit Essentials* (Lake Mary, FL: Internal Audit Foundation, 2013), 139.
2. Deloitte Development LLC, "The Broken Triangle? Improving the Relationship Between Internal Audit, Management, and the Audit Committee," deloitte.com, 2010, https://www2.deloitte.com/content/dam/Deloitte/uy/Documents/audit/El%20Triángulo%20roto_Auditoria%20Interna_Comite%20de%20auditoria_Gerencia.pdf, accessed October 7, 2018.
3. Ibid.
4. This section on the relationship triangle was excerpted from "The Broken Triangle," Deloitte.com. Accessed (November 14, 2013) at: https://www.deloitte.com/assets/Dcom-Uruguay/Local%20Assets/Documents/Auditor%C3%ADa/El%20Tri%C3%A1ngulo%20roto_Auditoria%20Interna_Comite%20de%20auditoria_Gerencia.pdf.
5. IIA Audit Executive Center, "Strong Foundations: A Pulse of Internal Audit Supplement Report," wwwglobal.theiia.org, https://global.theiia.org/knowledge/Public%20Documents/AEC-Strong-Foundations-A-Pulse-of-Internal-Audit-Supplemental-Report.pdf, (accessed December 3, 2018).
6. Richard Chambers, et al., "The Relationship Advantage: Maximizing Chief Audit Executive Success," Korn/Ferry Institute and The IIA Audit Executive Center (March 2011). Accessed November 14, 2013, at: http://www.kornferryinstitute.com/sites/all/files/documents/briefings-magazine-download/%20The%20relationship%20advantage%20Maximizing%20chief%20audit%20executive%20success%20.pdf.
7. IIA Standard 1111: Direct Interaction With the Board, International Professional Practices Framework (IPPF) (Lake Mary, FL: The Institute of Internal Auditors, 2013).
8. Daniel Coleman, *Emotional Intelligence* (New York: Bantam, 2012).
9. "The corporate director and succession planning," Korn/Ferry Institute. Accessed at: http://www.kornferryinstitute.com/sites/all/files//documents/briefings-magazine-download/The%20corporate%20director%20and%20succession%20planning%20%E2%80%93%20Nine%20points%20to%20consider%20when%20preparing%20for%20SEC20Bulletin%2014E%20.pdf.

Chapter 6
When in Doubt, Follow the Risk

1. Peter Bernstein's examples were cited in *Internal Auditing: Assurance and Advisory Services,* Third Edition (Lake Mary, FL: Internal Audit Foundation, 2013), 4–2.
2. COSO ERM Framework, *Enterprise Risk Management – Integrating with Strategy and Performance*, © 2017 Association of Certified Professional Accountants.

3. International Professional Practices Framework (IPPF) (Lake Mary, FL: The Institute of Internal Auditors, 2017), 137.

4. Averages calculated from The IIA Audit Executive Center's Spring 2012, 2013, and 2014 Pulse of the Profession surveys of internal audit trends in North America. After 2012, respondents were afforded the opportunity to reflect IT coverage percentages separate from "other." IT coverage has averaged about 11 percent since 2013.

5. The IIA Audit Executive Center, 2018 North American Pulse of Internal Audit, "The Internal Audit Transformation Imperative" (Lake Mary, FL: The IIA Audit Executive Center, 2018), 29.

6. Pulse of the Profession 2013: Time to Seize the Opportunity, March 2013, The IIA Audit Executive Center.

7. The Institute of Internal Auditors, Emerging Trends and Leading Practices Survey, Spring 2011.

Chapter 7
We Must Audit at the Speed of Risk

1. Richard J. Anderson and J. Christopher Svare, *Imperatives for Change: The IIA's Global Internal Audit Survey in Action* (Altamonte Springs, FL: The Institute of Internal Auditors Research Foundation, 2011).

2. Ross Tilly, et al., "The Role of Internal Audit in Addressing Emerging Risks" (September 26, 2016), www. Kmpg.com, https://home.kpmg.com/au/en/home/insights/2016/09/internal-audit-emerging-risks.html, accessed November 24, 2018.

3. NC State University Poole of College Management, Online video, "Identifying and Evaluating Emerging Risks," www.erm.ncsu.edu, https://erm.ncsu.edu/library/article/identifying-and-evaluating-emerging-risks, accessed November 24, 2018.

Chapter 8
Disruption Drives Innovation

1. This section on Innovation Behaviors is adapted from "How can innovation transform internal audit?" PricewaterhouseCoopers, 2009. Accessed at: http://www.pwc.com.au/assurance/assets/Innovation-Internal-Audit-Nov09.pdf.

2. *Internal Auditing: Assurance and Advisory Services*, Third Edition (Lake Mary, FL: Internal Audit Foundation, 2013).

3. This section on common challenges in implementing innovations is adapted from Glen L. Gray and Maryann Jacobi Gray, *Enhancing Internal Auditing Through Innovative Practices* (Lake Mary, FL: Internal Audit Foundation, 1996), 7–17.

Chapter 9
Communication Must Be Continuous

1. "The IIA Global Internal Audit Competency Framework," The Institute of Internal Auditors, 2013. Accessed at: https://na.theiia.org/aboutus/Public%20Documents/The%20IIA%20Global%20Internal%20Audit%20Competency%20Framework.pdf.

2. Daniel A. Goble, Lauren E. Shaheen, and Raymond Jeffords, "Questions for Internal Auditors," The Institute of Internal Auditors. Accessed at: https://global.theiia.org/iiarf/Public%20Documents/Questions%20for%20Internal%20Auditors%20%20-%20Chattanooga.pdf.

3. IIA Practice Guide, Interaction with the Board, August 2011, The Institute of Internal Auditors. Accessed at: https://na.theiia.org/standards-guidance/Member%20Documents/11759_PROF-Interaction_with_the_Board_PG.pdf.

Chapter 10
Failing to Plan Is Planning to Fail

1. IIA Practice Advisory 2210.A1-1, Risk Assessment in Engagement Planning, International Professional Practices Framework (IPPF) (Lake Mary, FL: The Institute of Internal Auditors, 2013).

2. Ibid.

3. Ronell B. Raaum and Stephen L. Morgan, *Performance Auditing: A Measurement Approach*, 2nd Edition (Lake Mary, FL: Internal Audit Foundation, 2009).

4. *Internal Auditing: Assurance and Advisory Services,* Third Edition (Lake Mary, FL: Internal Audit Foundation, 2013), 12-3–12-5.

Chapter 11
Fight the Temptation to Over-Audit

1. Comptroller General of the United States, Government Auditing Standards 2018 revision, (Washington, DC: US Government Accountability office), 2018.

2. *Sawyer's Guide for Internal Auditors, Volume 1, Internal Audit Essentials* (Lake Mary, FL: Internal Audit Foundation, 2013), 186.

3. Comptroller General of the United States, Government Auditing Standards 2018 Revision, "Fieldwork Standards for Performance Audits" (Washington, DC: U.S. Government Accountability Office), 190.

4. The IIA Audit Executive Center, "Technology Laggers vs. Embracers: CAEs Discuss Technology Performance Gap," white paper (September 2012).

5. *The IIA CIA Learning System, Part IV* (Lake Mary, FL: The Institute of Internal Auditors, 2007), 64.

6. Leslie K. John, Alessandro Acquisti, and George Loewenstein, "Strangers on a Plane: Context-dependent Willingness to Divulge Sensitive Information," *Journal of Consumer Research* 37, no. 5 (February 2011): 858–873.

7. K. Huang, M. Yeomans, A. W. Brooks, J. Minson, and F. Gino, "It Doesn't Hurt to Ask: Question-asking Increases Liking," *Journal of Personality and Social Psychology* 113, no. 3 (September 2017): 430–452.

Chapter 12
Better Never Than Late

1. Lawrence B. Sawyer, Mortimer A. Dittenhofer, and James H. Scheiner, *Sawyer's Internal Auditing: The Practice of Modern Internal Auditing*, 5th Edition (Lake Mary, FL: Internal Audit Foundation, 2003), 690.

2. Andy Sher, "TVA Identifies lavish spending," *The Chattanooga Free Times*, May 3, 2001.

Chapter 13
Culture Is Often the Culprit

1. NACD, "NACD Calls on Boards to Elevate Dialogue on Corporate Culture," www.globalnewswire.com, https://globenewswire.com/news-release/2017/10/04/1140652/0/en/NACD-Calls-on-Boards-to-Elevate-Dialogue-on-Corporate-Culture.html, accessed November 30, 2018.
2. 2016 Q3 Duke Quarterly CFO Global Business Outlook survey.
3. Tracey Keele and Rebecca Stockely, *Five Steps to Tackling Culture* (KPMG LLP, 2017), www.kpmg.com, https://assets.kpmg.com/content/dam/kpmg/be/pdf/Markets/five-steps-to-tackling-culture-new.pdf (accessed November 29, 2018).

Chapter 14
No One Is Immune to Ethical Lapses

1. Howard Sklar, "Infernal Audit: When Internal Auditors Go Bad," February 24, 2012. Accessed at: http://www.forbes.com/sites/howardsklar/2012/02/24/quis-custodiet-ipsos-custodes/.
2. International Professional Practices Framework (IPPF) (Lake Mary, FL: The Institute of Internal Auditors, 2013), 4–6.
3. Max H. Bazerman and Ann E. Tenbrunsel, *Blind Spots* (Princeton, NJ: Princeton University Press, 2012).
4. Cynthia Cooper, *Extraordinary Circumstances* (Hoboken, NJ: John Wiley & Sons, 2009).
5. Ibid.
6. Emily N. Strauss, "'Easing Out' the FCPA Facilitation Payment Exception," I.C.1: "The Facilitation Payment Exception," p. 241. Accessed at: http://www.bu.edu/law/central/jd/organizations/journals/bulr/volume92n4/documents/STRAUSS.pdf.
7. Cynthia Cooper, *Extraordinary Circumstances.*

Chapter 15
Always Remember—We Are Auditing People, Too

1. "Fraud Detection and Prevention," The Institute of Internal Auditors Ottawa Chapter. Accessed at: https://chapters.theiia.org/ottawa/Documents/Fraud_Detection_and_Prevention.pdf.
2. "Report to the Nations on Occupational Fraud and Abuse," 2012 Global Fraud Study, The Association of Certified Fraud Examiners. Accessed at: http://www.acfe.com/uploadedFiles/ACFE_Website/Content/rttn/2012-report-to-nations.pdf.
3. Report to the Nations: 2018 Global Study on Occupational Fraud and Abuse. Copyright 2018 by the Association of Certified Fraud Examiners, Inc., https://s3-us-west-2.amazonaws.com/acfepublic/2018-report-to-the-nations.pdf, accessed December 4, 2018.
4. Ibid.
5. Michael Capote and Cecil Greek, "Theorist Paper: Donald Cressey." Accessed at: criminology.fsu.edu/crimtheory/2004/Cressey.doc.

6. Ryan Hubbs, "Fraud brainstorming," *Fraud Magazine*, July/August 2012. Accessed at: http://www.fraud-magazine.com/article.aspx?id=4294973852.

7. Rudyard Kipling, "If," quoted in *Kipling: Poems* (New York: Everyman's Library, 2007).